FOR ⌇
FROⲘ
JOHN

CHRISTMAS '87
All our LoVE To You!

ATLANTIC
MONTHLY
PRESS

Out of Control

*The Story of the Reagan
Administration's Secret
War in Nicaragua, the
Illegal Arms Pipeline, and
the Contra Drug
Connection*

OUT OF

CONTROL

Leslie Cockburn

A MORGAN ENTREKIN BOOK
THE ATLANTIC MONTHLY PRESS
NEW YORK

Published simultaneously in Canada
Printed in the United States of America

FIRST EDITION

Library of Congress Cataloging-in-Publication Data
Cockburn, Leslie.
    Out of control: the story of the Reagan administration's secret war in Nicaragua, the illegal arms pipeline, and the Contra drug connection/Leslie Cockburn.—1st ed.
    p. cm.
    ISBN 0-87113-169-2
    1. United States—Military relations—Nicaragua. 2. Nicaragua—Military relations—United States. 3. Counterrevolutionists—Nicaragua. 4. United States—Foreign relations—1981- . 5. Nicaragua—Politics and government—1979- . I. Title.
E183.8.N5C63   1987   87–24070

The Atlantic Monthly Press
19 Union Square West
New York, NY 10003

Design by Laura Hough

First printing

For Andrew, Chloe and Olivia

FOREWORD

This book grew out of an investigation for CBS News, spanning three years, into the covert operations in Central America. For much of that time, the investigation was a collaborative effort, resulting in four broadcasts aired in 1985–87. My partner in each of these endeavors was CBS News correspondent Jane Wallace. We were joined in 1986 by Ty West, a CBS News associate producer and a brilliant investigator. The three of us broke the story of Oliver North's network for CBS News in June 1986.

As we moved on from the story of the arms pipeline and secret contra training bases into the darker world of drug trafficking in the supply network, we enlisted former Associate Press reporter Brian Barger. The four of us probed the use of major drug traffickers as a source of contra funding and as U.S. government-approved suppliers of contra aid. We broke the story for CBS News on the guns-for-drugs trade and the involvement of the CIA.

Jane Wallace and I traveled many times to Honduras, Nicaragua, and Costa Rica; all of us spent days on end in Miami, Washington,

North Carolina, California, and Alabama in pursuit of the real story of the White House covert network.

On the Iran side, I was fortunate enough to cover several stories in the Middle East in 1981–83. I was well aware of the Israeli arms trade with Iran at that time, and knew some of the arms merchants involved.

At the close of the Iran-contra hearings in August 1987, Ronald Reagan told the nation that all of this must be put behind us. If that is to be the case, it is essential that the American people know exactly what it is we are being asked to forgive and forget.

ACKNOWLEDGMENTS

I owe my greatest debt to my husband and fellow journalist, Andrew Cockburn, who edited and substantially revised this book at breakneck speed to make these events comprehensible to all.

My agent, Andrew Wylie, and editor, Morgan Entrekin, encouraged me to write the story and remained enthusiastic and supportive throughout.

In the course of pursuing the story there were those, other than my closest CBS colleagues as discussed in the Foreword, who gave me sources, confirmations, and support. Carroll Doherty, the Washington investigator and CBS News consultant, gave me key sources and encouraged me in 1985, when very few people knew or cared about this story. Courtney Hood, CBS bureau chief in Managua and the owner of the only punk sunglasses ever seen in Zelaya Province, was an inspiration. Scott Wallace of *Newsweek* supplied crucial information on the southern front.

There were a handful of journalists, among them Alfonso Chardy, Robert Parry, Knut Royce, Frank Greve, and Pat Lynch, who were diligently probing the White House operation long before the story became a popular issue in November 1986. Their work inspired me to press on. On Capitol Hill, Jack Blum, Dick McCall, Donna Martin, Mike Walker, and Pete Stockton all provided encouragement and advice. Others in the administration and elsewhere supplied vital information, but they will thank me for being left anonymous.

At CBS News, quite apart from those who worked directly with me, there were others whose support was absolutely indispensable. When I first came to executive producer Andrew Lack with a fractured tale of mercenaries, secret weapons shipments, and White House money he displayed considerable faith and courage in not immediately showing me the door. Many months later, when our first story about Oliver North's operation went on the air, to the accompaniment of indignant administration denials, Lack stood firm in his support, as did senior producer Tom Yellin and CBS News president Howard Stringer.

CBS editor Nobuko Oganesoff gave much of her life over two years to the story. There could have been no substitute for her particular skills and energies in rendering a complex drama comprehensible to the audience.

Cameraman Manny Alvarez, the proprietor of Underwater Sports, the best dive shop in Miami, and soundman George Bouza accompanied Jane Wallace and me on all of our most hazardous expeditions. Their indomitable courage and wealth of experience in Central America and Miami were irreplaceable contributions to the enterprise. Their brilliant humor was no less vital in sustaining us all in some very dark moments indeed.

Copy editor Ed Sedarbaum did not allow an impossible schedule to interfere with an exacting eye for detail.

On the domestic front, Jennifer Gorman kept our house from falling apart during the ordeal of writing this book.

Finally, I must thank my parents, who showed me the world at an early age and nurtured my curiosity.

"Nothing works against the success of a conspiracy so much as the wish to make it wholly secure and certain to succeed. Such an attempt requires many men, much time, and very favorable conditions. And all these in turn heighten the risk of being discovered. You see, therefore, how dangerous conspiracies are!"
—Francesco Guicciardini
Ricordi Politici (1528–1530)

"Fawn—next time with fewer people."
—Robert McFarlane
Note to Fawn Hall, April 22, 1987

Out of Control

Chapter One
ELEPHANT HERD

"I could feel the steps of a giant animal."
—Contra Commander Enrique Bermudez
March 1985

On September 1, 1984, a convoy of Cessna "push-pull" aircraft took off from a CIA-controlled air base in Honduras and flew south over the Río Coco, the river that marks the northern border of Nicaragua. The three American planes had been recently transferred from the Air National Guard in New York to a top secret Pentagon operation codenamed "Elephant Herd." The light aircraft, bristling with rocket pods, were minutes away from their target, a Nicaraguan military training school. After they crossed the border, the planes were joined by an American Hughes 500MD helicopter, fitted, like the other aircraft, for combat.

Below them lay rugged volcanic mountains carpeted with jungle and bathed in murderous heat. The landscape, crisscrossed with dirt tracks linking the scattered villages, was the scene of a bitter war that was now entering its fourth year. Ostensibly, the war was a Nicaraguan affair between the Sandinista government and the contras, who were attempting to overthrow them. But the contras had been created and nurtured by the U.S. from the very beginning. The

1

biggest operations of the war, the attacks on Nicaraguan oil installations and the mining of the harbors, had been carried out by the CIA using U.S. military personnel, with the contra leadership being informed only after the fact and instructed to take the credit. The little air fleet cruising south that September day was in the same tradition, for the operation on which they were bent was once again inspired, planned, and executed by Americans.

At two-thirty in the afternoon, a few minutes after crossing the Río Coco, the raiding force attacked their target, a military training school at the little town of Santa Clara, firing twenty-four rockets in all. Antiaircraft fire from the ground was heavy enough to bring down the helicopter in flames, killing the three-man crew. The Cessnas made it back to Aguacate.

In some respects the attack was typical of this war: ill-planned and poorly executed, it killed more civilians than combatants. In other ways the attack marked a departure, for it was the first time that a Sandinista army training base had been targeted. More significantly, it was the first time evidence that Americans were in combat had been left behind.

The following day marked the fifth anniversary of the founding of the Sandinista People's Army. As Soviet-made T-55 tanks, amphibious personnel carriers, SAM missiles, and cannon paraded through the streets of Managua, Defense Minister Humberto Ortega announced that two of the bodies that had arrived at the morgue were "burned beyond recognition," but that the third might be an American.

There had been other recent signs of direct American involvement in the war. A week before, Sandinista soldiers had shot down an American C-47 cargo plane. The previous January a U.S. Army OH-58 reconnaissance helicopter was shot down when it strayed across the border into northern Nicaragua. Although the pilot managed to crash-land just inside Honduras, he had been killed by continuing fire from the other side of the border. But the evidence in the Managua morgue was the most explicit so far. "It was a light-skinned man, between 30 and 40 years old, of medium height and build, with brown hair graying at the temples. The body was badly bruised and wore a torn T-shirt in mottled green camouflage colors," reported John Lantigua in the *Washington Post* after viewing the unburned corpse. He added, as if in response to the obvious question: "The Reagan administration has pledged it will not send Americans into combat in Central America."

* * *

Americans have been fighting and dying in combat in Nicaragua for more than a century, ever since, in fact, the country's strategic location astride the Central American isthmus became of interest and importance to U.S. authorities. In 1855 William Walker, a native of Nashville, Tennessee, arrived in Nicaragua at the head of a band of mercenaries with the mission of securing American business interests there. Initially contenting himself with the command of the Nicaraguan army, by 1856 Walker had declared himself president, and was promptly accorded diplomatic recognition by the Pierce administration in Washington.

Walker had, however, made the error of double-crossing his original business sponsor, the robber baron Cornelius Vanderbilt. Vanderbilt accordingly financed and supplied a rebellion that deposed and defeated Walker's forces, forcing the ex-president to flee on a U.S. Navy warship. Walker did not give up easily. Rounding up more mercenaries and money, he made three attempts to retake Nicaragua. The last effort, in 1860, was to be an invasion of Nicaragua from a base in Honduras. Captured by the British, who had a big role in the region in those days, he was handed over to the Honduran authorities and shot.

The adventurer's demise did not by any means bring an end to foreign intervention in Nicaragua. The U.S. Marines landed in 1894, '96, '98, and '99 to safeguard American property from local turbulence.

In 1909 the U.S. government backed a conservative movement opposed to the government of José Santos Zelaya, whose nationalism was viewed with disfavor in Washington and on Wall Street. When two U.S. citizens were caught laying mines in the San Juan River and were executed by Zelaya's troops, the U.S. seized the excuse to intervene in force. Zelaya resigned, and a government more respectful of American interests was installed.

The way was set for a more permanent American presence in the country, since U.S. and European investments and loans were now very large, and it seemed possible that a foreign power—the kaiser's Germany was the big threat in those days—might establish a beach-. head there. Consequently the government was handpicked by the U.S., and Americans took over control of customs collection and the national railroad in order to ensure prompt servicing of loans.

This state of affairs caused some local resentment, which turned into armed rebellion against the American-sponsored government.

In 1912 the marines landed again. The rebellion was put down at the cost of a few American and many Nicaraguan dead. The marine commander, Maj. Smedley Butler, an efficient officer who never let his sense of duty interfere with a realistic appreciation of the situation, watched the government troops celebrate the victory by looting and getting drunk and wrote to his wife, decrying "a victory gained by us for them at the cost of good American lives, all because Brown Brothers, bankers, have some money invested in this country." Shortly afterwards the Taft administration ordered Butler to make sure that the U.S.-favored candidate was returned to power in the upcoming presidential elections. This he did, afterwards informing his wife that "Nicaragua has enjoyed a fine 'free election,' with only one candidate being allowed to run . . . who was unanimously elected. In order that this happy event might be pulled off without hitch and to the entire satisfaction of our State Department, we patrolled all the towns to prevent disorders and of course there were none."

The marines remained in Nicaragua, save for one two-year interval, until 1933, their presence creating its own justification by the rebellions and civil strife it helped to provoke. In 1927, however, the Americans decided to set up a local force to keep order among the populace. It was called the Guardia Nacional, but it was insufficient to deal with the formidable threat to the status quo in Nicaragua that emerged at the same time.

Augusto Sandino, the son of a prosperous peasant farmer, had become radicalized while working outside the country for American corporations. He returned in 1926 with a tiny force dedicated to getting rid of the U.S. occupiers. Initially his troops suffered heavily from the marines' use of air power, at that time a novel instrument of counterinsurgency. On the first such mission, against the northern town of Ocotal (not far from Santa Clara), the bombing and strafing killed several hundred fighters and civilians. As a result Sandino adopted guerrilla warfare tactics against both the marines and the new National Guard—with some success. By 1933 the U.S. decided to pull the marines out. Sandino then agreed to stop fighting and come to terms. He was murdered shortly afterwards by members of the National Guard acting at the direction of its U.S.-appointed commander, Gen. Anastasio Somoza.

Somoza, whose role and position were succinctly and accurately

4

summarized by President Roosevelt as "our son of a bitch," founded a dynasty that was to rule Nicaragua until 1979. The key to control was the American-trained National Guard, whose brutal repression of dissent brought decades of peace and prosperity for the Somoza family, their supporters, and foreign (mostly U.S.) investors. The Somozas indeed managed to amass one of the world's largest private fortunes.

In the early 1960s a group of young leftist revolutionaries founded the Sandinista National Liberation Front, named for the old nationalist guerrilla. They enjoyed little popular support in the early years, but in 1972 a massive earthquake leveled the capital city of Managua. Both the ruling Somoza—another Anastasio, nephew of the original—and his National Guard reacted in grimly predictable fashion. The president stole most of the foreign aid that poured in after the quake, while the guard dynamited collapsed buildings rather than rescue survivors trapped inside. These excesses helped to galvanize the opposition, and the Sandinistas grew in strength and popular support. The ruler fought back savagely, unleashing his guard to massacre at will. By 1979 Somoza had alienated the conservative middle classes and the church, and even the U.S. had officially ceased all military aid.

The American public, whose interest in Nicaraguan affairs over the years had been less than intense, took note of the TV pictures depicting the desperate dictator's efforts to maintain control by bombing the poorer quarters of his own cities (often using Cessna O2 push-pulls). When a National Guard detachment was ill advised enough to cold-bloodedly execute ABC network correspondent Bill Stewart while his own cameraman recorded the event for the evening news, the game was up. The Carter administration abandoned both Somoza and a last-minute scheme to preserve the National Guard as an institution.

Somoza and large numbers of guard officers and their men who managed to escape retribution at the hands of the populace made their way abroad. The Sandinistas swept into power.

Somoza was assassinated in Paraguay the year after his fall, but the Guardia lived on. The officers and men of this beaten army who had gotten out through their own efforts or those of sympathetic Americans and others gradually regrouped in Miami and in the Central American countries bordering Nicaragua. They did not have to wait long for help.

In November 1981, CIA Director William Casey met with Argentine Chief of Staff Gen. Leopoldo Galtieri to lay plans for arming and training the contras, using veteran trainers from Argentina's "dirty war" against its own population. The decision to promote war in Nicaragua had been taken earlier that year. Within six weeks of his inauguration, President Reagan had approved a presidential finding, which is the way that covert actions become legal, to give the nascent contras $19 million. A November 1981 national security decision directive refined and laid down the long-term plan, proposing that the U.S. "support the opposition front through formation and training of action teams to collect intelligence and engage in paramilitary and political operations in Nicaragua and elsewhere. Work primarily through non-Americans to achieve the foregoing, but in some circumstances CIA might (possibly using U.S. personnel) take unilateral paramilitary action."

The "non-Americans" that the sponsors had in mind were primarily the exiled remnants of the old Guardia, renamed the Nicaraguan Democratic Force—FDN in Spanish—under the military command of Col. Enrique Bermudez, whom Somoza had trusted enough to keep as his military liaison in Washington.

The exiles had first called themselves the 15th of September Legion, characterized by a secret U.S. Defense Intelligence Agency report as "a terrorist group." Even after regrouping as the FDN, several individuals specifically accused of terrorism were promoted. The FDN's chief of intelligence, Ricardo Lau, had, according to the former Salvadoran intelligence chief Col. Roberto Santivanez, "received payment of $120,000" for organizing the murder of Archbishop Romero of El Salvador in 1980. The fact that a high contra official had executed the archbishop of El Salvador did not diminish the White House's zeal for its fledgling "democratic resistance." (Administration officials conceded to the author that Lau was still running contra intelligence as late as June 1985, well after he had supposedly been forced out because of his lack of concern for human rights.)

Use of characters such as Lau was, unfortunately, more of the pattern than the exception in the contra war. The U.S. problem with the contras, from the beginning and throughout, was that they were by and large the very same group who had been trained by the United States to protect the interests of the Somozas. Methods and techniques developed for a ruthless dictatorship already in power are not necessarily the best way to create a popular insurgency. Though this fact might appear obvious, the CIA never seemed to get the point.

Just before the U.S. presidential elections in 1984, Edgar Chamorro, a disillusioned member of the Directorate of the FDN, leaked a CIA contra training manual to the American press. The manual, *Psychological Operations in Guerrilla Warfare,* clearly advocated a strategy of terror as the means to victory over the hearts and minds of Nicaraguans. Chapter headings such as "Selective Use of Violence for Propagandistic Effects" and "Implicit and Explicit Terror" made that fact clear enough. The contra pupils whom it was intended to instruct were told of the most effective use of assassinations, preferably in the form of public executions, to impress Nicaraguan villagers. "Neutralize" was the actual euphemism employed, but its meaning left nothing to the imagination. The little booklet thus violated President Reagan's own Presidential Directive 12333, signed in December 1981, which prohibited any U.S. government employee—including the CIA—from having anything to do with assassinations.

The fact that the manual had been leaked by Chamorro, who had been the authorized spokesman for the FDN—and had, indeed, been selected for the FDN Directorate by the CIA—meant the document could not be dismissed as a fraud. The president nevertheless did his best to explain this outrage away, calling the affair "much ado about nothing." "Neutralize," he explained, meant simply telling people in authority in Nicaragua "you are not in charge anymore," an interpretation that must have come as news to the psywar specialists over at CIA. The other line of defense adopted was to portray the document as the work of overzealous personnel, mere temporary contract employees, who had gone ahead without the authorization of senior agency officials. Despite the administration's protestations of innocence, some of the CIA employees who were disciplined turned out to be quite senior indeed. Duane ("Dewey") Clarridge, the man who had been drafted from the CIA station in Rome to run the contra war, and had indeed commissioned the manual, was transferred. His reassignment was hardly a demotion, since he was put in charge of the European desk at CIA Operations Directorate headquarters. His deputy, a career agency employee named Vincent Cannistraro, was likewise transferred, to the National Security Staff office of Lt. Col. Oliver North. Joe (or José) Fernandez, another agency official who worked on the manual, was promoted to station chief in Costa Rica.

As it so happened, the manual that caused such a storm in Congress and the press when it was released had already been sanitized. It had originally been handed to Edgar Chamorro for distribution to

7

the troops, but he had found parts of it so especially unappealing that he had censored them. The original text included such advice as creating "martyrs" and, interestingly enough in the light of later revelations, "hiring professional criminals."

Chamorro has made it very clear that the contras were eager recipients of such tutelage. "I have been very close to the contra side," he recalls. "I am saying that our atrocities toward prisoners or toward civilians were routine. I mean it was a matter of intimidating people or using practices of terrorizing the country so people will fear you and will eventually support you out of fear. They were approving, condoning, the practical use of terror.

"The targets were people working for [Sandinista] government agencies, like cooperatives, or people who belonged to health clinics or people who were teachers or bank employees. Very often their ambushes are for people who are civilians, who are working on roads or, perhaps, on the harvest . . . they will attack anything that moves, you know, in areas near a combat zone, women or children or adults." Such methods, according to Chamorro, were entirely consistent with their training: "They were trained to kill communists, and this is an important thing because they might react in a situation where the only good communists are dead communists. So they will kill people who they don't have to kill, women and children. Sometimes terror is very productive. This is the policy, keep putting pressure until people cry 'uncle.'"

To complement the manual the CIA trainers had given the contra troops something else. When Chamorro went to the FDN he "found that among the things the CIA used to give us was a big knife. . . . It's called a commando knife, and our people, everybody wanted to have a knife like that, to kill people, to cut their throats. What is very sad in this kind of war is that sadistic tendencies don't diminish. They become stronger. People who are sadistic become more sadistic and more brutal and more cruel."

One could see living evidence of this process in remote regions of Nicaragua, such as Siuna and Paiwas, in early 1985. As well as the numerous reports of straightforward killings, there were an alarming number of cases of mutilation. It was particularly painful to hear, from two sets of children whose parents had been killed in contra attacks in different regions, that the victims' faces had been peeled off. In one case a mother, the other a father.

Despite repeated claims to the contrary in Washington and elsewhere, it appeared that not all the contra rank and file were willing volunteers. "Our commandantes have used force to make young people join us on a large scale, even threatened to kill them if they would not follow," Chamorro explained in an interview. "These people later on became soldiers. Some desert, but many of them stay fighting. They are scared to leave, or they have nothing else to do, or this gives them status."

The contra commanders routinely brutalized their own recruits, willing or otherwise, a fact that, according to Chamorro, was of much more concern to the CIA trainers than what was being done to children and other representatives of the "enemy." Discipline was routinely enforced, Chamorro added, by keeping people without food or tying them to trees, or raping female recruits with the help of the famous commando knife. The CIA, says Chamorro, was fully informed: "In 1983, 1984 they knew everything, they were monitoring all actions. They were exposed to all atrocities, abuses. I talked to the CIA, the station chief, to the deputies, of what I knew, and also to Mr. Kilpatrick, the person who helped us with the manual. He got very furious when he saw the actions of our commanders against our own troops. But I never heard him complaining about abuses committed against the enemy."

The FDN's military commander, former National Guard colonel Enrique Bermudez, always emphatically denied that the contras committed atrocities against civilians, or used kidnapping as a recruitment method. He was rarely pressed on such unpleasant questions, but in a May 1985 interview he did admit that there might be "isolated" cases of rape, mutilation, and kidnappings. He conceded that no one had been disciplined for such behavior. To anyone prepared to travel the back roads of Nicaragua, however, the evidence of bereaved and scarred victims, not to mention escaped kidnappees, was all too easy to find.

The contras were left in no doubt that their actions had the backing of the United States. As Chamorro recalls, "We talked only to high people in the CIA, and those people used to say that the White House knew very well what was going on. The person who was in charge of the FDN, of the 'project' as they call it [Duane Clarridge], used to tell us that they were briefing the president of the United States once a week." Indeed, as it was possible to discover in Tegucigalpa in the spring of 1985, the chilling truths about contra atrocities and recruitment methods were well known not only in the CIA but in the rest of the burgeoning bureaucracy of the contra war.

Corruption, the other unwholesome aspect of the contra cause, was also much in evidence, both at that time and later. As a White House envoy noted in a letter to his boss in March 1986: "There are few of the so-called leaders who care about the boys in the field. This war has become a business to many of them." If aid were to be renewed by Congress, "It will be like pouring money down a sink-hole."

The abiding problem for the Reagan administration was that ordinary Americans knew or sensed enough of what was going on to want no part of it. The administration had come to power determined to banish the "Vietnam syndrome," meaning people's reluctance to get involved in any more military adventures in the third world. But according to public opinion polls, the Nicaraguan war was consistently opposed by roughly two-thirds of the population. So the purposes and methods of the war had to be kept secret. A very large-scale military operation three hours' flying time from Miami would have to be covert, with official U.S. involvement muffled by layers of "deniability."

The most the administration would initially admit to was that it was supporting efforts to interdict arms supplies from Nicaragua to the guerrillas in El Salvador. But there was already enough evidence surfacing in the press of more far-reaching U.S. objectives to prompt the House of Representatives to vote unanimously in December 1982 to prohibit the spending of any taxpayers' money "for the purpose of overthrowing the government of Nicaragua." On the other hand, as long as the goal was simply stopping the alleged Salvadoran arms traffic, the money could keep on flowing. The same month that Congress made this neat distinction, the CIA was telling the exiles that they could expect to overthrow the Sandinistas by July of 1983, a statement that was not, naturally enough, communicated to the Congress. As scandals such as the assassination manual hit the headlines, Congress moved to place further restrictions. For many on Capitol Hill, the mining operation was the last straw.

The discovery that the CIA had laid mines in the Nicaraguan harbors of Porto Corinto, Porto Sandino, and El Bluff between January and March of 1984 caused a massive uproar when the news became public that April. (The story had in fact been broken months before by Jane Wallace on the *CBS Evening News,* but it was not until Congress confirmed it, and thereby made it "official," that the rest of the press felt bold enough to go along.) The operation had been conceived by the director of the CIA's Latin American Division, Dewey Clarridge, a career agency official who had been given the contra account by CIA Director William Casey and who made up in energy what he lacked in knowledge of Central America (or Spanish). His predecessor, Nestor Sanchez, was moved to a high position in the Pentagon, from where he made sure that the Department of Defense continued to give cooperation to the contra war. The contras, it transpired, had been informed only after the fact of what the CIA was doing and were instructed to take the credit. One contra leader was dragged from his bed at two A.M., handed a press release by a CIA contact, and told to read it over the contra radio before the Sandinistas broke the news.

The mining caused outrage in the international community. The government of France offered to assist in clearing the mines. Condemnation at home was equally fierce. Senator Barry Goldwater, the chairman of the Senate Intelligence Committee, expressed his own irritation in a pithy letter to William Casey:

> Dear Bill,
> All this past weekend, I've been trying to figure out how I can most easily tell you my feelings about the discovery of the President having approved mining some of the harbors of Central America. It gets down to one little simple phrase. I'm pissed off. . . . This is an act violating international law. It is an act of war. For the life of me I don't see how we are going to explain it.

In 1984 the Congress ratified the famous Boland Amendment, which, on the face of it, should have put the U.S. government out of the contra war for at least the twelve months following October 12, 1984, the date when it became effective.

The amendment stated that "no appropriations or funds made available to the Central Intelligence Agency, the Department of Defense or any other agency or entity of the United States involved in intelligence activities may be obligated or expended for the purpose or which would have the effect of supporting, directly or indirectly, military or paramilitary operations in Nicaragua by any nation, group, organization, movement, or individual."

The debate over Boland was in fact a continuation of the argument that had been going on in Washington ever since U.S. support for the contras had first been publicly revealed. The Republicans and Democrats who supported the administration repeated familiar charges that the Sandinistas were funneling arms on a massive scale to the revolution in El Salvador. The opposition in turn pointed out that there was little or no evidence of significant military support by the Sandinistas for the guerrillas in El Salvador. Indeed, the senior CIA analyst on the subject, David MacMichael, had publicly announced that the intelligence community possessed no evidence whatsoever that any large-scale traffic had occurred since 1981. More fundamentally, the opposition posed the basic question of what business the United States thought it had trying to overthrow the government of Nicaragua.

For the moment the opposition prevailed, despite passionate complaints from the administration. But this setback had not come as a surprise for the White House. Plans for circumventing congressional prohibitions had long since been hatching in the recesses of the national security community.

One of these plans was called Operation Elephant Herd. It had been authorized by President Reagan back in June 1983 to get around any future restrictions on aid, and was to be carried out jointly by the Pentagon and the CIA. The operation was designed to channel military equipment secretly from the Pentagon's inventory to the CIA for use in support of the contras. When, in December of 1983, Congress announced a legal cap of $24 million in aid for the contras, Elephant Herd swung into action, providing $12 million worth of military supplies above and beyond the limit. Through a simple exercise in creative accounting, the Pentagon declared any equipment requested by the CIA to be "surplus," with no dollar value. That was how the planes used at Santa Clara had been obtained. Among those who planned Elephant Herd was a young marine major on assignment to the White House named Oliver North.

The following May, North, now promoted to lieutenant colonel, had been formally introduced to the Directorate of the FDN by Dewey Clarridge. According to Edgar Chamorro, who was present, Clarridge had presented North with the words "If something happens in Congress, we will have an alternative way, and to assure that, here is Colonel North. You will never be abandoned."

Over the next two and a half years North was to be part of a concerted effort by the United States government to live up to Clarridge's promise. Laws on everything from the export of arms to the importation of narcotics to the recruitment of mercenaries, as well as the Boland Amendment, were consistently and methodically broken. By the end, the inner circle of planners at the White House and CIA had put into operation a scheme by which secret wars (and other covert operations) could be conducted without being subject to control by Congress or the wishes of the voters.

North had gone down to Honduras the day before the Santa Clara raid with orders from his boss on the National Security Council, Robert McFarlane, to exercise "absolute stealth." Dead Americans and a wrecked helicopter inside Nicaragua hardly constituted stealth, and when North returned to Washington, he wrote a careful memo to McFarlane, explaining that none of it was his fault. After noting that the helicopter had gone along for "command and control," North explained that both he and Clarridge had "urged that the operation be postponed because the rockets necessary for the attack had to be saved for potential use against the next arms delivery." He reported that contra leader Adolfo Calero had not authorized the raid to take place that day, and that "the loss of the only operating FDN helicopter on the Northern Front is a serious blow. . . . It may therefore be necessary to ask a private donor to donate a helicopter to the FDN."

There is every reason to doubt that the raid was conducted without the knowledge of senior American advisers as the chastened colonel claimed. A sophisticated flight map found on board the helicopter showed that the Hughes 500MD had flown from Jamistran, a base constructed by the U.S. military in Honduras. The map also showed routes fanning out from Aguacate, a base built and operated by the CIA in Honduras, and the point of origin of the Cessna O2 push-pulls used in the raid. This suggests that the raid could not have been launched without clearance from someone high up in the chain of command, someone who could give orders to Americans.

In his "after-action" report to McFarlane, North talked about the Americans who were involved as "non-official assistants." That category would have had to include members of the Twentieth Special Forces Group of the Alabama National Guard, the unit to which one of the dead men in the Managua morgue belonged. His name was Dana Parker, a thirty-six-year-old undercover detective with the Huntsville, Alabama, Police Department. He was also commander of the First Detachment, A Company, Twentieth Special Forces Group. After his death was reported, Huntsville officials confided to a local reporter that Dana Parker had been a "paid assassin, who had killed three Cuban government officials and got wasted trying to kill another one."

As it turned out, two of the bodies in the crash were American. (The third was a Nicaraguan contra.) The man who had flown the helicopter had been a thirty-six-year-old pilot from Memphis named James P. Powell. Powell had flown helicopters in Vietnam, where he had earned numerous citations and survived at least three crashes. In the two years before he died he had been less than forthcoming even to his family and close friends about his precise occupation. He had told a variety of conflicting stories about being an oil rig supply pilot, or flying helicopters for the TV series *Airwolf,* or working as a flight instructor. All of these turned out to be totally untrue. The oil rig company he mentioned denied that he had ever worked there, *Airwolf* had never heard of him, and he was not qualified as a fixed-wing flight instructor. When Powell had set off for Central America, he had made a detour on the way, to Gainesville, Florida, home of a Twentieth Special Forces detachment. He had flown there in a plane belonging to a Jack Moreno, who made himself scarce around the time of the Santa Clara raid and was described by his father as being "in the insurance business, I think," a job description that brings smirks to the faces of old CIA hands.

In his memo, North appended some "proposed press guidance." It is fair to say that this part of the operation worked beautifully. CIA officials notified Senator Daniel Patrick Moynihan, deputy chairman of the Senate Intelligence Committee, that the two Americans killed in the crash were "mercenaries," part of a group of seven who had left New Orleans the week before to join the contra effort. The dead men, they stressed, were private citizens with no official ties.

Senator Moynihan dutifully relayed the message that the agency was "looking into the circumstances surrounding the raid and the downing of the helicopter, as well as the involvement of the American mercenaries."

Within a week the raid was being described in headlines as a "Tragic Latin Expedition" mounted by a lone-wolf paramilitary group called Civilian Military Assistance with a voluble spokesman in the form of Tom Posey, an Alabama grocer and former marine who helpfully posed for interviews in a "Zero Hour for Communism" tee shirt.

"CMA," Posey told a crowded press conference, had been founded in July of 1983, first to "help out" the army in El Salvador, and then the contras. The group was described as a ragtag band of

Vietnam vets and Alabama national guardsmen who felt "something should be done" to help the beleagured contras. It was all very "down home," dollar bills collected in jam jars, travel by Greyhound bus, meals of C rations, and not a cent in compensation. There were quaint tales of hopeful letters posted to Central American military officials, supplies dispatched by parcel post to U.S. military attachés for forwarding to the needy, members banging on doors at embassies to get a hearing, and shipments of "canteens, first aid pouches, foot powder . . ." Their first mission to the contra camps had been in January of 1984. "We'd just gotten a brand-new bunch of uniforms," retailed Posey; "we figured we could save five hundred dollars in airline tickets and freight costs if we were to fly ourselves down there."

The scenario of gung-ho veterans turned "freedom fighters," determined to aid their ideological brethren with their few scant resources, made for good copy on this patriotic if somewhat eccentric group, and most people were content to leave it at that. Within two weeks the initially skeptical reports about the murkier aspects of the Santa Clara raid had died away. Yet there were enough clues on the record to invite speculation about the involvement of the CIA. The involvement of the Alabama National Guard itself had an interesting precedent. Just over twenty years before, Alabama national guardsmen had been recruited by the CIA for the abortive Bay of Pigs expedition. As one veteran of that affair remarked with a residue of bitterness in 1984, "They called us mercenaries too." The connection was rendered even more interesting by the fact that most of the more active members of CMA had strong ties not just to the Alabama Guard, but to its Special Forces contingent, part of the Twentieth Special Forces Group.

Two weeks after the raid Senator Jim Sasser of Tennessee threw what could have been a monkey wrench into the cover story by writing both Defense Secretary Caspar Weinberger and CIA Director William Casey to inquire as to the whereabouts of three Cessna O2s, formerly belonging to the New York National Guard, that had been declared "excess" the previous December. The response, so the senator informed reporters, was that the planes had been flown to Air Force Logistics Command at Andrews Air Force Base. From there they had been turned over, in February 1984, to "Project Elephant Herd." Elephant Herd was described at the time as a "multi-service tasking" involving several different branches of the military. They had then been turned over to Summit Aviation, a Delaware company with a long history of close cooperation with the CIA. One of Summit's specialties is the conversion of the civilian version of the Cessna O2 for military use. Sasser's inquiry and the response vanished into the files of the Senate Intelligence Committee. The *Washington Post* noted that "the nature of these transactions has raised questions about possible cooperation between the Defense Department and the CIA to circumvent an explicit Congressional ban on supplying arms and equipment beyond the $24 million specifically appropriated to the CIA for aiding the rebels during this year."

The questions were pertinent enough, if rather less than persistent. But the answers were there, scattered in the tracks of the elephant herd stamping over Central America.

Thus the basic elements for the new-model "underground" covert operation were now in place. It was to be concealed behind a cover of "private" groups, whose activities would mask the involvement of North and his superiors as well as providing publicity and money for the contra cause.

The private aid network that now sprang up to fill the supposed vacuum left by the congressional aid ban certainly included some colorful characters. In Tegucigalpa, the capital of Honduras, CIA personnel, mercenaries, and the burgeoning U.S. military establishment were joined by a flood of philanthropists, mostly from the extreme right. One group, particularly taken with the plight of Miskito Indian refugees from Nicaragua, shipped down tons of shoes that they insisted the Indian children should wear, as well as an aerobics instructor to cheer the wretched in their squalid camps.

Overall, close to twenty privately incorporated U.S. groups shipped an estimated $5 million in what was described as humanitarian aid to the contras in the twelve months prior to April 1985. It was a rich assortment, including one group that had previously provided mercenaries for the white supremacist Smith regime in Rhodesia, and another that included in its international membership, according to a congressional study, "at least one neo-fascist party whose chief served in Mussolini's government." The Reverend Sun Myung Moon's Unification Church was caught up in the fervor of charity through its political offshoot, Causa International, as was Operation Blessing, a spin-off of the Reverend Pat Robertson's Christian Broadcasting Network.

It appears that not everyone involved was motivated by charity, since considerable portions of funds raised for this humanitarian assistance for the contras never even left the United States. In April

1985, for example, the director of Friends of the Americas, a Louisiana state representative named Woody Jenkins, chaired a $250-a-plate fund-raising dinner in Washington. The lavish affair was sponsored by the Nicaraguan Refugee Fund, which had not at that point supplied much money to refugees or anyone else in Central America. Nevertheless the turnout was impressive. President Reagan was the keynote speaker, and the sponsors included J. Peter Grace, Nelson Bunker Hunt, Joseph Coors, and W. Clement Stone. Alleged victims of communist atrocities were on display for the affluent crowd. The president made an emotional speech, though he got mixed up in his atrocity stories. In terms of gross receipts the evening was a grand success, raising upwards of two hundred thousand dollars. However, out of this sum, precisely one thousand dollars of humanitarian relief actually made its way to the intended beneficiaries. The rest, according to an audit by the Nicaraguan Refugee Fund, went to caterers, florists, and the public relations men.

The aid network was, in essence, a smoke screen, a point explicitly admitted in 1987 by retired Gen. John Singlaub. Singlaub was the high priest of the aid network, his weather-beaten face flanked by jug-handle ears a familiar image on television. His function, as he explained to the select committees investigating what had belatedly become the contra scandal, was to serve as a "lightning rod." As such, he and others like him worked wonders. After the truth of what had really been going on had partially leaked out in 1987, one journalist who had labored long and hard to research the private aid network ruefully recalled that "I never stopped to think why it was so easy to cover this story, why all the doors on private aid were so easy to push open."

With the press thus distracted, it was easy to conceal other sources of supply for the now illegal war. One of these was the Department of Defense, using the simple device of routing munitions to the contras via cooperative third countries. In the spring of 1985 both a high-ranking Honduran general and a State Department official privately confirmed the fact that U.S. military aid to the contras, routed via the governments of Guatemala, El Salvador, Israel, Taiwan, South Korea, and of course Honduras, was running at a minimum of $80 million a year.

The easiest place to get a sense of the ongoing U.S. commitment to the war was Honduras. With the border of Sandinista Nicaragua only a short drive away, no one had to wonder why the gringos had dug in for the duration. Honduras had been effectively torn in half, with the contra-controlled territory running like a frayed ribbon along the Río Coco that marked the southern border. Though the civilian directorate of the contras preferred the amenities of life in Miami, the military leadership had made it their bunker.

Since 1983 the Pentagon had spent well over $100 million on an ongoing series of exercises. Ahuas Tara II, Kilo Punch, Granadero 1, Bigger Focus 84, and Kings Guard had involved thousands of American troops. U.S. Navy Seals were training in the Gulf of Fonseca, just off the coast of Nicaragua. The impoverished countryside was remorselessly bulldozed to make way for an archipelago of "temporary" bases and airstrips capable of accommodating large transport planes loaded with tanks. As the second poorest country in the Western Hemisphere, the country was happy to play host, soon living up to its reputation as the "USS *Honduras.*" Any squeamishness or stirring of nationalist sentiments among Honduran politicians and generals was speedily smothered by the torrent of aid. In the capital of Tegucigalpa, famed for the steep nosedive of its airport approach, the reins of power led not to the local presidential palace downtown but to the sprawling American embassy high up on the hill. Destitute children and prostitutes discreetly positioned themselves outside the entrances of the Holiday Inn and the Hotel Maya to solicit the burgeoning American clientele. Rambo movies and the sub-Rambo variety that only seem to get distribution overseas packed the cinemas. The strip outside the expanding American air base at Palmarola was lined with brothels, and the happy relationship was only briefly disturbed by the appearance of AIDS. The profusion of troops from different American units and services—Special Forces, air force, national guards—crowding the streets and bars of Tegucigalpa gave the place the atmosphere of sixties Saigon. Of course this time around it was all much closer to home. The Texas National Guard flew in mountains of beef to throw a barbecue that was the talk of Honduras, while the crowded bars sprouted satellite dishes to pick up the ball games from the States.

Some of the American military teams passing through were less overt than others. Members of these groups tended to wear civilian tropical shirts with casual open collars and carry fake business cards with engraved addresses for nonexistent companies. Their cropped heads and military bearing gave them away. When not out in the countryside conducting mysterious reconnaissance missions they amused themselves in the casino, or lounged by the pea-green pool. One such delegation installed themselves at the Maya Hotel in

Tegucigalpa in early May of 1985. This particular group was a potpourri of the various branches and services of the American military, with the added cachet of an envoy of the Office of the Joint Chiefs Staff. It was a lull in the military exercise season. Universal Trek 85 and Ahuas III, elaborate affairs involving army engineers, armored units, marine landings, and airborne assaults, were just winding down, and the next big exercise, Cabanas 85, was not due to open until June.

The mission of this group, as was apparent from their somewhat unguarded conversations in the restaurant and by the pool, was to scout locations for even more airfields and, more interesting, to work on contingency planning for the invasion of Nicaragua. It was equally apparent that the military's thinking on this rather major question was sharply divided along parochial service lines. The air force representatives sipped their beers and lobbied passionately for a strategy based on precision bombing strikes on various key targets around Managua. The army men argued with equal force for a graduated invasion, to commence with a landing on the Atlantic coast of Nicaragua and the establishment of a base at Bluefields, where the conservative English-speaking population might be expected to lend their hearts and minds more readily to being liberated. The navy was no less heated in pleading the wisdom of using the fleet to blockade the country while Seal teams sabotaged coastal installations.

One evening, as this elevated debate raged over dinner at the long table at the back of the Fisherman's Inn, an army Special Forces man surreptitiously passed me his card. The engraved message on the front described him as a salesman for a firm in Fayetteville, North Carolina, the home of Fort Bragg. The firm did not exist, but the message scrawled on the back was about something very real indeed. It asked for a private meeting to discuss the southern border of Nicaragua, where that country meets Costa Rica.

Later that evening the officer spread a large-scale map across the overshampooed carpet of his hotel room floor. Carefully, he drew a circle around a small town called Los Chiles, just inside Costa Rica. There was an operation going on there, he said, that deserved a close look. Speaking slowly and somewhat elliptically, clearly torn between a reluctance to divulge classified information and a desire to bring into the open something of which he disapproved, he described a war effort that was very "black," that is, covert. He himself had been down in Costa Rica, ostensibly overseeing the military training of the Civil Guard, but he had also gone on missions inside

Nicaragua. There were, he said, a group of American citizens, of Cuban descent, based in Los Chiles and fighting inside Nicaragua. The land actually on the border was American owned, and a group of "gringo" mercenaries had been training contras there. "They're not ours," he added quickly, meaning they were not part of the Special Forces. If there was an "incursion" by Sandinista forces against this group at Los Chiles, the United States would be obliged to step in. It was a "flash point" where the long-expected confrontation between the U.S. military and the Nicaraguan army might occur; a necessary step in the blueprint for the invasion.

The officer did not explain why he was telling me this, but he made it quite clear that something was about to happen. An assault on American property that would be a provocation so outrageous as to make direct U.S. military intervention inevitable. Whatever his reasons, he had provided the first inkling of an operation that was a key element in the most secret part of the undeclared covert war against Nicaragua—the development of the southern front in Costa Rica, the means of getting America into the war.

Chapter Two

THE SOUTHERN FRONT

"The southern front was the sine qua non. North agreed with that. Casey agreed with that."

—Gen. Richard Secord
August 19, 1987

T he Special Forces officer had one additional item of information about the mysterious operation in Costa Rica. Some of the mercenaries involved had been arrested by the Costa Rican security forces two weeks earlier. Neither he nor anyone else could have known it at the time, but this development was to trigger a series of events that would eventually lay bare the intimate and illegal connection between the "private" war and the very highest levels of government.

Prior to the intrigues spawned by the contra war, Costa Rica had been a quiet, benign little country, mild in every respect by comparison with its more colorful neighbors, Panama and Nicaragua. Journalists in search of a cliché often refer to it as the Switzerland of Central America (which the English novelist Graham Greene once remarked is "a libel on Switzerland"). Its rich farmland and gently rolling hills are reminiscent of the San Joaquin Valley in central California, and with both an Atlantic and a Pacific coast it has a thriving fishing industry. Pliant governments with democratic principles have put no obstacle in the way of Americans buying up huge tracts of land for cattle, sugarcane, citrus, and coffee. It is a matter of great pride to the Costa Ricans that they have no standing army. They bridled when former UN Ambassador Jeane Kirkpatrick advised them that a military buildup might help their chances of increased U.S. aid; they are content to leave all security in the hands of paramilitary police forces.

A standing joke among some American residents is, "You can't buy a Costa Rican official but you can rent one." While some officials are certainly for hire, the coexistence of left and right within the government structure—unique to Central America—has guaranteed healthy rivalries within the bureaucracy and a measure of independence from the U.S. that would be unimaginable for Honduras.

In 1985 the Costa Rican government was determinedly sticking to its official position on the war raging in Nicaragua: Costa Rica was neutral, and no one was fighting from its territory. This of course was flagrantly untrue and everyone in the region knew it. It was maintained because an admission of a contra presence in the country would justify Sandinista incursions. The reality was that the northern provinces of Costa Rica were dotted with contra camps and there was heavy American pressure for them to be allowed to stay there. So long as American aid and the myth of neutrality could be simultaneously sustained, there was no need to rock the boat. Within the government and the disparate security forces—the Civil and Rural Guards, not to mention DIS, the Intelligence branch—there were sharp political arguments about the direction in which Costa Rican neutrality should lean. The Civil Guard and DIS, which enjoyed close relations with the CIA, tended to favor wholehearted support for the contra cause, while the Rural Guard tended to support the notion of genuine Costa Rican neutralism.

Up until early 1984 this southern front of the war had been the exclusive province of the charismatic contra commander Eden Pastora, who rejoiced in the nom de guerre of Commander Zero. Pastora had been a hero of the revolution that ousted dictator Anastasio Somoza. In the aftermath, however, he had been shunted aside from the front ranks of the Sandinistas and consigned to relatively minor government posts that, in his view, did not match his contribution to the war effort. From disgruntlement he moved to active opposition to the Sandinista Directorate, within which the Ortega brothers and Tomás Borge were now in the ascendant. Daniel and Humberto Ortega took over the posts of president and defense minister. Borge, the senior guerrilla leader of the group, became minister of interior.

Pastora eventually moved south and established himself as head of a contra force known as ARDE, based in Costa Rica. He was a larger-than-life figure, handsome, provocative, and difficult to pin down. However, while adamantine in his opposition to the Sandinistas, he absolutely refused to have anything to do with the much larger contra group in Honduras, the FDN. The FDN was controlled by former "Somocista" (as Pastora called them) officers and men of the infamous National Guard. Pastora had fought for years against the Guardia, who were now enjoying the lavish support of the CIA. But he too needed support from the CIA, though he was loath to admit it. It came in profusion after his break from the Sandinistas, in the form of aircraft, military supplies, and cash delivered, at least on one occasion, in a suitcase. "It was $230,000 or $250,000," Pastora later recalled.

Pastora's refusal to cooperate with the FDN was not only irritating to Washington; it also caused political problems for the administration. The contra war had to be sold to Congress and the public as the struggle of an opposition united against the regime in Managua. Pastora was a very public reminder both of the lack of unity and of the dubious antecedents of the FDN "freedom fighters." By 1984 the message from Washington was clear. Pastora had to be reined in. At the beginning of May he was given an ultimatum: join up with the FDN within thirty days or the aid would be turned off.

On May 30, the day the deadline expired, Pastora held a press conference at an isolated jungle camp at La Penca, just over the San Juan River in southern Nicaragua. His planned speech about his determination to remain independent and not bow to pressure from the CIA was abruptly cut short by a powerful bomb explosion, which killed three of the journalists present and wounded eighteen others.

As we shall see, the bombing and the question of who was responsible had repercussions that reached far, far beyond Costa Rica. Most immediately, however, it marked the end of Pastora's fractured relationship with the CIA. As Pastora bitterly recalls, the aid was cut off, and the agency stole his vital aircraft and a helicopter. Most important, key ARDE commanders were lured away to a new FDN faction in the south that would do as it was told. "Commander Zero" took on new meaning as a name, and by the spring of 1986, when he requested political asylum from the government of Costa Rica, his organization had already been effectively destroyed.

The incident that was to lay bare the workings of the organization that had destroyed Pastora and that was intended to replace him

23

was so obscure that it merited coverage only in *Soldier of Fortune* magazine. At dawn on April 25, 1985, a group of Costa Rican rural guardsmen led by a Colonel Badilla walked into a remote contra training camp hidden in dense jungle three miles from the border and picked up five gringo trainers. The mercenaries, who had always enjoyed cordial relations with Costa Rican law enforcement, were surprised and shocked to be driven straight to La Reforma prison in San José and charged with violating Costa Rican neutrality and possession of explosives. They had not only trained contra fighters, but had themselves fought inside Nicaragua.

The two Americans, two Englishmen, and one Frenchman had considered themselves part of an operation sanctioned by the U.S. government and were angry that they should be sacrificed to satisfy political appearances. The night before, word had come over the Voice of America on the camp radio that Congress had once again turned down military aid to the contras.

Once they realized the seriousness of their predicament, that they faced a trial and a five-year mandatory sentence, the group split on whether they should start talking publicly about what they knew. Three of the mercenaries, a crusty former Florida highway patrolman named Robert Thompson, a Frenchman named Claude Chaffard, and an Englishman named John Davies, were resolved to sit tight and keep their mouths shut. After two months of rice and beans in their third-world jail, however, the remaining pair, Steven Carr, a middle-class twenty-six-year-old from Naples, Florida, and Peter Glibbery, a British army veteran, eventually decided that they had been betrayed and abandoned. They started talking to the local and international press.

It was an extraordinary story; so extraordinary indeed that no one paid any attention. At least one taped interview, recorded in July 1985 for a major American network, sat gathering dust on a shelf for months before anyone bothered to look at it. The fact that the U.S. embassy in Costa Rica routinely told inquiring journalists that the mercenaries' tale was pure make-believe did not help their credibility.

In summary, their story was that that they had been working for an American named John Hull, who owned or managed eight thousand acres along the Nicaraguan border and was one of the largest ranchers in Costa Rica. Hull, insisted Carr and Glibbery, had told them explicitly that he was the "FDN-CIA liaison in Costa Rica." Hull had also told them that he was receiving ten thousand dollars a month from the National Security Council to maintain and supply two contra camps. One of these, where the mercenaries had been arrested, was on Hull's land. The other lay just inside Nicaragua, near the Costa Rican border town of Los Chiles.

Glibbery talked about a tall, boyish visitor from Washington named Robert Owen who had gone with him and Hull to redirect a contra arms supply plane that had landed at the wrong airstrip. Glibbery had asked Owen who the plane's pilots were. "Salvadoran air force," was the casual reply. "Wow, what a jacked-up operation," the mercenary had thought at the time.

Carr recounted how he had been brought to Hull's ranch via Fort Lauderdale, in Florida, where he had joined a chartered aircraft loaded with six tons of weapons. The plane had flown to the Salvadoran air base of Ilopango, where U.S. military had watched as the cargo was unloaded by Salvadoran military personnel for transshipment to the southern contra front.

Hull was the "boss" of the war in that area, the mercenaries insisted. Not only was he directing military operations for the group taking over from Pastora, he was also, according to the mercenaries, paying the commanders. The money, they had been told, was coming from the National Security Council. They were less sure of the role of the mysterious Robert Owen, the visitor who had seemed so well briefed on the arms deliveries. "He seemed like a messenger from Washington," thought Glibbery.

All the time the two prisoners were recounting their bizarre tale to unreceptive audiences, they were under tremendous pressure both from their fellow mercenaries and from rancher Hull to change their story. Hull, they said, suggested that if they would agree to say they had been paid by local journalists, agents of the Nicaraguan government, the Cubans, and/or the KGB to spread such lies, they would get food parcels and legal help. A friend of Hull's, an Illinois rancher, delivered a sterner warning: Their lives were in danger. They talked too much. John Hull meanwhile told anyone who would listen that the mercenaries were either pathological liars or paid agents. Despite these threats and blandishments, Carr and Glibbery continued to tell their story with total consistency and in staggering detail to the press, the FBI, the U.S. Justice Department, and finally the U.S. Senate.

Peter Glibbery had taken a circuitous route to the contra war. Born and raised in the grimy British city of Birmingham, he had served for four years in the British army, and had served a stint in

Northern Ireland. He had left Her Majesty's service because he had decided that there was more chance of adventure in the South African forces. He served there for a year, in the reserves, but found the lack of action disappointing. It was then that opportunity beckoned.

"I was in South Africa back in 1984. I heard through a contact in the United States that there were jobs going in Central America." The message was: " 'If you're interested, get yourself over here and we can organize something.' I was in South Africa with another Englishman, John Davies. We left before Christmas '84, flew to the United Kingdom, spent Christmas with our folks. We flew out of the U.K. fifteenth of February for Newark, caught a bus down to Birmingham, Alabama. We made contact with a guy called Frank Camper."

Frank Camper ran a paramilitary training school in Dolomite, Alabama. The Recondo School offered two-week courses in basic weapons training and explosives for, as Glibbery put it, "anyone who pays," adding that he considered it far inferior to his own professional training in the British army. Above and beyond the courses, Camper's school functioned as a kind of mercenary clearing house where contacts could be made and addresses exchanged. Glibbery was more respectful of this aspect of the operation: "Frank Camper's boys have operated in South Africa, the Lebanon, Afghanistan, Honduras, Nicaragua, Costa Rica, so they are getting around a bit."

The school had received a brief public notoriety when two Sikh terrorists, recent graduates, put a bomb on board an Air India 747 bound from Montreal to London. The FBI, according to Glibbery, had asked Camper to cooperate in a sting operation against the Sikhs by offering to sell them explosives. The sting had somehow failed, and over three hundred men, women, and children aboard the plane had died. Camper's ties to various U.S. government agencies, including the FBI, the Defense Intelligence Agency, and the CIA, were well known in mercenary circles. Glibbery himself had traveled down to South Africa in 1983 with a Recondo graduate who claimed that he had been commissioned by Camper to collect information on the South African armed forces for the Pentagon's Defense Intelligence Agency.

It was in just such an official context that Camper presented a possible mission for Glibbery and Davies in Central America.

"Frank was saying that the CIA were interested in recruiting us to spy on the FDN in Honduras. He said, 'They think you're different from the guys who normally go down there, and they think you'll be able to provide them with better information.' So we said, 'What are the pros and cons?' And he said, 'Well, the pros are, you'll probably get paid for any information you provide. The cons are, if the FDN finds out what you are doing, they'll probably waste your ass.' " It appeared that the CIA was mistrustful of their FDN protégés' combat reports from Nicaragua and wanted an alternative source. After a few days in Dolomite they and Camper drove up to the Birmingham Gun Show, where they were introduced to Tom Posey, the leading light of Civilian Military Assistance. Posey and CMA were still very much in business five months after the fatal helicopter crash at Santa Clara had exposed them to public scrutiny. Glibbery and Davies were given a thick wad of official-looking forms to fill out. A week later a man knocked at the back door of Camper's gun shop and introduced himself as Sam Hall, come to take them to Decatur, Alabama, for their marching orders.

Hall, the brother of an Ohio congressman, later earned his fifteen minutes of fame when he was picked up as he photographed a Sandinista military base outside Managua in late 1986. This was not long after another American, Eugene Hasenfus, had been shot down and captured while flying military supplies to the contras. While Hasenfus admitted to working for the CIA, and was treated as such, Hall was universally cast as an eccentric loner. The Sandinistas indeed subsequently released him on the grounds that he was allegedly "mentally unstable."

Glibbery's encounter with this curious figure paints a rather different picture. For example, according to Glibbery, once in the car Hall produced an orange folder containing "a picture of him in a wetsuit, aboard a submarine, with all these navy guys around. There's a picture of him in Israeli paratrooper gear complete with parachute and R-4 rifle, standing with a bunch of Israeli paratroopers. This wasn't faked, because there was a row of C-130 Herculeses in the background on the tarmac, all with a Star of David. He said, 'I went into Lebanon in 1982.' " There were indeed pictures of Hall in Beirut (wearing a United Nations beret this time), as well as in El Salvador and South Africa. Glibbery and Hall traded South African stories. Hall claimed to have been hired by the South Africans to bring back some schoolchildren who had been kidnapped over the border into Botswana. "There's a picture [of Hall] leaning by an African waterhole, and you've got to know what an African waterhole is like. He'd been wounded and he had this battle dressing over his jaw. He had the scars yet." Glibbery, who had had a lot of experience with mercenaries and pseudomercenaries, was impressed. "It was like he jumped from one job to the next, and that doesn't happen to the best professional soldier. We thought, 'Perhaps this guy is who he appears to be.' " The assumption seemed especially reasonable because Glibbery and his partner thought they were on their way to spy on the FDN contras for the CIA.

It was the final page of Hall's dossier that most impressed the two mercenaries. "Langley, Virginia, letterhead, okay? And he's saying, 'Forget you ever saw this.' " The letter reminded Glibbery of the British Official Secrets Act: " 'You must not communicate anything you see or find out about . . .' " It was signed and countersigned. " 'Curiouser and curiouser,' said Alice in Wonderland. We just drove up to Decatur, Alabama."

Posey told Glibbery and Davies that their references had checked out and briefed them on the next leg of their journey to Central America. He gave them the number of a Howard Johnson's hotel in Miami, where they were due the following Saturday, March 9, 1984, and said, "You're going to contact a guy called John Hull. John Hull is a farmer in Costa Rica. He helps the contras." En route back to Camper's place to pack, Hall, according to Glibbery, regaled his passengers with more personal details: his wealthy parents had left him money, he had conquered a problem with drugs, he was a father of two.

Hall was keen to join the trip to Miami, but Camper wanted his help for what turned out to be the abortive sting operation against the Sikh terrorists. "What he needed was a guy to pose as an arms dealer to sell them explosives, and that was what Sam Hall was for."

The next day Glibbery and Davies caught a Trailways bus at three in the afternoon for a twenty-one-hour trip to Miami. On arrival they called the Howard Johnson's at the Miami airport, where Posey had told them John Hull would be waiting for their call. There was no reply in Hull's room. "We went for a walk, walked around for an hour, came back, phoned again. Hull had checked out two or three days before. We thought, 'Oh, God, there's been a cock-up.' " However, the switchboard operator suggested they phone back after three, when her relief came on, because she would probably know where Hull had gone. At three-fifteen there was better news. Lilly on the switchboard knew that Hull had gone to Orlando and would be back that evening. She suggested they come on over and wait. "She checked us in, said there was no charge. She said there's a 'guerrilla rate,' which was something like seventeen bucks a night instead of sixty bucks, but 'don't worry about it. The movement is taking care of it.' [The so-called guerrilla rate was in fact a private accommodation on the part of Hector, the night manager, according to the FBI. Needless to say, Howard Johnson executives were kept in the dark about this scam.] We crashed. *First Blood* was on the television, which was the last thing we needed."

Hull arrived as they were tucking into hamburgers and French fries in the hotel restaurant later on. "Lilly introduces us [to] this old guy, and he's very standoffish." He was flanked by an Oklahoman, Larry Huff, described as a business associate, and a young Miami Cuban, Felipe Vidal, who was obviously involved with Lilly, the helpful switchboard girl.

The new recruits were questioned about their competence with weapons, "sixty-millimeter mortars, fifty-caliber Browning machine guns." They were shortly joined by another mercenary, Claude Chaffard, who was later to be arrested and jailed in Costa Rica with the others. Chaffard, as they later learned, had been sponsored by a Bostonian named James Keyes by means of a ten-thousand-dollar donation to Posey's group. It seemed that Keyes had been a member of the OSS, the World War II precursor of the CIA, and had also served in the CIA under George Bush, with whom, so the mercenaries were given to understand, Keyes was still in contact.

It was at this point that they learned that they were headed for Costa Rica rather than Honduras. When the group, along with Hull's Costa Rican common law wife, Margarita, gathered at the airport early the next morning, Glibbery and Davies found that they did not have enough money with them to make up the difference in airfare, but, as Glibbery recalled, "Hull makes up my ticket with his Gold Card. He then buys Claude Chaffard's ticket with his Gold Card."

Glibbery recounted the VIP treatment he and the others received once they landed at the San José airport. The colonel in charge of airport security met them and walked the group through immigration. He saw to their bags, "gray military rucksacks, gun-cleaning kits. We weren't there for a fishing holiday."

Once Larry Huff had hired a car—Margarita had taken Hull's for some business in San José—they set off for Muelle, John Hull's vast *finca*, or ranch, which stretches thirty miles in from the Nicaraguan border.

The road that the two mercenaries took to their newest war that day leads north from the sleepy capital of San José through Costa Rica's volcano country before entering the dense rain forest. After the turnoff for Ciudad Quesada, the nearest town to Hull's property, the winding road is dotted with villages and roadside stands selling cut roses, *gomas* (rubbery candies), biscuits, and nuts. In the village of Zarcero the spires of a cathedral rise above a park of yew bushes carved into fantastic shapes—dinosaurs and creatures straight out of a package of animal cookies. Farmhouses with rusty red roofs pepper the rich terraced hillsides.

Ciudad Quesada itself is the gateway to the San Carlos Valley. Gringos and wealthy Costa Ricans wearing cowboy hats roar about in expensive jeeps, in town for business before returning to their big cattle ranches or sawmills or coffee plantations that surround the town. Farmhands relax in the square, crowned with the local version of a Greek temple.

Although Hull keeps an office in town, his red-tiled *finca* a few miles down the road is the headquarters of the enormous holdings that make him the most prominent rancher in the valley. The way Hull tells it, he came down in the late 1950s from Indiana with his father in their own plane. They were armed with a soil-testing kit, for what is now thousands of acres of rich farmland was then dense forest. They found that the soil was rich and hired local peasants to clear it. Today the name of John Hull stands out next to his airstrip on large-scale maps of Costa Rica. A rosewood box in the house holds the wills of ten generations of John Hulls, back as far as his English ancestors. He still keeps land, and indeed an American wife, back in Indiana. Margarita keeps house for him in Costa Rica.

Hull's ranch house is functional rather than ostentatious, but the stuccoed living room looks out through open arches to a magnificent volcano that occasionally puffs smoke at dusk. The San Carlos River, reputed to have fresh-water sharks, flows below the terrace around the back. The grounds are thick with parrots and giant iguanas, which sometimes cause trouble when they get into the water tank and cut off the supply. When Hull is not too busy with running the ranch or the war, he enjoys alligator hunting.

Hull himself is an imposing figure. About six foot tall, and always deeply tanned, he carries his sixty-four years well. Rarely without an armed bodyguard when he is at home, he has a certain air of authority. The Spanish in which he barks orders at his men is overlaid with a pronounced Indiana drawl. His rules prohibiting strolls in the garden after curfew are backed up by attack dogs and guards with orders to shoot to kill. His justification to visitors for such siege conditions is that he has his own security to consider, which in light of his activities is probably prudent.

Soon after Glibbery, Davies, and Chaffard arrived at this bucolic retreat they were introduced to five or six contras who had come to the ranch for "rest and recuperation," as it was described to them. As Glibbery puts it, "They'd come out of the bush after a month or so, so instead of eating rice and beans they'd get to eat rice, beans, cheese, and eggs." The mercenaries were told that they would be eating with the contras rather than up at the house with Hull. After a couple of days they met Jesus, a military commander with the FDN contras, who clearly took his orders from Hull.

Glibbery describes his first foray into Nicaragua as a casual affair. Hull simply said to him, "Go up to the camp, see what's going on, and do a survey. Tell me what the guys are like, what they need to be trained in. Tell me what you need to make the men an effective force." Then the three mercenaries, along with a couple of contras, set off for the guerrilla camp inside Nicaragua, about fifteen kilometers east of the border crossing of Los Chiles.

The roads, which had been paved as far as the ranch, eventually turned into deep red dirt tracks that, depending on the season, can become dust traps or muddy troughs. The heat was intense, and as they left the farmland and entered the jungle, the humidity became almost unbearable. The turnoff to the camp from the main dirt road was conveniently marked by a drinks stand, where thirsty contras came for a beer or Coka. This was near the actual border now, a sparsely populated no-man's-land that was constantly watched by Costa Rican border patrols.

They headed deep into the rain forest. Tree monkeys and brilliantly colored parrots squawked high overhead, and the tapping of the woodpeckers sounded exactly like distant machine gun fire. Jaguars lurked in the undergrowth, but the main fear for anyone walking along the path was of claymore mines buried underfoot.

The small rebel camp was just a few hundred yards from a peasant hut that marked the border. There were about forty Nicaraguan contras in residence, along with Jesus, the commander, whom they had already met. But, to their surprise, there was another officer at the camp, an American. "Commandante Pedro" had come from Miami, a Cuban-American. Even to Glibbery's critical eye he seemed a thorough professional. Once upon a time he had fought with Che Guevara before changing sides. He had been fighting for twenty-five years, in places as far afield as the Congo.

"Aren't you getting a bit tired of this?" asked Glibbery.

"I'm getting that way," was the reply.

Apart from their small arms the little band had light 60-mm

mortars and rifle grenades. Their heaviest weapons were Russian RPG-7s, light antitank rockets. But Glibbery the former British army regular found the level of basic training shocking. He spent most of his visit cleaning rifles. Although Pedro appeared to know what needed to be done, "he wasn't willing to pass on the professionalism to the other guys," the Nicaraguans.

The group relied for intelligence almost entirely on what the Costa Rican civil guardsmen passed on from their interrogations of the thin stream of refugees crossing the border at Los Chiles. This intelligence tended to be of high quality. A few days after Glibbery arrived at the camp, Pedro showed him a plan he had worked out, based on a fresh report from a Civil Guard sergeant, for an attack on the closest Sandinista position three kilometers away. Glibbery was impressed; the contents of the weapons pits, the number of Sandinista soldiers who slept in each building, even the construction materials of the buildings themselves were all carefully laid out. Twenty contras were sent to carry out the attack. "We cleaned their weapons for them, tested them, and sent them on their merry way." The net effect of this offensive was that the Sandinistas came and mortared the jungle camp for the next two nights, forcing everyone who was left to move back across the border to another site.

Soon thereafter they had a visit from a senior contra. A Dr. Donald Lecayo arrived down the jungle road in a white Range Rover, introducing himself, as Glibbery recalls, as "the main political guy" for the FDN contras in the south. Lecayo told the mercenaries that in Somoza days he had been the lawyer for Coca-Cola in Nicaragua, where his boss had been Adolfo Calero. Calero was now the political leader of the contras and the liaison with the United States. (It subsequently transpired that a considerable portion of the $27 million voted by Congress for humanitarian aid to the contras had passed through the hands of Donald Lecayo and Thelma Lecayo.) Glibbery and the others were left with the impression that Lecayo was a "get-things-done man, which was good."

After a few days more the mercenaries finished up their reports and returned to the ranch, where they found the proprietor pacing his verandah in an angry mood. "We said, 'What's wrong John?' He said, 'That son of a whore, that cocksucker Jesus has fucked up.' " The CIA had earlier sent down six packs of C-4, a powerful U.S. military plastic explosive, to blow up economic targets in Nicaragua. Jesus had been given the mission. But he had idled the time away and not done anything, claiming that he had buried the explosives so he could use them later. Now, as Glibbery recalled, Hull explained, "We're supposed to blow up the power lines in Costa Rica that feed Nicaragua with electricity. And I sent Jesus out to do this job and he comes back three days later, spent all the money I gave him to carry out the operation, and the bastard says he can't remember where he buried the explosives." Hull's suspicion was that Jesus had really sold the explosives and spent three days on the beach with his girlfriend.

Glibbery had come to appreciate who was in charge of the contra operation in this part of the world on both the military and political fronts. "Hull was ordering them to make attacks or not to make attacks. He supplied funds to Lecayo to enable him to run his political operation. Hull didn't go to them, they came to him. He was the boss." The evening after the outburst over the commander's incompetence, however, Glibbery got an inkling of Hull's impressive connections at a much higher level.

There was no phone at the house, but behind the bar on the cool verandah there was a radio hooked up with Hull's office in Ciudad Quesada. When the mercenaries had been there just over a week, the office radioed: "John, there's been a phone call from the United States, very important. They'll ring back in an hour, and you get yourself down here to take the phone call." Hull immediately got in his car to take the call. When he came back he threw his keys down and announced: "That was my friend on the NSC."

"What's the NSC, John?" asked Glibbery.

"Oh, the National Security Council. I've got a friend on the NSC."

Glibbery did not pursue the matter, thinking, "Okay. This guy is a multimillionaire and I'm nobody, I'm a grunt. Whatever he wants to tell me I will listen to, but I'm not going to press him."

The following morning, however, Hull was more expansive on his White House connection. He informed Glibbery that "this guy on the NSC sends ten thousand dollars a month to my bank account in Miami, and God help me if the IRS ever finds out about it because if they do, I'll never be able to explain where the money is coming from."

The Briton has a typically pithy way of explaining Hull's unprompted confidences: "The thing about John Hull is that he only opens his mouth to change feet. He's a pretty talkative guy and he's the wrong guy for the job."

Over the next month of his involvement with the Hull operation Glibbery kept his questions to a minimum. He was busy enough shuttling back and forth between the contra camps and the ranch, filing reports with Hull on the state of contra training. Hull's invariable response was to say, "Well, I've got to go into San José and I'm going to deliver this to my boss." He had made it clear on numerous occasions that "the guy he went to see was CIA, the local CIA man, and the word came back that this guy in San José was quite impressed with the reports we were all writing."

Hull's friend was Joe Fernandez, the CIA chief of station in Costa Rica, who went by the code name of Thomas Castillo. The military professionals' reports being relayed to him by Hull in the spring of 1985 were of special interest to Fernandez. Although Eden Pastora had survived the La Penca bomb attack the previous year, the CIA had abandoned all support of his organization and was instead supporting the new FDN faction, which, as Glibbery had already observed, was taking its orders from John Hull.

As this shift in support had become apparent after La Penca, in the summer of 1984, Pastora had gone to Fernandez to complain that Hull's men had stolen his helicopter and some of his aircraft. Fernandez had cut off the fuming guerrilla, making it very clear that Hull worked for him, for the CIA, and Pastora was on no account to take action against his former supplier. Pastora heeded the warning, although he was still bitter about the theft of his vital air wing. The helicopter had stayed with the CIA in Costa Rica, while the aircraft were withdrawn to El Salvador.

This being the period of the Boland Amendment, such active involvement of a senior CIA official such as Fernandez in contra affairs was of course highly illegal. After Col. Oliver North fell from grace and from his post at the NSC in November 1986, Fernandez was suspended, then fired. It had become embarrassingly clear that throughout Boland the station chief had been busily aiding the weapons pipeline to the contras, and had a direct and secret line of communication with North. The FBI informed the agency that they had found damning communications between Costa Rica and the White House in North's files, which reportedly discussed how much trouble they could find themselves in if their activities became known. Nor could it be argued that Fernandez was operating outside the control and knowledge of the CIA hierarchy, since he had reportedly received clearance for his activities from two senior CIA officials, Alan Fiers, the chief of the Central American Task Force, and Clair George, deputy director for operations—the agency's clandestine branch. Indeed, Fernandez appears to have had official blessing from

34

the very highest levels. On April 23, 1986, Fernandez had attended a meeting at the White House. The other people present had been Oliver North, White House Chief of Staff Donald Regan, National Security Adviser John Poindexter, a Costa Rican security official (and his wife), and President Ronald Reagan.

Glibbery the humble mercenary was never to meet Fernandez, but after a few weeks he discovered that Hull's references to high-level contacts in Washington had not been idle boasting. About three weeks after he arrived, he and his English colleague John Davies were sent down to San José to hand over a list of what was needed at the camp to Dr. Lecayo, the supposed political chief of the southern FDN contras. "We needed mines, we needed M79 grenade launchers. All they had for wounded guys was Tylenol. You got shot and they gave you four Tylenol, so I put down saline, dextrose, battle dressings."

Hull had another job for the Englishmen to do. His orders were, "I want you to pick up this guy from the airport called Robert Owen. Can't miss him. He's about six feet four inches tall, broad guy. And don't tell him I told you this, but he's the FDN's public relations man in Washington."

The lanky Owen seemed genial enough. As Glibbery remembers, they all spent the evening at Hull's house in San José, where Owen passed the time by grilling Dr. Lecayo on whether the FDN contras had been involved in a "fund-raising" bank robbery. Lecayo strenuously denied it.

When they got back to Muelle, Hull's ranch, Owen seemed right at home. Hull's first question to his visitor was, "Any messages?"

They appeared to have a lot to discuss. As Glibbery recalls, "John normally goes to bed at nine o'clock. They were talking until two or three in the morning. I got the impression that Rob Owen was a courier from the United States, bringing down information."

Though the mercenaries were getting a rather different impression, to the world at large at that time Owen was just a PR man who had worked for Grey and Co., the powerful Washington public relations firm favored by powerful Republicans and right-wing foreign regimes, before leaving to open his own firm, I.D.E.A. Inc. I.D.E.A. shortly landed a $50,000 contract from a State Department entity called the Nicaraguan Humanitarian Assistance Office, set up to distribute $27 million appropriated by Congress for the contras. Actually, Owen's real job was as a courier and bagman shuttling back and forth between Washington and Central America with messages and money. The $50,000 contract, according to an NHAO staffer, was "a payoff."

The Saturday after Owen turned up, a little red-and-white Maule aircraft touched down at the strip just a few yards from Hull's house. A pair of contras emerged and reported that an aircraft bringing down arms "from the north" had landed at the wrong strip, and they needed Hull to fly out and guide them to the right place. Glibbery and Owen went along for the ride, the six-foot-four Owen only just managing to squeeze himself in.

After flying for about twenty-five minutes on a course, noted the ever-alert Glibbery, of approximately 290 degrees magnetic, they landed next to a Brittain-Norman Islander aircraft "registration number Xray Charlie, zero zero six." The cargo included a .50-caliber machine gun and pamphlets from the U.S. Army General Warfare School. Glibbery was more interested in the pilot. "There was a Latin in an air force uniform with wings over his left breast, so I sort of spoke quietly and said, 'Where's this guy from?' "

"Oh, he's Salvadoran air force, this [shipment] came down from El Salvador," Owen replied offhandedly. Glibbery reflected that if the Salvadoran air force was providing a pilot to fly an aircraft all the way down to Costa Rica with a shipment of arms, "you kind of get the impression that this is part of the big picture."

Actually, Glibbery was seeing more of the big picture than he knew, for the Maule aircraft on which he had flown out to the arms plane was one of a number of such aircraft purchased by Gen. Richard Secord, beginning about the time that the contras ran out of official CIA aid in the summer of 1984.

Owen's inside knowledge didn't seem to stop at Salvadoran pilots. He and Glibbery chatted about Tom Posey, the jam-jar patriot, with whom Owen appeared to be on friendly terms. They also discussed a Miami Cuban contra named Rene Corvo, who was coming down to take over from Commandante Pedro, who was going on leave. Owen chuckled at the thought. "Rene Corvo's crazy," he told Glibbery. "You'll know what I mean when you meet him."

Soon after this enlightening conversation Owen returned to Washington to report. Thanks to the researches of the Iran-contra committees, we know more about the discussions that kept Hull up long past his bedtime, because Owen immediately wrote up his impressions in a memo to his boss, Oliver North. It was addressed to "The Hammer," one of North's many somewhat theatrical code names, from "TC," Owen's totally apt code name, The Courier.

The subject was "The Southern Front," a project, according to TC, that was riddled with problems. "Lack of leadership" was matched by "lack of coordination between several small groups now operating." The goal was to find an "alternative to Pastora," and Owen was busy vetting every possible candidate. Owen noted that the camp belonging to "the Cubans and Calero's people" was under the day-to-day command of a Nicaraguan named Jesus, but "overall is under the wing of Pape." It is likely Pape was their code name for John Hull or a contra commander under his supervision. According to Owen, Jesus lacked leadership potential. (In view of the episode with the explosives, this may have been an understatement.) Owen added in an update to North a few days later that the core group of the new front would include Donald Lecayo and Fernando ("El Negro") Chamorro as the military commander. El Negro, unfortunately, was a drunk and most of his deputies were corrupt. "The concern about Chamorro is that he drinks a fair amount and may surround himself with people who are in the war not only to fight, but to make money." In addition to this there had been some "past indiscretions" on the part of this standard-bearer of the contra struggle: "drug running" and "sale of goods provided by the USG [the United States government]."

Despite this rather sobering assessment of the troops, Owen managed to close on a brighter note. "Weapons and ammunition can be purchased on the black market to start. AKs [Soviet assault rifles] go for about $300 apiece. . . . Once things get moving they believe material can be either airdropped or flown into small fields. This was done and is still being done to bring supplies into Pastora and the other groups. There are strips big enough to land a DC-3 on." "Pape," wrote Owen, "has broken down the camp that was under him into four small camps and thus spread the men around. He is waiting for equipment to start coming in from El Salvador. Morale is good and the men will start working in small teams."

Such a comprehensive view of the "big picture" was more than the attentive Glibbery, and even perhaps the Special Forces leaker in Honduras, had available. But Glibbery had already seen and heard enough to know more than was good for him. He was about to be joined by someone with his own quota of dangerous knowledge.

Chapter Three
THE PIPELINE

"Everybody's covering their tracks; but there are a few things they can't explain away."

—Steven Carr
June 1986

Peter Glibbery certainly knew a lot more about the total involvement of Hull, the American embassy in Costa Rica, and certain parties in Washington in the contra's southern front than did the Congress. As far as Congress was concerned, no one from the CIA or any other government agency was allowed to lend military support to the contras, be it money, training facilities, or arms. But Congress was being ignored without much difficulty in view of the lack of diligence of the so-called oversight committees. The arms were flowing down the pipeline, and Steven Carr came along with them.

Carr was the son of an IBM executive, though his home life was far from ideal. His parents were divorced, he had a blind sister, and his older brother had come back traumatized from Vietnam. Steven joined the army himself (post Vietnam), but was discharged for drinking too much and taking drugs. He settled down to studying carpentry, dealing cocaine, and getting into trouble—he forged several of his mother's checks and then, much to their surprise, turned himself in to the local police in Naples, Florida. He was fair, with a slight build and a sharp sense of humor that quickly degenerated into cynicism. On his left shoulder there was a tattoo, a skull with a dagger in its mouth surrounded by red flames. It said, "USMC Death Before Dishonor," though Carr had never been a marine.

Before he came to Central America, Carr had sported his own brand of idealism. He wanted to fight in a war and was determined to find one, whether through the French foreign legion, the South African army, or the contras. "I was too young to go to Vietnam," he said, "and I know that probably sounds crazy. My brother went to Vietnam; I was raised on John Wayne movies. I wanted to be in combat, to see it, you know: 'Am I going to run away? What am I going to do? Freeze up?' I guess many people have said that for many different wars. . . . It meant that much for me to find out about me."

In 1984 Carr made a trip to Costa Rica. He hoped to find someone who could give him entrée into the tight-knit world of the contras and their supply network. He found the right man.

Bruce Jones was ostensibly just a landowner, another good old boy transplanted to northern Costa Rica like his friend, neighbor, and business partner John Hull. Unfortunately for him, Jones was even more talkative about his contra activities than Hull. When he was featured in a *Life* magazine spread entitled "A CIA Man in Costa Rica," with full-color glossy photos of Jones fording the San Juan River with the fighters, the Costa Rican government felt obliged to deport him. His friend Hull always valiantly tried to maintain that the photo was faked and that Jones had in fact simply been kneeling in a creek no deeper than a bathtub.

However, before Jones indulged himself with the photographer and got thrown out of the country, he had had enough time to introduce Steven Carr to the right people.

Carr returned to Miami armed with introductions, and moved into the Howard Johnson's across from the Miami airport—the one with the guerrilla rate. He spent two months there, meeting people in the network and collecting supplies, including heavy weapons, from various depots around Miami.

The men in charge were Miami Cubans, full-fledged members of Brigade 2506, the organization founded by veterans of the Bay of Pigs invasion force. Brigade members have never forgiven President Kennedy for what they regard as his betrayal in not committing U.S. military might to their aid on the beach all those years ago. Their ties with the CIA have, however, always remained close since the days when the agency put together the Bay of Pigs invasion force, then the JM/Wave assassination program, and then the hit-and-run program of Operation Mongoose, all failed attempts to unseat or eliminate Fidel Castro.

"The 2506 Brigade got the rooms [for just seventeen dollars a night, of course]. We never paid for it," Carr explained. "2506 picked up the tab. Everybody knew what we were doing in that hotel, everybody. We were in the bar every night getting trashed out, Bruce Jones running around with his *Life* magazine, shouting, 'Brooke on the outside, Bruce on the inside.' "

The brigade was not just a collection of wilted middle-aged Miami businessmen with paunches, elegant wives, and a sense of civic duty. They maintained a paramilitary wing. Its members were young and they were actively training in south Florida to fight in Central America. The anticommunist fervor passing from father to son in the Miami Cuban community would make Jesse Helms blush.

In early March 1985 Steven Carr and several others collected six tons of weapons from safe houses in Miami. The man in charge of the operation was Rene ("Renecito") Corvo, a wiry Miami Cuban in his thirties who was widely thought to have CIA protection and had earned the nickname of the Poison Dwarf. The man who supplied the bulk of the weapons, according to Carr and at least one other participant in the operation, was Francisco ("Paco") Chanes, a loyal brigade supporter who was in the shrimp-importing business. He was widely alleged to handle other imports as well, and when Carr went to the Chanes house to pick up a load of weapons, he saw something that would later come back to haunt him: three kilos of cocaine. "Chanes controlled the money," according to Carr.

Corvo too had a respectable stash of weapons. Carr later confided to Glibbery that "Corvo took Carr to his mother and father's house in a panel van. The back bedroom was stacked with arms— sixty-millimeter mortars, a box of G-3 rifles, and apparently a box of M60s. Nine M16 rifles, a fifty-caliber machine gun. They went through to the garage and there was a twelve- or fourteen-foot-long twenty-millimeter cannon, complete with rounds." According to an FBI file on the shipment, the cannon came with 150 rounds of ammunition, and the mortars were packed with 80 to 100 rounds each.

In Carr's view the 2506 must have had a heavyweight source for this arsenal, not just a local gun merchant who drilled out serial numbers. "If you really look hard maybe you can get an AK. You're not going to get a cannon and mortars on the street, and certainly not in a consistent supply like they were."

40

Once the crates were loaded up in vans, the convoy headed for Fort Lauderdale, where, according to customs records, Corvo paid fifteen thousand dollars for a charter from a company called Florida Air Transport. When the time came to depart from Fort Lauderdale, the pilot was ready on the apron with engines running when Carr drove up in the panel van. They opened the back doors and loaded all the weapons. Carr later reported that he had seen Corvo paying the pilot eight thousand dollars for the trip. The destination was Ilopango military air base in El Salvador just outside the capital. Carr was aboard, taking the next step in his search for combat. Also aboard were Rene Corvo and Robert Thompson, a man who affected mirrored Rayban sunglasses and cowboy hats and who portentously announced himself as having been a "state trooper, chief of police, and criminal investigator for the state attorney's office in Orange County, Ninth Judicial Circuit, State of Florida."

Carr was fully aware of the implications of a plane heavily laden with arms leaving Fort Lauderdale with no questions asked and arriving at a heavily guarded military base, full of American military, with, again, no questions asked. He was reassured by the American military presence at Ilopango. "There were seven American air force personnel watching the whole scene of unloading into trucks from the plane our twenty-millimeter cannon, fifty-caliber machine guns, mortars, high explosives, medical equipment, uniforms, boots. They witnessed the whole thing and didn't say a word, like it happened every day. Somebody had to arrange it. I was very surprised; I thought we were going to land at a dirt strip and be sneaky about it. Not these guys, they were right aboveboard. 'We're doing this, and aren't we great about doing it!' "

The party was greeted by the base commander himself. Corvo introduced them all, watched by the incurious U.S. Air Force personnel.

A year later, in the spring of 1986, the U.S. embassy in Costa Rica was asked to comment on Carr's assertion that there was an active arms supply route for the contras through Ilopango. The blunt reply was that Carr had fabricated the story, which was a "fantasy." When they were asked for evidence to back up their dismissal of Carr's detailed allegations, the embassy stiffly replied that they were unable to discuss intelligence operations. In the fall of 1986, however, Eugene Hasenfus told the story again, and as he had just been shot down with a planeload of arms deep in Nicaragua, it was impossible to dismiss his admissions as fantasy.

Carr was billeted with the family of a Salvadoran air force officer. They waited for a week in El Salvador before moving on to Costa Rica. The original plan had been to ride down with the aircraft bringing the arms and land covertly in Costa Rica, but instead they flew commercial, landing at San José airport with all their personal military gear.

Once in Costa Rica, Carr was introduced to Hull, who imparted the customary confidence that he was the CIA-FDN liaison in the country. Hull demanded Carr's and Thompson's military service serial numbers "to verify with the CIA who we were, to make sure that we weren't communists trying to infiltrate their movement."

The arrival of Corvo produced a brief argument in Hull's contra command. Corvo, with the credentials of Brigade 2506 and his reputation as a CIA operative, considered it his prerogative to take over operations at the camp maintained by Hull just inside Nicaragua. He had, after all, marshaled the supply of weapons down to the camps.

"They were having a power struggle, who was going to be commander," recalled Glibbery later. "Hull said, 'I want Jesus to be the commander; he's the FDN guy sent down from the north,' and Corvo was saying, 'No, I'm the commander and these are my people. We started this camp; you're just feeding them.' " To which Hull rather tartly replied, "You're right, if I hadn't been feeding them for three months they'd all be starved by now."

The pile of new equipment in the weapons tent that Corvo had supplied resolved their differences. Glibbery was delighted, although he was skeptical of the military credentials of the new arrivals, Carr, Thompson, and the Miami Cuban.

Back in Miami there were in fact quite a few people who were skeptical about this particular Cuban. Robert Owen may have chuckled about Corvo's being "crazy," but in Miami districts like Hialeah there were those who were less indulgent, even in houses where an automatic weapon was as common as fitted plastic covers on the sofa. At least one legitimate organization raising money for genuine humanitarian aid for the contras had cut its ties with Corvo, who its members believed stole money and dabbled too often in the cocaine business. One couple heavily involved in contra support, Hilda and Joe Coutin, claimed that Corvo and his wife had threatened to kill them for making disparaging remarks about his activities.

The Coutins were running the Broadway Boutique at the time, a Miami fashion shop with a unique inventory: ladies' clothing in the front, weapons and military gear in the back. Carr and Thompson had shopped there before heading south, and Tom Posey was a friend. Joe Coutin had been the post commander of the Cuban Legion when Corvo had turned up soliciting funds for the families of Cubans off to fight for freedom in Central America. The legion members initially gave generously, until they decided to send a couple of members down to Costa Rica to check on Corvo's progress. The two returned with dismal tales of involvement with drug smugglers, not to mention the fact that legion money was being squandered on women and "Bavarian beer" in San José. As Hilda virtuously puts it, "All those nice people that believed in freedom, and really believed in the freedom fighters, felt used."

Once Coutin-Corvo relations were severed, the Coutins started to receive bloodcurdling threats from the wayward former recipient of their charity "because Corvo knows very well that my husband and the people from the Cuban Legion know too much about their activities in Costa Rica."

As it so happened, the Coutins had a career on the side as FBI informants, and Hilda reported to the bureau what was going on. Nothing happened, the FBI's response to Hilda on the subject of Corvo being that "he is wanted by the FBI and even by the authorities from Costa Rica." Yet Corvo was shuttling freely between Miami and the contra camps in Costa Rica. As Hilda surmised, "I don't really think the FBI want him that much, or if they do, someone is trying to hide something."

Meanwhile, back at the ranch, Corvo had asserted his authority over the contra contingent and was now anxious to launch an attack on the Sandinistas. According to Glibbery, Hull tried to dissuade Corvo from making the raid. "Hull told him not to do it because of an upcoming vote in Congress. He told him the publicity would be bad [should any of the Americans get killed] and [would] blow the chances of forty million dollars." Corvo pretended to agree, and then went ahead anyway.

Among the twenty contras or so who followed their leader into action were the newly arrived Americans, Robert Thompson, the former highway patrolman, and Steven Carr, who was at last about to fulfill his dream of going into combat. They were headed for a Sandinista outpost called La Esperanza.

When Carr got back he looked, according to Glibbery, "like

death warmed over." All he would say initially was that "we shot up the place," but he had discovered that war is not a bit like a John Wayne movie.

Immediately after the attack (in which, according to various reports, between thirty and seventy soldiers and civilians were killed) the gallant Corvo had dashed for home with only half his force, leaving the rest, including Carr and a wounded man, still inside Nicaragua. The exhausted Carr told Glibbery that it had taken him "fifteen to sixteen hours to get out, by which time Corvo and his group were just finishing the food that the Costa Rican Civil Guard had provided for the entire raiding party."

Corvo's cheerful greeting to the stragglers was, "Hi, what took you so long?" which did not increase his popularity. Just then a Costa Rican came by to tell them that they had better move away from the border because there were two hundred Sandinistas in hot pursuit. They had to cross the Río Frío to get away and, as Glibbery recalls, "the first man on the boat wasn't the wounded man; it was Rene Corvo, leaving Carr and the wounded man to be the last men back across the river, which left a slightly pissed-off Carr even more fuming."

Safe on Costa Rican soil, the group made their way to the border post at Los Chiles and telephoned an extremely agitated Hull. His first question to Thompson was, "Are you guys [the two Americans] okay? Is either of you wounded? . . . Shit, we got a report from the CIA that one of you had been killed inside Nicaragua." (Hull was so sensitive to the presence of the two Americans that he would never allow them to sleep at the ranch, dispatching them to his office in Ciudad Quesada every night.) Fortunately for the enterprise, there were no dead Americans left inside Nicaragua that day.

By now Carr was rapidly losing his earlier illusions about the operation: "Corvo came down and he wanted to do something because they're big on the macho image. He was gonna say, 'I attacked here, I did this.' So he was in a hurry to go get his attack off and then go home and brag about it."

Nor was he impressed by the sluggish day-to-day routine of the war: "They moved the camp around occasionally; we'd pack up all our stuff and move about two kilometers down the road, then they'd send over a couple of mortars which were totally ineffective [although] the contras knew exactly where the Sandinistas were. See, the commanders are still going to get paid. The refugees are still going to get fed, and it's either they're sitting around in a refugee depot and get fed or they run around with a weapon and they feel like they're really going to do something. [But] when it comes down to going on patrol, you wouldn't believe how many people would say, 'I'm feeling bad.' "

By the time Carr's contra career came to an end with his arrest by the Costa Ricans he had seen enough to convince him that the American dollars sustaining the war had been squandered: "They're throwing their money away by giving it to a lot of FDN commanders, because they are all theives—they're selling dreams, and they're getting the money for it, but they're keeping it. It's sticking right in their pockets." He had some sympathy for the foot soldiers. "They wanted leadership, and they weren't getting any leadership from their commanders, from the FDN. The commanders fight among themselves [about] who's going to steal the biggest amount of money this month: 'Well, I need a few tires on my brand-new Range Rover.' "

The number of weapons out of the six tons that he had brought down from Florida that actually made it into the field further fueled his suspicions about the profit aspect of the war. "My feeling is that a lot of things were getting lost in the shuffle and were being sold privately."

Carr's worm's-eye conclusions were shared and confirmed by others far away. Robert Owen, who had his own tincture of idealism, lamented to Oliver North in a 1986 memo that the contra leaders regarded the war "as a business." Even Congress sometimes got the point. When the House Subcommittee on Western Hemisphere Affairs and the General Accounting Office attempted in the spring of 1986 to audit the $27 million awarded by Congress to the contras in late 1985 for humanitarian assistance, they found that two-thirds of the money had vanished, much of it into bank accounts in the Cayman Islands. Of the money the investigators could track, very little went to buy battle dressings and the like. Miami condo associations, fashion shops, Visa card accounts, and Israeli bank account numbers filled the pages of the subpoened bank records. Nevertheless, such evidence of corrupt mismanagement did not stop Congress from pledging $100 million more of the taxpayers' money. Meanwhile, former contras were complaining of a flourishing black market in contra arms, some of which were being sold to the leftist guerrillas in El Salvador. Since President Reagan had for years justified his support of the contras—in public at least—on the grounds of stopping Sandinista support for the Salvadoran rebels, this was ironic indeed.

*   *   *

Carr and Glibbery took their dangerous knowledge with them when they and the other mercenaries were carried off at the end of April 1985 by Colonel Badilla to La Reforma prison in San José. Badilla told no one of his plan. He was acting, so he later told reporters, on the direct orders of the interior minister, a member of the neutralist faction in the government at that time.

Once Hull's former military trainers began to talk, which they did after three months behind bars, Hull knew he had a problem. During repeated visits to the prison he attempted to extract statements from the prisoners that would state that every word of their incriminating stories had been fabricated for money at the behest of either journalists or foreign intelligence agents. In return for this concession he offered a supply of edible food and the promise of a quick release. Glibbery steadfastly refused, though the offer certainly looked appealing from his side of the bars. Carr, after he had spoken to what he calculated as seventy journalists, eventually caved in and signed a statement retracting his entire story. As he later told CBS News, "I did it for a basket of food." Despite Glibbery's obduracy he too was eventually freed on bail. By May of 1986 the mercenaries' story had reached the ears of a U.S. senator (John Kerry), whose office was beginning to ask questions. It appears that Hull thought a unilateral gesture—a thousand dollars in bond money for all five prisoners—might win Glibbery's favor, and silence. Glibbery, however, though glad to be free, was in no mood to shut up.

To anyone who came to ask for his comment on the prisoners' tales, Hull portrayed his relationship with the mercenaries as innocent, well-meaning hospitality. In June 1986, sitting on his cool tile verandah with his diminutive sidekick Alvaro hovering nearby and a bodyguard or two in the wings, the master of Muelle emphatically denied that any of the events as described by Carr and Glibbery had ever taken place. He did admit having met the mercenaries: "They came through here on their way. We talked to them. They stayed overnight. They had breakfast here, and they wanted to know where to go and which road to take to get to the northern border. I know that they were going to train anticommunist forces because that's what they told me they were going to do and I assumed they were telling the truth. As far as I'm concerned, they're welcome. If they got shot, I'd be glad to take them back through here to get them medical attention, to get wounded people in here and get them to the hospital. And I've never made any secret of that. It's been absolutely open."

There was the awkward matter of Hull's having posted bond for the prisoners, including Glibbery. His explanation for having bailed out a group of mercenaries he had met casually seemed a trifle thin: "It was a humanitarian gesture," all part of the humanitarian efforts for the contra cause made by this "transplanted Indiana boy."

Hull insisted that he had no role whatsoever in any NSC/CIA operation: "I'm a rancher, a farmer and absolutely nothing else. Our efforts have been strictly humanitarian. We've tried to help the people. I set up a program where we gave twenty thousand pairs of glasses to underprivileged Costa Ricans. I have sent a child to the States for an open-heart surgery that was dying." So far as the contras were concerned, he had no involvement, only opinions: "Ask any Nicaraguan anywhere and he'll tell you today that it was a thousand times better under Somoza than it is under the present dictatorship of the left."

His opinions on his talkative pair of ex-employees (Carr had retracted his signed statement) were equally pronounced. Carr and Glibbery were paid liars, and their paymasters were the communists. "This is a communist disinformation campaign to try to smear the reputation of the CIA, to try to smear the reputation of our own government," he proffered. "As far as I'm concerned, there are communists here. As far as I'm concerned, there are communists in our own government. There are communists everywhere."

While Hull delivered this succinct political analysis he had at his side Robert Thompson, the former Florida police officer, one of the jailed mercenaries who had not betrayed him by going public. Sipping a cool *fresca* in the brutal heat, Thompson stoutly maintained that he was not a mercenary at all, merely an aspiring journalist. While making the rounds of Hull's property, he carried Hull's gun.

The problem for Hull was and continues to be that there are too many people around, not to mention documents, that confirm and supplement the detailed recollections of Carr and Glibbery. As a result he had had to gradually modify his initial indignant denials of extrahumanitarian involvement. In the spring of 1987, for example, he finally admitted to receiving arms and running contra camps. By summer 1987 he had admitted that he was indeed a former CIA operative.

According to Eden Pastora, the contra commandante who was

gradually frozen out of the southern front (with added impetus from the La Penca bomb), Hull was overly modest. He had been very important in Pastora's war effort while the commandante still enjoyed the patronage of the CIA. Hull had stored and transported weapons for Pastora's forces. Pastora had used Hull's farms for his camps. Hull had taken delivery of arms shipments for Pastora at his ranch—"the largest part came from the CIA, arms that were brought from Miami." These shipments were by no means isolated gestures of goodwill. The arrangement lasted, said Pastora, "for years." After La Penca, when Pastora was in a state of some irritation with Hull, the CIA station chief had warned him not to touch Hull, as Pastora recalled, because Hull was CIA and was indeed "responsible for the CIA in northern Costa Rica."

Pastora remembered the role of the Poison Dwarf, Rene Corvo, along with another Miami Cuban, named Felipe Vidal, in arranging the arms shipments from Miami.

Vidal, who operated under the code name of Morgan, had been with Hull on the first encounter with Glibbery and Davies in the Howard Johnson's in Miami. On the Brigade 2506 posters plastered around Miami featuring a group shot of brigade members taken in a Nicaraguan jungle, Vidal was center stage, just below Rene Corvo. Vidal used to describe how his father had taken part in the Bay of Pigs operation and had been executed by Castro. Glibbery and Carr had also encountered him at the camps, where he was a frequent visitor. Carr used to refer to him as "Hull's pet bulldog." Glibbery considered him affable enough, "until you know what he does for a living," something Glibbery found out when he found a powerful crossbow in a cupboard at Hull's place in San José. Hull said it belonged to Vidal, explaining, "I think he's a hit man." Some in Miami had the same impression, rumoring that his price for a hit was ten thousand dollars. He may have other lines of business, since he has been arrested at least seven times in Miami on drug and gun charges, all of which were apparently dropped.

This is not to say, however, that Vidal is a rogue elephant. "He works for the CIA," says Pastora matter-of-factly. "One time we captured him and he started screaming that he was from the CIA." This might have been a convenient appeal by a man about to be shot, except that many others well versed in the murky world of contra-CIA politics confirm the claim. Vidal's connections appear even higher. Just as the worlds of Georgetown and Cuban Hialeah commingle in the persons of Robert Owen and Rene Corvo, so too does the sinister Vidal have his connections in the respectable corridors of the State Department.

Vidal and Owen have been accused of working together to divert substantial sums from the much pillaged funds of the Nicaraguan Humanitarian Assistance Office. A clerk who worked for Creaciones Fancy, a San José store, has identified Owen as having picked up a fraudulent receipt for fifteen thousand dollars' worth of uniforms and boots in 1986 (items considered humanitarian by Congress), which would thus provide a cover to spend fifteen thousand dollars on something else. Franklin Reed, a member of a small Costa Rican–based contra faction, claimed Vidal used these funds to buy weapons to lure fighters away from the crumbling campaign of Eden Pastora. The FBI opened an investigation of the diversion, with no discernible result.

Pastora is emphatic that it was Vidal, along with Corvo and Hull, who "robbed our helicopter" and "promoted desertions among our comrades in order to destroy us militarily because we didn't want to be CIA soldiers."

This sabotage, the commandante assumed, was coordinated in Washington. Six months before the world learned to appreciate the central role of Oliver North in executing U.S. foreign policy, Pastora was complaining that "everything that has happened to us moves around Oliver North. It's a gratuitous hate. We can't explain why."

Hull used to claim that he had never met Oliver North—"I understand that he's a fine young man." North, even while still in office, was less circumspect. When asked whether he had called Hull in late March 1985 (a reference to the NSC call that caused Hull to drive into town as noted by the observant Glibbery), North said simply, "I'll have to check my diary."

When the staff of the Tower Commission got around to checking North's diary they discovered that in fact North had had several meetings with Hull, along with Robert Owen and other lieutenants of the National Security Council's secret network. Likewise the Owen memos turned up by the congressional Iran-contra committees discredited the vehement denials of anything more than a passing friendship with the young PR man that Hull had maintained back in 1986 when he said he had "no idea who the fellow works for. We were friends, we met a few times and that's all there is to it." By May of 1987 Robert Owen was reading to the committees doggerel dedicated to his hero—"The knowledge that on this troubled earth there still walk men like Ollie North . . . In our lifetime you have given us a legend"—for which Hull speedily claimed authorship.

Given this record of veracity, it is interesting to note Hull's professed lack of connection with the likes of Corvo and Vidal: "I have met Rene Corvo, I might have met him twice. . . . He came into my office when he had a court trial here in Ciudad Quesada. We sat around the office for an hour or two just chatting. But I have no connection with Rene Corvo. I have no connection with the drug business." The part about Corvo's court trial is true; he was tried for pistol-whipping a Costa Rican underling in a bar in Los Chiles after the La Esperanza raid. Hull's explanation for Corvo's choice of his office as a place to relax rather than a restaurant or café was, "It's cheaper there. He can sit there free."

Likewise, Hull had met Vidal, but just, so he claimed, as a fighter passing through. He had also had a brief encounter with Tom Posey of Civilian Military Assistance. "I did tell Tom that if he had any people that were wounded or sick, this place was open for humanitarian reasons."

The most vehement denials of all are of course reserved for anything to do with Carr and Glibbery. They maintained that Hull had brought up the subject of his bank account in Miami and how it was used to funnel money from the NSC. Hull stated in response that he had no Miami account. Carr, however, had once received a small birthday check from his father. He had cashed it with Hull, who deposited the check in his Miami account at Marine Midland International. When a top Florida private investigator questioned the bank about this account he was told that bank employees had been instructed not to give out information on this account.

Asked why he had paid for part of Glibbery's ticket to Costa Rica with his Gold Card, Hull quickly denied ever having possessed an American Express card, but airline records show that indeed he had paid for the ticket. Asked about his stays at the Howard Johnson's motel at the Miami airport, Hull hedged at first, claiming that he did not know Miami well and could not remember where he stayed. He then conceded that perhaps he did stay at the Howard Johnson's. "If it's the place where we usually go, which I assume it is, I think we stayed there two times in the last four, five years."

* * *

Early in 1986 two FBI agents turned up at La Reforma prison to have Glibbery and Carr tell their story. Kevin Currier and George Kiszynski were treated to a full account of the gunrunning, illegal arming and training of the contras, stories of Americans fighting inside Nicaragua, and the evidence of White House participation. Currier and Kiszynski were joined by Jeffrey D. Feldman, the assistant U.S. attorney for Miami.

Feldman, by Carr's account, had chosen to play rough. He opened the conversation by shoving a piece of paper at the young American, who had now been behind bars for a year, with the brusque instruction to "sign this."

"I said, 'What is it?'

" 'This acknowledges that you were read your rights and that you don't want an attorney present.'

" 'No, I want to talk to a lawyer before I talk to you guys.'

" 'I didn't come two thousand miles and waste all this money and time to have you tell me this.' He badgered me into a corner, basically saying, 'If you don't talk to me now, you're screwed, buddy.' "

Carr was reluctant to incriminate himself with details of the arms shipment and the raid on La Esperanza. In a letter to his brother from prison, Carr said he had heard on the radio that upwards of seventy Nicaraguans had been killed. But when Feldman "blew up" and theatened Carr with federal prison, Carr gave in; as he stated later, "I told him everything."

Feldman had a copy of the Costa Rican arrest sheet. "What is on this that you know was on the plane?" he demanded.

"Well, the sniper rifles, the sixty-millimeter mortar, the flak jackets." Feldman marked the items in yellow with his highlighter. "All you have to do is get the weapons, check the serial numbers, and you've got Miami right there. And you've got Tom Posey for the .308 sniper rifle."

Feldman seemed particularly interested in John Hull. "I told him about the NSC," Carr recalled, "you know, the money, and his friend, and the FDN and how he was manipulating everything. [How] John Hull told us he was the CIA liaison and the FDN liaison and—hah, hah—he can't trust the Nicaraguans with the money." Feldman threw down a piece of paper and asked Carr to draw Hull's ranch house. "I was a carpenter; I can draw floor plans. I drew him a floor plan of [the] house. And he was kind of upset about that, you know. I didn't understand it." For further proof, Carr directed Feldman to the prison visitors' books where John Hull had been obliged to sign in on his frequent visits to talk Carr into shutting up. "This is the same John Hull that's been saying he doesn't know us. So why is he visiting us?"

Feldman seemed disturbed when given the bloody details of the La Esperanza raid in Nicaragua. "He's cussing like a marine: 'You killed people?'

"'Yeah.' I'm looking at the guy, going, 'Oh my God. If I have to go in front of this guy in a Miami courtroom I'm really screwed.'"

After Carr spilled the whole story, he pressed this assistant U.S. attorney on why he was so aggressively gathering up the evidence. Feldman explained that there was an "ongoing investigation."

"He told me he was after the guns, the drugs, and John Hull."

Chapter Four
MIAMI, CUBA

"I would say that Miami is more of a threat to the United States than Nicaragua."

—Edgar Chamorro
June 1986

B y the mid-1980s Miami had shed its image as a sunbaked purgatory for aging retirees. Money was pouring into this faded retreat with its peeling deco buildings and package-tour hotels. It was Latin money, for Miami was fast becoming the capital of Latin America, and an increasingly sophisticated and dangerous city. Behind the glistening facades of the new skyscrapers shooting up lay Casablanca. The exiles who flocked there hailed from every political faction of every political conflict in Central and South America, and the former dictators and their generals kept company with arms merchants and druglords. These immigrants, whether active or retired in their various lines of business, brought billions of dollars into the local banks.

The pillars of the Latin community were and are the Cubans, who have regarded the place as a surrogate Havana ever since they abandoned the real thing to Fidel Castro. Spanish has overtaken English as the language of the city, and Cuban entrepreneurial energy is matched only by the kick of the elegant little cups of Cuban coffee that are a staple in every Cuban neighborhood.

The hatred in this community for Castro, and by extension all leftist revolutionaries, made it easy for the community to identify with and support the Nicaraguans who arrived after the fall of Somoza. The businessmen and bankers who made up the core of the contra leadership made Miami their headquarters. The Cubans, who saw the struggle in Nicaragua as a prelude to their own return to Havana, were their natural benefactors. The events surrounding the Bay of Pigs, the last attempt at a Cuban contra war, had taken on mythic proportions in the community, and Nicaragua had played a part in that epic by providing the embarkation point (under prodding from Washington) for the abortive invasion. Somoza himself had waved Brigade 2506 off from the dock, asking them to bring him back a hair from Castro's beard. Now that Castro had literally embraced the nine commandantes who made up the Sandinista leadership in Managua, the exiles shared an enemy that blurred into one.

While waiting to return to their respective Jerusalems, they settled down to the business of making money. Two lucrative trades fueled by the volatile situation in Central America provided plenty of opportunities: drugs and arms. As it became as easy to order a machine gun as a cigar, Brickell Avenue, with its towering buildings each more fantastic than the next, became known as "the avenue cocaine built." Laundered money that traveled from Miami to the Caymans or the Bahamas and back took shape as condo developments. Any attempt at law enforcement in this environment was hampered by the amount of cash available for million-dollar bribes.

Given its atmosphere, inmates, and location, it is not surprising that Miami has become a focal point for the murky world of covert operations. Even the innocent traveler flying into the Miami airport can catch a glimpse of this aspect of local life. Off to the side of the main runways, well away from the passenger terminals, is a motley collection of aircraft hangars and cinder-block offices known locally as Corrosion Corner because of the somewhat aging DC-3s and DC-6s parked on the tarmac in front. The planes often carry no company markings, and an alert observer might note the frequency with which the tail numbers get changed. This is the home of companies like Southern Air Transport, Conner Air, and Vortex, carriers of strange cargoes to strange places.

The CIA has always retained close ties to the Cuban community, even after efforts to destabilize Castro and his regime by sabotage or assassination had been discontinued. The Cuban community has served as a resource pool for agency operations from the Congo to

Vietnam. In the 1980s they had become the "Unilaterally Controlled Latino Assets," as the CIA put it, for the war in Nicaragua. Members of Brigade 2506 and its offshoots were proud of their agency ties and considered their involvement in this covert war an especially patriotic service. When an operation was afoot, word passed amazingly quickly on the street, and every true-blooded member of the brigade, from bank presidents to doormen, was ready to play his part.

Jesus Garcia was neither a bank president nor a doorman, but as an officer in the Dade County jail he was as willing as any to do his bit for the Company and the cause. He was to discover, however, that the CIA and the U.S. government do not always repay the loyalties of trusting souls.

Until the summer of 1985 Garcia was a typical enough Miami Cuban. Built like a middleweight fighter, he had served as a prison officer with an unblemished eleven-year record after he completed an army tour in Vietnam. The Garcias and their three daughters lived in a modest walk-up in Hialeah, and were as devoted to "the cause" as any of their Cuban neighbors.

Garcia was the booker at the Dade County jail, which meant that he became acquainted with scores of people in the underworld. He had become a walking data bank, knowing who could forge papers, who could commandeer a helicopter, who could tap a bank account in the Caymans. Among those who crossed his professional path were some who might be criminals by conventional standards, but who fit differently into the context of Miami society. A cocaine dealer who had contributed funds to anti-Castro or anti-Sandinista resistance charities, for example, was entitled to respect when booked at the Dade County jail. A gun merchant who had smuggled a few weapons to the freedom fighters deserved good treatment; a drug pilot who had actually flown them south was held in high esteem.

When Garcia booked Tom Posey of Civilian Military Assistance for carrying a concealed weapon at the airport, he knew he had a celebrity on his hands. "I understood he was a freedom fighter; I had remembered him from *Nightline*, Ted Koppel. So instead of putting him in a cell like everybody else, I put him in a room and treated him special."

Posey was out within hours, but the Cuban prison guard and the Alabama mercenary stayed in touch. They had mutual friends in the

Cuban community and Garcia offered his services should the freedom fighter ever need an extra hand. By and by Posey did need an extra hand. "We got together and he introduced me to several people."

It was February 1985, and the airport Howard Johnson's was overflowing with guests registered at the guerrilla rate, Steven Carr, Robert Thompson, and Bruce Jones among them. Although their links with Brigade 2506 were through senior men, Rene Corvo and Francisco Chanes, they were happy to sign on Jesus Garcia to help them gather and load the weapons that were due to be flown out of Fort Lauderdale on March 6.

Garcia was much less happy with a more unorthodox operation that he says was then under discussion by Posey, Corvo, Jones, and others.

"They came to me with a plan to hit the American embassy in Costa Rica. They had an idea this would start a war between Nicaragua and the United States."

Had the target been a Cuban embassy or a Sandinista official, Garcia would probably have obliged. But the plan as unfolded over drinks at the Howard Johnson's gave Jesus grave forebodings over the potential death toll in such an attack. He could certainly understand the logic behind it, particularly later on, when he read that the U.S. ambassador in Managua had warned the Sandinista government that any incident at an American embassy in the region would compel the United States to take action.

Even while he says he was being shown a detailed plan of the San José embassy by Posey and being told about the C-4 explosives stored in a room upstairs, Garcia felt sure that this bizarre plot must have had some sort of high-level clearance. "The embassy plan was blessed from the White House. There were too many big people involved in this. In order to hit a U.S. embassy even us Cubans who are here in Miami would normally out of courtesy notify the CIA."

The plan had a yet more Byzantine twist, for it included the assassination of the ambassador himself, Lewis Tambs. Tambs was to be transferred to Costa Rica from Colombia in July, and the announcement had already appeared in the press. Tambs had caused grave irritation to the leading lights of the Colombian cocaine business by what they regarded as his overly enthusiastic attitude toward cleaning up the trade. One of the two major drug families in Colombia, the Ochoas, had accordingly placed a million-dollar bounty on the diplomat's head. The Howard Johnson's clique and their confederates planned to serve the higher purposes of U.S. foreign policy and the somewhat more mundane concerns of the Ochoas in one fell swoop.

Garcia had no trouble believing in this aspect of the plot either; he had considerable knowledge of the operating procedures of the Colombians from his prison duties. However, he wanted no part of it. He would restrict his contribution to the more mundane task of helping with the arms shipment.

Thus it was that Garcia, along with Steven Carr, went to the house of Francisco Chanes, a proprietor of Mr. Shrimp and Ocean Hunter, two companies officially engaged in importing shrimp from Costa Rica. At Chanes's house Garcia, like Steven Carr, saw three kilos of cocaine.

Once the weapons had all been accumulated, as Garcia recounts it, the community celebrated. Such a party, it is fair to say, could only happen in Miami. It took the form of a picnic at the paramilitary training ground used by Brigade 2506: "We got together on a Sunday for a party. The arms were gathered, the plan was going to be set in motion, and all of us just celebrated that day. You had Nicaraguan [contra] leaders there, you had Miskito [contra] leaders, you had Cuban leaders." Cuban girls in rainbow chiffon dresses danced to scratchy music. Young brigade soldiers in fatigues sprinted through training exercises in the background, looking for all the world like a photo opportunity at a contra base in Honduras. The elders of the community moved through the crowds exchanging greetings and making deals while their wives tended the buffets of Cuban delicacies. It was the synthesis of Miami society and the war.

After Jesus Garcia saw Rene Corvo and his assistants Steven Carr and Robert Thompson set off for Fort Lauderdale with the arms shipment on March 6, 1985, he returned to his humdrum tasks at the jail. He heard nothing from his mercenary friends for the next four months. Then, on July 21, he got a call from Tom Posey.

Posey wanted to know if Garcia had a valid passport, because he had "work" for him in Central America. Later that day Joe Coutin, the Cuban Legionnaire and FBI informant, called. Garcia knew him as "Tom Posey's right-hand man" in Miami. Coutin told Garcia to go out and get a Mac 10, a small but deadly rapid-fire submachine gun, and a silencer. Garcia thought this a reasonable enough request, particularly because he knew that Coutin was working with Posey and was considered a freedom fighter. "I felt there might be a tie with intelligence. Although no one ever said that he was Central

Intelligence, there must be some tie." As Garcia remembers, he was told to hold on to the Mac 10 until he received a call from someone passing through en route to Honduras, on a mission: "There was someone leaving for Honduras at seven A.M., if I'm not mistaken, on the ninth of August."

On the evening of August 8 the Garcias got a phone call from the airport. The mysterious man passing through had arrived. Garcia picked him up early the next morning.

The visitor introduced himself as Maj. Alan Saum, and he had an airline ticket for Honduras in his pocket and all the right credentials, including a recommendation from Tom Posey. Garcia phoned Posey to confirm: Saum was legitimate.

The major, however, soon started mentioning more important connections than Tom Posey. "Saum said he had come from the White House. I had known about Oliver North. [This statement was made in May 1986, six months before North's name was public knowledge.] Well, not only did I know about him, he was pretty famous, Oliver North." Saum called the White House from the airport. It was a short call, but the Garcias were nonetheless impressed. Back in the modest Garcia home in Hialeah the well-connected visitor made a lot more calls. As Garcia's phone bill confirms, Saum made three calls to Tom Posey, one to a number in Honduras, and one to Gen. Vernon Walters, U.S. ambassador to the United Nations and former deputy director of the CIA, at his office in New York.

Sitting in the Garcias' living room, with the Mac 10 hidden in the next room, Saum proposed another embassy hit. This one was more palatable to a loyal brigade member, for the targets would be the Cuban and Soviet embassies in Managua and the scheme supposedly had very high-level authority indeed. "Vice President George Bush's baby, that's what he called it."

Jesus Garcia made his judgments on the basis of what he had seen of this network before. He had, after all, seen them move six tons of weapons without a hitch from Miami to Fort Lauderdale and on to Central America. He also felt he had let the team down by bowing out of the American embassy plot. "I didn't want to get involved in the first hit, the American hit. I thought I owed it to him, so I agreed on hitting the Russian and Cuban embassies." Garcia would do whatever was required to make the venture a success.

Settling into the Garcias' tiny apartment, his flight to Honduras abandoned, Saum began discussing whom they might recruit for the mission to Nicaragua. They spent the next four days plotting "George

Bush's baby." There were false papers to attend to, airplanes to hire.

None of this was to come to pass because, on August 13, Major Saum betrayed his recruit. He led D. C. Diaz of the Miami police and Kevin Currier of the FBI straight to the closet where the Mac 10 was stored. Jesus Garcia was charged with attempting to sell a machine gun and silencer. The corporal from the Dade County jail was soon behind bars at MCC, the Metropolitan Correctional Center. Instigating a conspiracy to attack foreign embassies in a foreign country could be considered a serious offense, but there were no charges against Saum.

The ungrateful guest fled the Garcia home, but he left behind a collection of documents that were revealing indeed. Apart from his unused ticket to Honduras for August 9, there were the names and numbers of American and Honduran generals, including a Gen. Gerry Curry of Chesapeake, Virginia, and Gen. Walter Lopez, who was at that time the chief of staff of the Honduran armed forces. There was also a number for a senior member of Vice President Bush's staff, Lt. Col. Doug Menarchik. There was a "Captain Lookie" [sic] with the words "Honduran Intelligence" scrawled next to it (Captain Luque was at that time a Honduran army liaison to the contras.) A Col. David Aldeck was listed under two numbers for General Walters. There was a reference to Alfonso Callejas of the FDN contra force. There was the address of Gen. Gustavo Alvarez Martinez, the Honduran strongman. A business card belonging to a George P. Wittington of Henderson, Kentucky, turned up, which is interesting in that George P. Wittington is one of the big American landowners in Costa Rica.

It should hardly come as a surprise that there was also a number for John Hull. There was also an Avis rental car contract for one A. Saum, "U.S. Military," with an Evansville, Indiana, address. Evansville is just down the road from the American home of rancher Hull.

Among the more personal documents left behind was a copy of Saum's birth certificate, giving his date of birth as December 16, 1956, and a U.S. military I.D. card under the name of David Oliver and issued by the DMZ Police, Korea, on June 25, 1970. There were also photographs in this bizarre file. One of Saum himself, looking beefy and clean-cut, one of Tom Posey standing in front of a memorial for the Cubans who died in the Bay of Pigs, and a picture of "Cathy," a fresh-faced graduate in marketing from the University of Evansville.

Cathy's résumé was also among Saum's papers. Her talents

ranged from Fraternity Sweetheart to a 4.0 average in "international marketing, finance, distribution, economics and foreign relations." Along with the résumé there was a copy of a letter from Saum to Tom Posey on the subject of Cathy dated July 25, 1985: "This is a letter per request 8.15 Thursday 25 July. Enclosed is information on a new recruit, what a lady. I need to get her into a training facility. I have been using her in intelligence gathering. She's been coded 'the seductress.' She will be a great asset." A letter from "the seductress" to Posey was enclosed with such lines as "I learn quickly, but the training afforded to me by the fact that I was born to the female gender should negate any questions that you might have about my efficiency in performing the tasks at hand." At the foot of Saum's letter to Posey was a postscript: "Tom, photos show Cathy no justice. She's training now in political assassination." Major Saum obviously had some very interesting and curious connections indeed.

Jesus Garcia was assigned a Miami public defender to take his case. It could have been any one of the lawyers who carry out such work. The luck of the draw turned up a young, well-scrubbed attorney named John Mattes.

Mattes, a native of Madison, Wisconsin, initially approached the Garcia case like any one of a thousand minor weapons charges that are a staple of the Miami courts. He could not have conceived at the time that the story of this petty criminal would become an obsession, but every time Mattes was ushered into the courtyard of the Metropolitan Correctional Center he was drawn deeper into a world of intrigue he could not decipher. The mysterious Major Saum who claimed to be an emissary of George Bush could have been just an imaginative con man. Perhaps he was not a major at all, and had garnered all the names found in his papers from phone books in Washington and Honduras. Yet Posey of Civilian Military Assistance had vouched for the man, and the FBI had not touched him.

The suppression hearing for the case of *United States* v. *Jesus Garcia* convened on October 31, 1985. The prosecution was in the hands of Jeffrey Feldman, the same man who later turned up in La Reforma prison in Costa Rica claiming, so said Carr, he was after "the guns, the drugs, and John Hull."

Feldman had little sympathy for Garcia, even though twenty-five fellow officers from the Dade County jail had come to testify on his behalf. The prosecutor, thought Garcia, seemed particularly anxious that there be no discussion in court of Garcia's extraordinary tale about the planned assassination of Ambassador Tambs.

Feldman did seem anxious to establish the link between Garcia, Saum, and Tom Posey of CMA, as though he were indeed going after a bigger fish. Garcia told his story, for the record, of Saum's scheme to hit the embassies in Nicaragua, a plan that was of course totally unrelated to the plot on the American embassy in Costa Rica. "He kept telling me," Garcia quoted Saum, " 'We are breaking the law; we are breaking the Neutrality Act.' But he [also] said, 'I am working with the White House.' He called the White House, I heard him. So I said to myself, Okay, we'll deal with this, for country. I'm a veteran."

Mercedes Garcia, who had been wary of inviting this stranger into her home, recounted that her husband had calmed her down by saying: "This is for love of country." She then told Feldman, "I know you will understand, and if you don't understand what a country means to a Cuban, you don't understand this case at all, sir."

Finally, the government produced their witness against Jesus Garcia. It was Maj. Alan Saum, who took the stand and corroborated the Posey link.

Q: Did you get the defendant's number from Tom Posey?

A: Yes, Decatur, Alabama.

Saum described his meeting with Jesus.

Q: ... in the morning on August 9, you met Jesus Garcia. What happened?

A: We just sat around the airport for approximately an hour or so. . . .

Q: What did you talk about?

A: Paramilitary operations, the weather, just about everything.

Q: And after you left Miami International Airport, where did you go?

A: To Mr. Garcia's home.

Q: What did you do there?

A: We sat around for a short while, discussing different things involving the Soviets' move into Central America. Then we had breakfast.

Saum maintained his jocular mood as he stated that his job was to gather intelligence on the operation, meaning the Decatur, Alabama, CMA–Miami Brigade 2506 nexus.

> Q: As far as your attempt to gather information on that operation, you told Mr. Garcia that you could obtain passports and papers, correct?
>
> A: Yes I did.
>
> Q: Was there any discussion about the firearms that would be brought into Nicaragua?
>
> A: As many as we could get.

It seemed curious that the presiding judge, the Honorable Clyde Atkins, did not see fit to release the minnow and bag the shark. Saum did not repeat any of his claims of White House affiliation, though the Garcia phone bills attested to his attempts to prove that he had friends in high places.

In the courtroom Saum stated that his employer in the intelligence business was a representative of the Honduran military, who in the court transcript appears as "Oscar Lackatina." It is likely that this is really "Oscar from La Quinta," a major contra base in Honduras. Saum went on to say that "I furnished the information to a man by the name of Sam," an intelligence operative.

Feldman made no effort to challenge Saum's curious claims of employment, and instead pressed his witness for more information on Tom Posey. Saum was happy to oblige: "Mr. Posey had the organization" that sent "firearms, money, boots, uniforms; whatever was needed by the Central Latin American rebels to help the cause, to fight the Soviet movement into Central America."

What was being described was a highly illegal operation, violating not only the Neutrality Act, which forbids activities directed against a country with which the U.S. is at peace, but also arms export laws.

It was Posey, according to Saum, who had given the information on how to get into the paramilitary groups in south Florida.

On cross-examination John Mattes demanded more information on the sketchy intelligence ties. Feldman objected, saying that such information was irrelevant. Mattes had checked Saum's military records and found that he had left the service with an honorable discharge from the marines, as a private. Mattes challenged the witness on why he had misrepresented himself on documents, such as the car rental form left behind at the Garcias, an act that happens to be a federal felony.

Q: You would commit a federal felony to gather information from private individuals?

A: Yes I would.

The admission that Saum had committed a felony, for which he was never charged, elicited a remarkable response from the judge: "I think it's clear that to obtain information in an alleged undercover capacity, he would misrepresent himself."

The court's blasé attitude toward Alan Saum, and its lack of sympathy for Jesus Garcia, shocked John Mattes. For him, the case had become far more than just an illegal-weapons charge. He prodded his client for more details. Who had sanctioned the arms shipments? Where were they going? Who would want to kill an American ambassador? What was the Cuban involvement with the contras? Why would someone want to see to it that Garcia was convicted of a crime and was therefore not a credible source of information?

Garcia believed that he had been "set up" either because of his refusal to go along with the embassy plot or simply because he had knowledge of it. "There are people here who are above the Constitution. I didn't know the federal system was like this," Garcia said. "I never dreamed."

Mattes took on an investigator, Ralph Maestri, who had been working for the Miami public defender's office for fifteen years. Together they laboriously followed up leads in the Miami Cuban community and in the murky world of the mercenaries that might account for the treatment of the humble foot soldier Garcia. Starting with the raw material of a six-ton arms shipment and an apparent plot to do away with a U.S. ambassador, Mattes was determined to build a case that the FBI could not refuse.

Gradually, one by one, he began to find witnesses who could and would corroborate details about the network. He heard about Carr and Glibbery sitting in their Costa Rican jail cells, desperate to be officially debriefed. Even Miami Cubans, locked in internal squabbles over operating methods and leadership, were willing to go on the record. Crucially, a man who had been a senior military commander within CMA agreed to talk about actual operations. As Mattes put it, "The United States government couldn't find enough investigators to go interview those people who are claiming publicly that they're involved in the arms network."

In January 1986 Mattes felt he had enough to make a federal case. "We turned all of that information over to the United States attorney's office . . . and urged them to follow up [with] subpoena documents." Soon he began to hear back from federal agents that his information was checking out: "Rooms had been rented, for instance, by people here in Miami in the early winter of 1985. People had come to Miami on their way into Nicaragua, people who were staying in Miami as a staging area, utilizing it to gather the weapons and gather the support necessary to move them into Nicaragua."

Then everything changed. In February 1986, the assistant U.S. attorney in charge of the case told Mattes that the Department of Justice "wasn't interested" in going any further with it. As Mattes delicately puts it, "That's when I think we began to have our doubts as to the interest level on the part of individuals in law enforcement. They started the investigation, and then the cover-up."

Mattes was devastated, but he did not give up. Instead, he flew down to Costa Rica and interviewed Glibbery and Carr.

According to Garcia, Carr had sat in on the discussions at the Miami Howard Johnson's back in early 1985. A year had gone by, and Carr had changed from a romantic idealist eager for battle into a sad and cynical inmate of a third-world prison cell. He was happy to talk about John Hull and the goings-on at the ranch. He had no problem discussing the blatant way the arms had been moved to Costa Rica from the United States. There were, however, some aspects of his adventures in the contra movement he was afraid to discuss. The embassy plan was one of them, though there was evidence that he had at least learned of it in Miami.

Glibbery had never been part of the embassy plan, but he recalled one intriguing incident from his time of service with Hull that interested Mattes very much indeed. Just after Easter of 1985, as Glibbery tells it, Hull had summoned him for a mission to pick up arms from a supply dump in a sawmill about an hour's drive from the ranch house along "very, very bad roads" and past a large Voice of America transmitter that lies on the edge of the ranch. A rendezvous had been arranged with the manager of the sawmill, who was a member of the right-wing Costa Rican organization Costa Libre, but when they got there the sawmill was locked and deserted. "Hull was cursing and swearing, saying, 'You can't trust those motherfucking Costa Ricans.' "

The following night things had gone more smoothly, and Glibbery was delighted with the cornucopia of guns and ammunition stored at the mill. Behind the mill, however, on the roof of a "brick bunker, a low one-story building," Glibbery found, in addition to various types of grenades, two claymore mines. "So I said to John, 'Hey, great, John, there's a couple of claymore mines up here,' and John Hull said, 'No, you better leave them where they are, we might need them for an embassy job later on.' "

This casual revelation had drawn silence from Glibbery. "I'm not going to ask questions," he later explained. "The guy had just shown me too many things."

The day Mattes returned he and Maestri, his investigator, went straight to FBI headquarters and begged them to follow up. "It was a well-organized network; it was a well-financed network, and it was a network where there were Americans—particularly an American in Costa Rica named John Hull, who seemed to be coordinating the operation in Costa Rica."

While at FBI headquarters Mattes got an indication that his investigation was at least being taken seriously at a high level. "The agent in charge of the case remarked to me that we had to wait there in order to provide the information regarding the gunrunning because he had to type up an investigative report on our activities and get that report telexed to Washington that day." This casual revelation posed an obvious question. As Mattes put it: "Why Washington would be interested in what a public defender and his investigator are doing remains, you know, a question that I don't have an answer to."

Whatever the answer was, it was not that Washington wanted a deeper probe, as Mattes soon found out. Two days later, he and his investigator were invited to the U.S. attorney's office in Miami, where they were faced with the same FBI agents and Feldman, the assistant U.S. attorney. "The words were, 'Get out. You're out. Stay out. You've crossed the line. You've gone too far.' They told us that if we went any further, we would see the inside of a grand jury room." Their purported crime was "obstructing justice."

"Going and getting information and evidence and trying to provide it to them somehow was obstructing justice." The lawyer was, reasonably enough, baffled. "Somehow I couldn't follow that logic. We were just shell-shocked. I mean, frankly, this is not the kind of thing that happens every day, when you're out trying to gather information to win your client a new trial. It's not a common experience that a United States attorney comes to you and says, 'Get out of trying to defend your client.' "

Coincidentally or not, this gag order was issued two days before President Reagan went on television to make a public appeal for his $100 million contra aid package up before Congress. The day after the speech, the House of Representatives began its debate on whether or not to resume contra military aid.

Meanwhile in Miami, a sentencing hearing was scheduled for Jesus Garcia. Mattes was eager to present his evidence on Oliver North's supply network and on Garcia's role in it.

He never got the chance, because the hearing was abruptly called off. Feldman asked for a continuance (a postponement), quoting a direct order from Washington. It has been subsequently reported that this order came from the office of D. Lowell Jensen, who at the time was the senior deputy to Attorney General Edwin Meese.

Feldman added insult to injury when Jesus Garcia's family received a death threat (a live mortar round was left in front of his home). Mattes had been dreading this happening because it could affect Garcia's readiness to talk to the FBI. But the assistant U.S. attorney's office said simply, "How do you know that bomb was intended for them?" Garcia, as his lawyer points out, "was willing to go forward to the FBI and disclose evidence of arms trafficking, criminal conspiracies, and he was willing to testify to that. The response he got from the community was a 105-millimeter mortar round."

Alan Saum had disappeared immediately after the trial—to Europe, as it subsequently turned out, although since he could not have afforded it himself, who paid for the trip is still unclear. When he returned, early in 1986, Saum was ready to talk, if only on the telephone. The usual medium of contact was his answering service in Indiana: Porky's Restaurant in Evansville. His rambling conversations were punctuated with, "I can't tell you about that," or "I'm going too far." He refused to specify his employers, though he did claim to be working for at least one government agency. In several lengthy calls he veered between the eccentric and the intriguing. Saum talked of working "on the front lines of democracy" and poured out free-associated reminiscences of trips to Switzerland, Libya, and Central America. He said he had "killed people" and had been wounded once "in Geneva."

More pertinently, Saum admitted that he had operated "under orders" to bring about Garcia's arrest. He acknowdged his relationship with John Hull, and said at one point that Robert Owen, the messenger for Lt. Col. Oliver North at the NSC, had been trying to reach him. He never explained his acquaintanceship with Lt. Col. Doug Menarchik, the military aide to Vice President Bush. All in all, thanks both to his mysterious contacts in high places and his eccentricities, Saum managed to remain an enigma. His former wife claimed that he had worked for the CIA, though she was unfamiliar with his job description. A woman in Evansville said Saum had entrusted letters from the White House to her. In the event of his death she was to send them to a Virginia address.

In June 1986 Saum disappeared again. Before his departure for parts unknown he told John Mattes, "I've been betrayed by everyone—they're going to bury me now." In April 1987 the burial ground that had been selected for him was revealed. In a letter with a Swedish postmark and a return address in Bet Shemesh, Israel, he described his current assignment: identifying pro-Soviet activists among Swedish writers and artists. The Swedish Artists' Guild, he had discovered, "sends delegates to Managua, Nicaragua, and paints anti-American and pro-Soviet murals on walls. And we thought Sweden was neutral. Are they neutral when they send money to fight the freedom fighters?" Major Saum was still in somebody's secret army. It was not clear whose but, judging by the fate of others who had been enlisted to serve the cause as foot soldiers, he was lucky to have been buried in Sweden or Israel rather than behind bars.

Joe Coutin, for example, proprietor of the Broadway Boutique gun shop, FBI informant, and Tom Posey's "right-hand man," was arrested on the charge of having converted a semiautomatic weapon to fully automatic, a federal felony. The weapon in question had then allegedly been used in the murder of the Drug Enforcement Agency's number-one informant, drug pilot Barry Seal.

Mrs. Hilda Coutin, also licensed to sell weapons, was livid. She claimed that her husband had applied through the proper government channels to convert the gun that had landed him in jail. This tough Cuban matron was invariably fully made up before breakfast and wore stiletto heels that could have been classified as weapons themselves. Hilda was firmly convinced that her husband had been set up by the authorities. She felt particularly incensed because of the couple's sterling work as FBI informants. They had kept the bureau fully briefed on local illegal activities ranging from gunrunning to cocaine smuggling within the contra aid network. If Joe was a disposable asset, then she felt no compunction to keep quiet about what she knew, and about what had been passed on to the FBI and the U.S. attorney's office.

Hilda opened up to Mattes about the clients of the Broadway Boutique. She described the meetings her husband and others in the Cuban network had had with members of Civilian Military Assistance to discuss the finer points of the war. There had been meetings with contra leaders as senior as Adolfo Calero himself, where everything but humanitarian aid was discussed. One of the military figures working with CMA who had taken part in these gatherings had used the code name Flacko. When Mattes found him, he was ready to start talking about the strategy that lay behind the secret army.

The man with the code name Flacko turned out to be Jack Terrell, a trim, erect individual with a southern drawl and the military attribute of never looking quite at home in civilian clothes. Terrell readily admits to a checkered past, including a spell as a juvenile delinquent (which earned him a conviction for being found in a stolen car), a prison guard, and an entrepreneur in various kinds of businesses. He is more reticent about his military experience, claiming that he learned his soldiering as a mercenary fighting for Ian Smith's Rhodesia. Yet in many ways, broad and subtle, one is left with the impression that he trained and served with some branch of the U.S. military. Just how and when that occurred, and when and if it stopped, is as yet an unanswered question.

His connection with Central America officially dates from 1984, when he joined Civilian Military Assistance to serve as a "senior military commander," functioning chiefly as an organizer of anti-Sandinista Miskito Indian forces. He alludes however to another mission on his agenda: Project Pegasus. This was to be a program of assassinations directed against key Sandinista leaders inside Nicaragua. Terrell remains studiously vague about just who had ordered this macabre initiative and who, beyond a reference to "covert funds," was paying.

In any event, Terrell arrived on the scene at about the same time as the Boland Amendment became law. Among the company he kept, this piece of legislation was never more than a joke. "During the time of the Boland Amendment, they could carry out clandestine activities in any fashion they wanted to and people in Washington could sit back and say, 'Well, if anything happens to these people, whether they were carrying out directly or indirectly any plan of our government, it's easy to be at arm's length and have this great big beautiful deniability factor."

He was always much amused by the notion, so easily accepted by much of the press throughout Boland, of private citizens out of the government's control. As he points out, private citizens do not just walk into a war. "That would be like me going to South Africa tomorrow and saying, 'Give me a gun. I want to do my thing.' You know, they'd laugh at you. If the United States wanted to stop you from entering a conflict, they would punch your card; you're out of it."

Terrell first met John Hull in December 1984 at a meeting in the Shamrock Hilton in Houston, Texas. The meeting had been set up by Adolfo Calero, the civilian leader of the FDN, which was and is the largest contra group. Hull came highly recommended. "He had been preintroduced to me by Calero, when the FDN wanted to form a new southern front in Costa Rica. He told me that he wanted me to meet with the CIA liaison to the FDN in Costa Rica, this being John Hull."

Another big-league player in the covert world flew in from Washington for the Houston meeting, none other than the lanky Robert Owen, whom Terrell came to know as "the bagman for Ollie North."

The topic under discussion at the Shamrock was a proposal to ship American personnel to the southern front of the contra war. Government funding for contra military operations had, so far as the public knew, been totally cut off for two months. Yet Terrell was left in no doubt that in December 1984 the tap was running. "In our meeting in Houston, I questioned the financing for putting American trainers in Costa Rica. I was assured by Mr. Hull and Owen that we would receive money from the NSC to the tune of ten thousand dollars a month for the operation at Hull's ranch in Costa Rica." The ranch operation was to be the incubator for a new FDN force that would assume control of the southern front, taking over from Eden Pastora, the contra leader who had refused to bend to the will of the CIA.

"We were discussing logistics for this type of operation in Costa Rica, which would have thirty Americans and two hundred plus Nicaraguans. When I questioned who was going to pay for the transportation for the Americans from the United States to Costa Rica, who was going to feed them, [provide] their lodging, base facilities, and things of this nature, then Owen told me, 'Well, I take ten thousand dollars a month to John Hull, from the NSC, for these types of operations. And if we need more money, that's no problem.'"

Terrell had no reason to question Owen's credentials. "Within these circles, you just don't walk in the door and say you're doing XYZ operation unless indeed you are." This assumption was correct. Owen was indeed a right-hand man of Lt. Col. Oliver North, and among his duties was reporting back on Terrell's activities. Flacko was primarily interested at that time in organizing the Miskito Indian contra groups who were fighting in Zelaya Province on the Atlantic coast of Nicaragua. As Owen informed North, "Flacko's long-term goal is to build up the Miskito and train them to the point where they can start taking land. The area he wants them to concentrate on is where there is a port and where one of the operating gold mines is. The ultimate plan is to open the port and take the gold mine. Once the port is open, a boat will sail from Miami directly to the port with men and supplies, drop them off and take out the gold which is captured."

There is a slight note of caution in Owen's report. It seemed that Terrell might have been getting a little too successful: "Flacko is also setting himself up to be the one who handles all financial support for the Miskitos. Thus everything going to them in terms of support from groups in the U.S. goes through him. . . . All this is being done under the guise of CMA."

Therefore, when Terrell was brought in on the planning for the southern front, he was already a major player in the contra support network: "Flacko has been working on getting the support of some of the Cuban community, including the Cuban Legion, the Cuban Independent Movement and Alpha 66. He hopes this support will be both financial and manpower."

The urgency to manufacture a new southern front, one that would be prepared to cooperate with the National Guard veterans leading the FDN up in Honduras, was important for public relations reasons. Congress was grumbling at the time that the contras seemed to be little more than an unwieldy collection of splinter groups, constantly at each other's throats. No less than six armies battled for turf along the Nicaraguan borders. The FDN shared the northern border with two Miskito Indian factions. In the south, two groups jostled with Pastora to control the southern front.

It had become difficult to sustain any illusion of a streamlined fighting force with one coherent objective amidst such disarray. "I was told that the FDN was under orders from the CIA to present a unified front with the entire contra operation," reports Terrell. "The FDN strategy was to come in and take over the southern front in Costa Rica, to consolidate it minus Pastora and ARDE [Pastora's group]. They were going to form a new entity there known as UNIR, and this would be the remnants of [contra leader] Alfonso Robelo's troops, which at that time numbered a hundred fifty-three, and the troops of Fernando ('El Negro') Chamorro into one group on Hull's ranch. They would import FDN commanders into the situation to legitimize it as far as looking like a Nicaraguan operation. The Americans would be training and calling the shots in the background, but they didn't want to make it look like a high-profile gringo operation."

Terrell brought a cynical eye to all this plotting and scheming, and he had a pithy way of expressing his reservations. He wanted to know why the unified command did not include Eden Pastora, or why this supposed coalition of splinter groups consisted of FDN leaders under another name. "Whatever you want to call this operation in Honduras, Costa Rica, and Nicaragua, the closest thing that the [contra] leadership have to a combat situation is when they put on their pinstripe uniforms and come to Washington to do combat for money."

This firsthand assessment of the realities on the ground were very much at odds with the press reports coming out of Honduras in 1984 and 1985, portraying a force starved for funds while uttering heartfelt paeans to democracy. The president of the United States took an even loftier view. Speaking of the contras, he declared in early 1985, "They are the moral equal of our Founding Fathers, and the brave men and women of the French Resistance. . . . We cannot turn away from them. For the struggle here is not right versus left, but right versus wrong."

Terrell, unlike the press or the president, had full access to the camps. The way he saw it, "You've got estimates ranging between five thousand and thirty thousand tough contra soldiers on this border, yet they hold not an inch of dirt. The only progress they've made is in purchasing condominiums. Their families live in the United States. They live in luxury, so it's business. Bottom line it's business. Why do you stop a war when people are getting very well off?"

Sitting in his White House command post, Lt. Col. Oliver North was getting the same message. Early in 1986, for example, his emissary Robert Owen dolefully reported that "there are few of the so-called leaders who care about the boys in the field. This war has become a business to many of them." Nor was he overly impressed by contra leader Adolfo Calero. "He is the creation of the U.S. government," wrote Owen resignedly, "so he is the horse we chose to ride."

Terrell also noted the distinction between the contra leadership and the "boys in the field." Speaking of the latter group he pointed out that "most of them don't even know why they're there. They are either formally conscripted or they come there because they have a place to eat. You see the social segregation, the standards of living that are so separate. The Sumocistas live like kings; they're on salary, their families are supported while the campesinos eke out whatever they can to survive." Given the amount of aid being donated for the cause, even the humble foot soldiers of the contra bands should have had at least the bare necessities of comfort and combat. But, as Terrell observed, it was simply being stolen. "One very glaring example was in La Quinta [the contra base in Honduras where Major Saum's friend Oscar was the supply officer]. I had known that the Cuban community, which has been the premier suckers in this whole deal, had donated hundreds and hundreds of cases of canned goods to the fighters. They were being warehoused at La Quinta. I saw this huge warehouse full of food and I said, 'Why is this food not going down [to the border camps]?' and I was told by one of the leaders, 'Don't you know that canned goods make a campesino sick?' and I'm thinking, 'This guy must think I fell off the turnip truck.'" Terrell soon discovered who was getting the Cuban charity, when he observed "the families of these commanders coming from their leased houses in Tegoose [Tegucigalpa] to this place to pick up the canned goods like they were shopping at Safeway."

(His observations were shared by some of the contra officers in the field who charged that the top military commanders were siphoning off cash at the expense of the troops. These officers described the use of faked receipts, black-market currency deals, and the substitution of cheap, poor-quality goods for top-quality supplies. Caesardo Martinez, the commander of the FDN's Jeane Kirkpatrick Brigade, was sacked in January 1986 after he complained about rampant corruption. He remarked bitterly to a *New York Times* reporter: "I think the entire leadership is corrupt." Enrique Bermudez, the military commander of the contras, was accused by disillusioned officers of stealing as much money as he liked with the assent and protection of the CIA. Another field commander, Marlon Blandon Osorno, told the *New York Times:* "The CIA told us that the general staff was taking the money that belonged to us." An alternative supply channel was briefly instituted and abandoned after complaints from Bermudez and the local CIA contingent.)

Terrell was astonished to see the amount of money passing through contra hands in Honduras. "I've been in their accounting office. I've seen filing cabinets full of hundred-dollar bills, suitcases full of money. I said, 'Why do you want aid from the United States when you've got bushels of money here?' They were laundering money. They gave us premium trade-in on money. When the lempira [the Honduran currency] was 2 to 1 to the dollar, we were getting 2.8 to 1 to bring American cash into the country. They were running a mill there of money; I brought in thousands myself."

Again, the high command in Washington was fully aware of what was going on. "These people don't know they are even in a war," Owen told North. "They think they are running a business."

Rather than clean things up, however, it appears that the contras' American directorate were more concerned with getting rid of Terrell, whose vocal and unflattering observations were becoming disturbing. By the end of January 1985 they wanted to force him out. "Best bet might be to dry up his funds, have someone talk to him about national security and put the word out he is not to be touched." Owen was mindful that doing this might tarnish the Band-Aids-and-jam-jar image of Civilian Military Assistance. "Posey has been doing the best he can to either sit on Flacko or deal him out, but that is not possible because right now Flacko knows too much and it would do no one any good if he went to the press. He has got to be finessed out."

In December 1984, however, when Terrell sat down with John Hull and Robert Owen and Adolfo Calero and others to talk about opening the southern front of the FDN, he was still a true believer. Not, of course, that he was unaware of the legal implications of what they were doing. As Terrell describes it: "Hiring mercenaries—that's neutrality violations. Running weapons, that's firearms violations. Plotting to kill people, that's conspiracy to murder." But with such distinguished company, Terrell felt perfectly at ease. After all, Owen was there. "He says, 'I am here representing the NSC and this is my contribution in dollars.' John Hull was saying, 'I am here; my contribution is you will use our airstrips, my farm, we will launch our operation from my ranch. I get the arms.' Calero says, 'I've talked to Langley [CIA headquarters]. We're coordinating this situation. This is where we go.'"

The "conspiracy-to-murder" aspect of the bargain, according to Terrell, had to do with Eden Pastora, the odd man out of this unified front in the south, and the *bête noire* of the White House. This point puzzled Terrell at the time. "I'm thinking, you know, you've got two hundred ten ragamuffin contras that they're trying to put together to put in Costa Rica, when you've [already] got a far greater organization in this area known as ARDE, led by Pastora."

When he raised this point, however, he drew a visceral response. "What do you know about Pastora?" Terrell replied mildly that he knew "a little."

Terrell recounts, "Hull starts in berating him [Pastora], 'You know this man is a communist? He flies the Sandinista flag in his camp. He deals with the Sandinistas. He sells them ammunition. He steals weapons and ammunition from us.' You know, every bad thing you can say. Then he said, 'He's got to go.' I said, 'What do you mean he's got to go?' 'We've got to kill him.'"

What Terrell did not know, was that Hull had worked hand in glove with this "communist" for years. As Pastora readily recounts, he had looked to Hull for jungle training camps. Hull had stored and transported weapons flown in from Miami by Rene Corvo and Felipe Vidal for Pastora. Hull had ferried Pastora's troops and Pastora himself in his aircraft. But by late 1984, because of Pastora's stubborn refusal to join forces with the former "Somocista" FDN forces in the north (or as some Pastora detractors put it, his refusal to join in a subordinate capacity), the relationship between the rancher and the dashing contra had turned sour. Hull began to bleed the Pastora organization, at the behest, so Pastora claims, of the CIA Costa Rica station chief himself. In addition to the theft of military hardware, the embattled leader found that his commanders were being bribed with promises of money, guns, and future promotion. Later on, Carr and Glibbery contributed to this process by stealing Pastora's jeep and fitting it, to general merriment at the ranch, with fake Illinois license plates.

Terrell was a trifle taken aback by Hull's vehement expressions of hatred against Pastora, and by Owen's acquiescence. He was nevertheless prepared to go along to the point of devising a plan for eliminating Pastora. It was to be an elaborate affair, a public execution just inside the southern border of Nicaragua. The execution team were to be Americans, Cubans, and Nicaraguan contras disguised as Sandinistas. Pastora would be hung.

Later that month, December 1984, the plotters met again in Miami at the well-appointed home of Adolfo Calero. According to Terrell, it was a full house. Not only were Terrell, Hull, and Owen present, but so were Calero, the military commander Enrique Bermudez, Aristedes Sanchez (another senior FDN contra), and the zealous CIA operative Felipe Vidal. Lounging outside on the patio was someone Terrell didn't know who "looked like he was from some Arab country." Vidal said his name was Amac Galil.

Once again the mention of Pastora evoked strong reactions. "When I brought up Pastora, Adolfo goes into this rage and states that Pastora had called him a homicidal Somocista son of a bitch." Calero's solution, according to Terrell, echoed Hull's: "He's got to go."

Later, in his diary, Terrell summarized the meeting this way:

> The termination of Zero [Pastora] discussed with Adolpho [sic], Aristedes, John Hull, Donald Lacy and a man not identified but told [he is with] 'company.' Many people involved. Some look like Cubans, some Nicaraguans, some Argentinian.—A.C. Adolfo Calero very upset with statements made by Pastora. Says he too Sandinista. Must die. Big problem.
>
> Asks me to put it together and not tell them how it will be done, just do it. Will have complete cooperation of all Costa Rican officials. Have several safe houses in C.R. under control of John Hull and Bruce Jones. Seems Rob Owen in on most of this. Am told he is private consultant and liaison man for U.S. (Company). . . .
>
> Must appear that Sandinistas did it. Discussion on capturing Zero and having men dress in captured uniforms. Am told this must be very visible hit and people must believe the Sandinistas did it. Am told to let Hull know when ready to move. . . . A.C. open to anything. He desperate. Wants and needs southern front.

Terrell had no illusions that he was getting into something that lacked official blessing. "You've got the hierachy of the FDN sitting there; you've got a representative, this guy Owen, from the NSC, CIA. So, you asked me if the U.S. government knew what was going on? They had to know from that meeting. Plus, Adolfo has told me on several occasions, 'Langley calls me five times a day,' and he's walking around with his little portable phone and this is fact."

During the meeting Felipe Vidal made a comment about the intended victim that meant little to Terrell because of his relative ignorance of Pastora's recent past. He said, according to Terrell, "We put a bomb under him the first time, but it didn't work because of bad timing."

The remark was very relevant indeed, because there had been a "first time," at a place called La Penca on May 30, 1984, and the bomb had worked well enough to kill eight people and seriously injure many more. While the Miami plotters were hatching their schemes, an unofficial investigation into La Penca was slowly uncovering the connection between the secret army and this bungled but bloody operation.

Chapter Five
LA PENCA

"It's upsetting that anyone would do something like that, just blow apart innocent people. We have begun to expect that kind of terrorism coming from certain sectors in the world. People generally don't think the U.S. government would be involved in that sort of thing."

—Tony Avirgan
May 1986

In the spring of 1984 Costa Rica was a backwater for the international press corps posted in Central America. The hub of the region was El Salvador where, when they ventured out of the Camino Real Hotel in the capital, journalists could find mutilated corpses practically at their feet, the work of the so-called death squads, the unfettered arm of the security forces. Whole villages had been massacred for alleged support of the leftist guerrillas. Even American nuns had been raped and murdered by the Salvadoran military. It was a brutal war, and at the time interest in its course had not yet faded among editors of the more powerful newspapers and the networks.

To a lesser extent, Managua was also a center of attention. The contra war was escalating and the Nicaraguan capital was a nesting place for stringers and young free-lancers who hoped to make their names out of the war. It had the feel of Saigon in 1964—a place where something was about to happen. The mining of the harbors by the CIA had upped the ante, and the important correspondents were shuttling back and forth between El Salvador and the Intercontinental Hotel, the mock-Mayan hotel presiding over the wasteland that once, before the 1972 earthquake, had been downtown Managua.

Covering the contra war rarely meant extended stays in the war zones. A quick dash up the Pan American Highway to Estelí or Ocotal on the northern border and the occasional foray to an isolated village with a Sandinista military unit yielded sufficient copy to satisfy editors at home. Any contact with the FDN contras was arranged in their host country, Honduras.

Costa Rica, by contrast, appeared to lack both the danger and the excitement of these countries. There was really only one story out of San José: Eden Pastora and his efforts to keep his contra movement afloat.

Although Pastora was maintaining his staunch opposition to uniting with the FDN (and thereby losing his independent military command), there were others in ARDE, as his army was known, who were less reluctant. Alfonso Robelo, for example, ARDE's chief political spokesman and a key contact with the CIA, was quite happy to make accommodations.

By May 1984 the dispute was coming to a head, with ARDE split between the supporters of Pastora and those who wanted to go with the FDN and Robelo. Up until this point Pastora, who continued to portray himself as a "true Sandinista," had never cared to admit that he had been taking aid from the CIA. But on May 23, in an interview with a Costa Rican radio station, he tacitly admitted the relationship by complaining of the agency's change of policy toward him: "There are strong pressures by the CIA. . . . They have blocked all help to us. For the past two months we have not received a bullet or a pair of boots, we have not received anything." What Pastora did not say publicly was that he had received a warning from the CIA at the beginning of May. He had been given thirty days to accept unity, or face the consequences.

Notwithstanding these threats, Pastora was determined to brazen it out. On May 29 he announced that he would be holding a press conference the next day. He could not, however, hold it inside Costa Rica, since the government was sensitive enough about its official neutrality to insist that he make his public appearances somewhere else, such as one of his camps just over the southern Nicaraguan border.

The next morning, May 30, about two dozen journalists arrived at the rendezvous for the long trip north, a hotel parking lot on the outskirts of San José. Among them was Linda Frazier, an attractive American working for the local English-language newspaper, the *Tico Times*. She had only recently gone back to journalism after taking time off to look after her family. Her husband, Joe, worked for a wire service and today he was off on assignment in Managua. Their ten-year-old son was left with a baby-sitter in San José. Susan Morgan, a British journalist, was there for *Newsweek*. Tony Avirgan, a free-lance reporter/cameraman, was stringing for ABC News at the time, and he had some difficulty persuading the ARDE officials on hand to allow him to come, since they had objected to his ABC reports on Pastora's problems with the CIA. Martha Honey, Avirgan's wife, was at that time the Costa Rica stringer for the *New York Times,* but she did not come along on the trip. She was trying to meet a deadline on an important story: the CIA's ultimatum to Pastora and its imminent expiration. Various other American, European, and Costa Rican journalists made up the party, including a taciturn Danish free-lance photographer named Per Anker Hansen, who had attached himself to a Swedish TV crew for the previous few weeks.

After some considerable confusion—no one ever gave the Pastora organization high marks for efficiency—the party piled into jeeps and cars and headed north, passing Ciudad Quesada and John Hull's vast properties en route. The atmosphere among the party was fairly lighthearted, for no one thought they were heading for a major story. Once they reached the San Juan River, which marks the northern border in that part of Costa Rica, they boarded two long dugout canoes powered by outboard motors. Per Anker Hansen appeared very concerned about safeguarding a large aluminum camera case he carried with him. Before getting on board the canoe he bought a plastic bag and wrapped the case in it, very carefully.

It was dark when they reached La Penca, a jungle camp two hours downriver and just inside Nicaragua. By the time they set up their equipment in the primitive wooden structure where they would hear Pastora, it had started to rain. Everybody reflected on the long and uncomfortable trip home in the canoes and over dirt roads turned to mud. Back in San José, TV Channel 6 had just broadcast an interview with Pastora in which he described the pressure on him to join with the FDN. "But," he had added, "the CIA will have to kill me first."

At that very moment, the local CIA station chief was meeting with two other men deeply interested in the contra war and Pastora's future in it: Robert Owen, who had arrived from Washington four days before, and John Hull.

Although Pastora tried to insist that it was now too late to start the press conference, the journalists immediately crowded around him. Hansen had parked his metal case close to where Pastora was standing, but then backed out the door, grumbling that his camera was not working.

Pastora had just begun warming to his subject, the treachery of the CIA and the FDN and his determination to remain independent, when a bomb exploded in the room. The tape from a camera that stayed running shows the explosion as a brilliant flash. The camera continued operating for a few seconds afterwards, recording dark shadowy bodies on the floor and the moans of those still alive.

Reid Miller, a correspondent from the Associated Press, was knocked back "about ten feet into a wall," as he later recounted. "The explosion seemed to come from the middle of the circle of journalists. It was 7:30 P.M. . . . I slid down a two-by-four brace to the ground then rolled into a narrow slit trench that had been dug nearby. Many of Mr. Pastora's men stood with their rifles slung, offering no help to the wounded and seemingly stunned. Many of the wounded, like myself, had crawled or stumbled from the building and were sitting or lying on the muddy riverbank."

Pastora, slightly wounded, was rushed from the scene by his men. He did not stop to help the others, or to order his men to do so. The bodies lay on the floor and on the mud for hour upon hour that night. Some, like Linda Frazier, were dying slowly while the attack was being reported on the news in San José. Miller describes in his dispatch how "Linda Frazier was pulled from the house almost an hour after the explosion and laid on a blanket nearby. Mortally wounded, she was to lie there another two hours before help came— a doctor and two nurses dressed in the green fatigues of Mr. Pastora's Revolutionary Democratic Alliance [ARDE]. She and all of the other wounded received an injection of antibiotics but little else. At one point I crawled over to her, unable to walk because of shrapnel wounds in my right leg. She took my hand, and I could see that she was talking to me, but I could not hear her words because the explosion had left me temporarily deaf."

The American embassy did nothing to help, though a helicopter airlift of rubber boats and emergency medical supplies might have saved Linda Frazier's life. John Hull, who had two aircraft at his ranch nearby, also remained aloof. When asked later why he had done nothing he invoked the foul weather as an excuse. But the rain had subsided by midnight and still no one came. Hull was of course meeting with the CIA station chief and Robert Owen that evening. While Owen admitted this to the congressional Iran-contra committees, he claimed that the little conclave did not hear about the bombing until three-thirty the next morning. It is curious the three men could have escaped hearing the news, when the story was running on TV and radio and the embassy had been alerted seven hours earlier. Owen left Costa Rica the next day.

Toward morning the last of the wounded were finally put on boats for the river trip and then driven over bad roads to the hospital in Ciudad Quesada. Tony Avirgan was covered in blood and bandages. Susan Morgan, badly wounded, was flown by Learjet to Miami. In all, three journalists were dead, as well as five of Pastora's guerrillas. Nearly thirty people were wounded, many seriously.

Per Anker Hansen showed no signs of injuries at La Penca, but when he arrived at the hospital he carried two shallow cuts on his arm and a modest amount of bloodstains. He sat in a wheelchair for most of the night, badgering the nurses for news of Pastora's condition. At one point he gave a ten-minute interview to a Costa Rican radio station describing his experiences of the blast. In the morning he persuaded his acquaintance from Swedish television to come with him back to San José. There he checked out of his hotel and disappeared.

The news of the bombing sent shock waves through the Central American press corps. The victims, as they well knew, could have been any one of them. There was no lack of suspects for what everyone agreed had been an attempt to kill Pastora. The roster included the Sandinistas, the CIA, the Cubans, the FDN, not to mention various German, Italian, and Basque leftist terrorist groups. One prominent newspaper quoted Pastora as blaming his erstwhile Sandinista comrades, despite the fact that according to reporters who were on the scene he had immediately and vocally blamed the CIA.

La Penca certainly marked the watershed in relations between Pastora and the CIA. From now on the aid cutoff was permanent. When Pastora went to Washington in July he was informed of this fact by Alan Fiers. The soon-to-be head of the CIA's Central American Task Force added insult to injury by revoking an earlier promise to pay the commandante's five-thousand-dollar hotel bill. Whereas before Pastora had depended on Hull for logistical support, the rancher now severed relations.

Pastora was inclined to see the malign hand of Lt. Col. Oliver North (whom he only met once) behind these actions. North, he believed, was bad-mouthing him around Washington, "saying that I traffic drugs, that I have a low military level, that I have to be destroyed, that he doesn't have any confidence in me. Everything that has happened to us unexplainably revolves around Oliver North."

In the immediate aftermath of La Penca, however, official Washington was quick to point the finger at Managua. Within twenty-four hours the CIA and State Department were telling journalists in Washington that the bombing had been carried out by the Basque terrorist organization ETA on behalf of the Sandinistas. Arturo Cruz, Jr., son of a contra leader who was on the payroll of both the State Department and the White House, was callous enough to name the dead Linda Frazier as the ETA agent who had planted the bomb. In fact no evidence emerged at the time or since to implicate the Basques in the assassination attempt.

Tony Avirgan, who survived the explosion with a mangled hand, severe burns, and "a big hole ripped out of my side," was another victim tarred by official comments. The U.S. ambassador to Costa Rica at the time, Curtin Winsor, Jr., let it be known that Avirgan was linked to the ETA. This remark actually prevented the wounded journalist from being flown to the U.S. for further treatment for some days after the bombing.

The bombing changed Tony Avirgan's life. Long after his wounds had healed he still carried in his mind the image of Linda Frazier's body shielding him from the direct impact of the blast.

"I was just sitting on a box, actually not very far from where the bomb was planted, drinking a cup of coffee. And I mean, it's not even nice to think about, but one of the reasons I wasn't killed was because there was another journalist, a good friend, who was standing right in front of me and she took the major impact of the blast and she was killed. I remember it very clearly. There was a very, very bright flash of light and a loud explosion so loud that it just kept ringing in my ears over and over and over again for a long time. At first I didn't realize what had happened. I felt my hair and eyebrows burning, and I thought it was just happening to me. I thought that maybe some pressure lamp had exploded and then I heard firing, a machine gun going off, which happened to be one of Pastora's guards panicking outside. Then I thought maybe it was a Sandinista attack and there had been a rocket that landed in the building. I started hearing the moans and the cries, it was really quite horrible. What was most horrible was not being able to help the other people who were injured and dying, to spend almost the whole night there just lying on the ground with others who were slowly dying next to me and just not being able to do anything for them." And so, even though the story had faded from the news within a few weeks of the bombing, Avirgan and Honey set out to find out who had been behind it, and why.

As an investigative team, the couple were well matched. Martha Honey, a small and determined blond, is endowed with a furious energy, prepared to pursue the most surprising sources and the most tenuous leads whatever the obstacles. Avirgan, tall and genial, is more considered in his approach, ready to carefully consider and analyze each piece of evidence before fitting it into the whole.

By the fall of 1985, a year and a half after the bombing, they believed they had their answer. It was an uncomfortable conclusion for two free-lance journalists with little protection raising two small children in Central America. As Avirgan puts it with characteristic understatement: "It's upsetting that anyone would do something like that, just blow apart innocent people. We have begun to expect that kind of terrorism coming from certain sectors in the world. People generally don't think that the U.S. government would be involved in that sort of thing."

Within a few days of the blast it was established by the Costa Rican authorities that the actual assassin had been the supposed photographer, Per Anker Hansen, and that the bomb, made up of C-4 plastic explosive and a radio detonator, had been concealed in the metal camera case that he had been at such pains to protect. Whoever he was, he was neither the real Per Anker Hansen, nor was he a photographer. The passport he had been using for at least a year had been stolen in Copenhagen in 1978. By the time the Costa Ricans closed the borders he was long gone.

After the first ten months of work, funded by a grant from the American-based Committee to Protect Journalists, Avirgan and Honey had accumulated a great deal of circumstantial evidence to suggest that La Penca had been a plot involving the FDN, right-wing Cubans, certain Costa Rican security officials, and the CIA. On the other hand, they were no nearer the killer and those who had given him his orders. It was at that point that pure chance brought them into contact with a source that led them to what they thought was the heart of the mystery.

On March 29, 1985, Carlos Rojas Chinchilla, a San José carpenter, stopped in for a drink at the Rendezvous Bar. The Rendezvous was tucked away in one of the crowded downtown side streets of the capital. It happened to be close to the American embassy, a drab office block distinguished only by the marine guards posted at the door and the television monitor scanning the entrance. Rojas, a pale and thin young *"tico"* (Costa Rican) whose wife ran a beauty shop, had slipped into the bar for a beer before catching the bus home. He was sitting alone at one of the tables when three men stopped to talk in the doorway.

After a moment, two of the men turned and left, heading in the direction of the American embassy. The third, a short, dark-skinned young man with a smooth round face and straight black hair, looked around the bar for a moment, walked up to Carlos, and proceeded to pour out an extraordinary story. He wanted help, he said, to escape from his companions, who he claimed were casing the American embassy for a bomb attack. He asked if Carlos would contact his brother, who was fighting with the contras. For ten minutes the young man, who said his name was David, spilled out his tale, all the while watching the door in case the other two came back. The mild-mannered carpenter sat wide-eyed, wondering why this was happening to him, an ordinary middle-class Costa Rican who had stopped in for a simple drink.

David said that he was a contra, part of a group of FDN Nicaraguans, North Americans, and Miami Cubans based at a ranch owned by an American named John Hull. He said the group intended to bomb the embassy, just as they had bombed La Penca, and he wanted no part of it. He needed a safe house, someplace to hide, and someone "on the outside" to reach his brother. Carlos demurred, saying that the tiny apartment above the beauty shop where he lived with his wife and child was an impossible hiding place. In any case Carlos, not unreasonably, was loath to get involved in something as strange as this. David scrawled down a number as a place where he could safely be reached if Carlos should change his mind.

Soon the two men returned and collected David. Carlos followed them out and watched as the three got into a large gray car without license plates.

Shell-shocked by his peculiar meeting, Carlos went straight to his wife and relayed the tale. She told him in no uncertain terms to keep his mouth shut and mind his own business.

Heeding this sound advice, Carlos continued on his uneventful life as a carpenter and part-time café manager until, on April 26,

1984, he read an item in the newspaper that caused him to reconsider. A group of mercenaries and a large cache of weapons had been picked up on John Hull's farm by the Costa Rican Rural Guard. President Luis Alberto Monge of Costa Rica had ordered the raid after the group had launched an attack inside Nicaragua (the raid on La Esperanza, Carr's first mission). Monge was in the middle of an election battle with Oscar Arias, who was hounding the president about the use of Costa Rican territory as a staging area for the contra war.

What Carlos read was in fact a report of the arrest of Peter Glibbery, Steven Carr, and the others. These names meant nothing to Carlos at the time, but as he read he realized that every detail— the ranch, the arms, the foreigners—conformed to what the mysterious stranger in the bar had told him. If he had been right on those details, perhaps there was something to the story about the plot against the American embassy. Carlos decided that he simply had to try to warn someone. After another conference with his family it was decided that the best course would be to find some American to whom they could tell the story—who could do with it what he chose—thus relieving the Rojas clan of the burden.

It so happened that Carlos's wife, the hairdresser, had an American client, and it was to her that they told the story. The woman turned out to be the secretary of Tony Avirgan and Martha Honey.

Honey and Avirgan immediately passed the story of the bombing plot on to the chief of security at the American embassy, who noted the bizarre information with little comment. Carlos, however, was by no means off the hook.

Since the carpenter'story meshed so well with what they already suspected, the two journalists were determined to follow up. They convinced Rojas to reestablish contact with David. At a series of clandestine meetings the reluctant contra continued his tale, relayed to the Americans by Carlos. He recounted how Hull's contra operation included Miami Cubans and his fellow rancher, Bruce Jones. In 1982 and 1983 Hull and Jones had transformed their farms into staging areas for drops of weapons supplied by the CIA for the contras. One CIA official was a frequent guest at the ranch. David remembered his name: Duane ("Dewey") Clarridge. David retailed how Hull and Clarridge were upset with Pastora for refusing the advice of CIA advisers and for rejecting the CIA's plan to fold the Pastora operation into a unified command run by the FDN in the north.

The plot to kill Pastora, said David, had been worked out at meetings in Honduras and Miami early in 1984 between Adolfo Calero, John Hull, Felipe Vidal, and Rene Corvo (the subsequent hero of La Esperanza), and an American called "Robinson Harley," described as belonging to the CIA.

David claimed to have actually met the assassin in Hull's company at the ranch. He was supposedly a Libyan, a professional killer who called himself Amac Galil. Galil, he said, had been recruited in Chile for the Pastora job by two ranking officials of the FDN and by a CIA man who posed as a journalist.

The entire operation had cost fifty thousand dollars, which, according to what David had heard, had been paid over by the CIA via the FDN contras.

David also confirmed that the assassination attempt had been actively assisted by a number of high-ranking Costa Rican security officials. He claimed in addition that Hull had helped Galil escape.

So far as the plot against the embassy was concerned, David made it clear that the group had not just the embassy, but a specific ambassador in mind: Lewis Tambs, whose appointment had been announced in January of 1985 and who was due to arrive in July.

This extended secondhand debriefing of David by Avirgan and Honey came to an end in the third week of July. As Carlos later described it to me, he and David had just finished a meeting in a San José park when a group of armed men grabbed the pair and forced them into a jeep, making them lie on the floor with their shirts over their heads. They drove for five or six hours like that, the last part on a rough and bumpy road. Finally they arrived at a camp on a farm, where they were left with a guard. Someone said, "Hull isn't here."

David told Carlos that they were almost certainly about to be killed and they had better do something, kicking the guard in the crotch as he said this. They ran for the jungle under fire.

The pair kept moving through that night and the next day, at one point, ironically enough, catching sight of Eden Pastora driving by on a country road in a white car. Finally a vegetable truck stopped and gave them a lift to the outskirts of San José. Carlos phoned Avirgan to come get them, but David made the unfortunate decision to continue running on his own. Neither Carlos nor the journalists ever saw or heard from him again.

It is fair to say that the whole extraordinary story, from the initial meeting in the bar to the glimpse of Eden Pastora in his white car, sounds more like a Gabriel Garcia Marquez novel than sober journalism. Fortunately, there is an abundance of corroborative detail to hand—even to the point of a confirmation by Pastora that he was indeed on that road on that date, in a white car.

On the embassy plot, for example, not only had Jesus Garcia been briefed on the subject in February 1985, but his wife, Mercedes, had given a statement to the police at the time of his arrest in August detailing exactly what he knew about the scheme. This was some time before Garcia came into contact with Honey or anyone else who could have primed him with David's story. Furthermore, Peter Glibbery's detailed recall of the night Hull told him that some claymore mines might be needed "for an embassy job" does at least suggest a general interest in the subject on the part of the ubiquitous rancher.

Soon after his arrest, Jesus Garcia had mentioned to John Mattes that he knew Galil as a character who hung out in a particular bar in Miami. Galil does indeed appear to have been in Miami in December 1984, which was when Jack Terrell claimed he saw him on the patio of Adolfo Calero's house during the meeting with Hull, Robert Owen, Calero, Vidal, and others familiar to our story. That was the gathering, it should be recalled, in which another attempt to kill Pastora was reportedly under discussion, and Felipe Vidal is said to have offhandedly remarked that "we" had put a bomb under him that had not worked because of "bad timing."

In May 1987, almost three years after La Penca, Alberto Guevara Bonilla, a former agent of DIS, the Costa Rican intelligence service, gave a sworn statement that two months before the bombing a photographer called "Per Anker Hansen" had turned up at a northern border post with a directive signed by the head of DIS. The order said that the man should be given transport for "journalistic tasks," not a service normally extended by DIS to the press. Guevara supplied Hansen with a jeep, and he had set off in the general direction of La Penca.

Three weeks before the bombing, "Hansen" turned up again. This time, said the DIS agent, he had an American with him, John Hull. They needed a powered canoe, in which they headed downriver toward La Penca. Guevara knew Hull well by sight, and he identified a photograph of "Hansen," taken at the time of the bombing, as Hull's companion on that day.

Unfortunately, such impressive confirmation of his story was of no use to David, for it appears that he was recaptured by his erstwhile colleagues, and this time did not manage to escape. Avirgan was told by a trustworthy source in the Costa Rican Civil Guard that an informant on Hull's ranch had reported that David had been brought back, tortured, and killed. Such an event seems to have been par for the course in contra circles in those parts. On August 25, 1985, Robert Owen reported to Oliver North that an execution had taken place on the southern front. Under the heading "Human Rights Violation," Owen wrote, "The internal investigation shows Chepon [a code name for contra commander José Robelo] did order the torture and the ultimate execution. It was decided Negro [contra leader El Negro Chamorro, whom Owen elsewhere described as a problem drinker with a following of drug smugglers] should decide what punishment he deserves and was supposed to decide by Friday."

Exactly who was tortured and executed is unclear, though it occurred at the time of the reported death of David. For Tony Avirgan and Martha Honey, not to mention Carlos Rojas, the point was immaterial, for they were getting very clear warnings that they themselves were in extreme danger.

"We began to receive telephone death threats," recalled Honey the following year, when the pressure had temporarily eased. "At first they were against Carlos. [They] said, if he told what he knew he would be dead. He began to see cars following him and people following him. Then we received several calls here saying that not only was Carlos in trouble, but we were also and we should stop our investigation.

"We managed to get Carlos and his family out of the country. They went to Norway, as refugees seeking political asylum. We sent our children away . . . I mean, it was really a terrible period. The Costa Rican officials we were working with put guards in our house. [They] were living here twenty-four hours a day. It was an unreal kind of situation."

The Rojas family came back after two months, thinking that the coast would be clear. They were wrong. At the beginning of 1986 the harassment and death threats started all over again. Carlos at one point received a note, melodramatically composed of words clipped from newspapers: "Carlos Rojas, if you, Tony Avirgan, Martha Honey or Edgar [Avirgan's soundman, another La Penca victim] continue with the investigation, it could be that you will die."

Avirgan and Honey were alarmed at the sophistication of the surveillance. They believed Costa Rican security men were involved, "particularly people in DIS, the Directorate of Intelligence and Security. We know that some of the cars that were following us were from this organization. We know that this organization has very close ties with John Hull."

They received information that the threats were coming specifically from those in the group involved in drug dealing. David had told Carlos that cocaine from Colombia was being transshipped for Miami on the several airstrips on Hull's ranch. He had specifically named Hull, Felipe Vidal, and Rene Corvo as being involved in the business, part of the proceeds of which were used to buy arms and other military supplies for the contras.

Again, there is much corroborative evidence for this accusation of David's. Felipe Vidal had actually been charged in Miami with drug running, and Rene Corvo has been accused by members of the Cuban community in Miami of trafficking in cocaine in Costa Rica. Most tellingly of all, CIA station chief José Fernandez admitted to the congressional Iran-contra committees in secret testimony that Vidal and Corvo were "our people" (CIA) and had a "problem with drugs," but that the agency had had to "protect" them.

In late January 1986 Martha Honey decided to alert the American embassy. "I went with three other women to the embassy. We asked specifically to talk to people from the DEA, the Drug Enforcement Agency, because we had information that those who were harassing us were involved with cocaine trafficking. We laid out to this DEA man what we had been suffering, expecting that as American citizens, which we all were, that we would be able to discuss with him what might be done. His response to us was, 'Well, ladies, my suggestion is that you find yourself a big friend and get a gun.'"

The embassy had been hostile to the pair ever since they had revealed their findings about La Penca at a press conference in San José in September 1985. "The U.S. ambassador said on Costa Rican television that we were traitors," recalls Avirgan with some bitterness. The ambassador was Lewis Tambs, whose life Avirgan had been attempting to save.

The journalists had warned the embassy about a possible bomb plot as soon as Carlos told them of his first meeting. Avirgan recalls going in and telling everything he knew to the chief of security. "He, without comment, took down the information and thanked me for coming in." Later, when other journalists questioned the ambassador on this point, the ambassador conveniently forgot that Avirgan had ever been to the embassy. In actual fact the State Department had stepped up security at the Costa Rican embassy because of reports that "teams of Latins" were surveilling the building.

Hull made no secret of his irritation at the persistent journalists, denouncing them as "agents of the KGB" at every opportunity. Not only did he have a tendency to crack somewhat tasteless jokes about La Penca to visiting journalists—"we wouldn't want that to happen today"—but also he did his bit to encourage the old canard about Avirgan's possible involvement. When I visited the ranch he produced a contra doctor who had treated some of the La Penca victims. A word with him, insisted Hull, would lead to new intelligence about the La Penca bombing. The doctor, who in fact was involved in Oliver North's supposed humanitarian aid project, recounted how he had treated Tony Avirgan and that the journalist had "not been wounded enough," a not so subtle innuendo that Avirgan had planted the bomb.

"It all seems so unprofessional," Martha Honey once told me. "This ragtag bunch of people that hang out at [Hull's] place are involved in horrible deadly serious actions, but in such a slipshod way. It's kind of like war on the cheap, not through American military people, but through people like Hull, who were hired at some point to run the operation on behalf of the U.S. It's sort of like the wild West. It's not the way we think of a war being run, but yet the consequences are so horrible."

In September 1985 Avirgan and Honey published the *La Penca Report,* summarizing what they had learned about the conspiracy. Hull immediately sued them for enormous damages. They began to devote most of their energies to preparing for the suit, due to come to court in Costa Rica in May of 1986. They made contact with John Mattes, whose own investigation into the curious case of Jesus Garcia had turned up so much evidence to corroborate the report and the existence of a secret army operating between Miami and Costa Rica.

It was only when a Washington attorney got wind of their story that their dilemma became a link in a much larger chain, one involving senior members of Oliver North's network, that stretched back into the past and far from Central America.

Chapter Six
THE OLD-BOY NETWORK

"We used to joke that truth is always stranger than fiction."
—Robert Owen to the Iran-contra committees
May 19, 1987

T he first time that most people heard the names Richard Secord, Thomas Clines, Felix Rodriguez, and Rafael Quintero was when the Iran-contra scandal burst into full flower in the winter of 1986. But these very people, and many others, had been named as key players in the contra business six months before in a lawsuit filed in Miami on behalf of Tony Avirgan and Martha Honey by the formidable legal counsel they had retained in December 1985.

Daniel Sheehan is hardly a conventional Washington lawyer. Unlike the armies of polished corporate attorneys who occupy commanding heights of the capital's power structure, Sheehan works from a ramshackle office in the slums. He is the general counsel of the Christic Institute, which describes itself as an "interfaith public interest law firm and public policy center." Its headquarters, though only a few blocks from the Capitol, are in the ghetto of Northeast Washington, the kind of place where taxi drivers insist you have the wrong address. Inside, cheerful and preoccupied assistants crowd the narrow corridors, not at all bothered by their shabby surroundings.

An impish Irishman with silver-flecked hair and a voice curiously similar to that of Oliver North, Sheehan sits at the back of this rabbit warren. His phone never stops, except when he unplugs it in what has become a reflex action whenever the conversation turns to sensitive matters. Despite his lack of the outward trappings of success, he has an impressive number of legal victories under his belt, including the famous suit against the Kerr-McGee Corporation on behalf of the family of the suspiciously dead Karen Silkwood, the suit against the Three Mile Island utility on behalf of the local inhabitants, the successful criminal defense of the staff of the Catholic bishop of Brownsville, Texas, on the charge of aiding Salvadoran refugees, and numerous others.

Sheehan likes to point out that he comes from a law enforcement background—his father was a prison guard—and that he considers himself a "public interest cop." A more significant influence on his legal career may have been the fact that he attended not only Harvard Law School, but also the Harvard Divinity School, and at one point seriously considered becoming a Jesuit priest. "I have never taken a case that I didn't believe in," he said one night in Martha Honey's kitchen, "never." Law, for Sheehan, has a great deal to do with right and wrong. That deeply held belief, combined with long hours and relentless optimism, has produced impressive results.

The Christic Institute and their general counsel became interested in the secret military plans and activities of the Reagan administration long before they heard of Tony Avirgan or Martha Honey or John Hull. In the spring of 1984, in the course of his defense of the Catholic sanctuary workers in Texas, Sheehan got wind of administration plans to lock up some four hundred thousand Central Americans who had fled as refugees to the U.S. were the president to declare a "State of Domestic National Emergency" at the same time as he ordered American troops into action in Central America. The operation was to be coordinated by the Federal Emergency Management Agency, which was headed by Louis Giuffrida, an old California crony of Ronald Reagan's, and would use the fifty state National Guard organizations as well as newly formed "State Defense Forces."

Sheehan later heard that in at least three states, Texas, Louisiana, and Alabama, these State Defense Forces had in fact been set up and were recruiting exclusively among right-wing paramilitary groups. In Louisiana at least, so Sheehan was told, these forces were to be used as a means of funneling arms to the contras. The arrangement was to siphon off half of the arms and equipment issued for their exercises and dispatch them straight to Central America. In Louisiana the weapons shipment was reportedly to be handled by a state legislator—who later became a prominent sponsor of "humanitarian" assistance for the contras.

Intrigued by this interesting news, Sheehan asked his sources to find out if the same thing was going on in the Texas and Alabama organizations. He was soon to hear that, so far as Alabama was concerned, it was indeed. The parties concerned were reported to be none other than Thomas Posey and his Civilian Military Assistance group (this was four months before the Santa Clara raid put Posey and CMA in the headlines). By the end of May 1984, Sheehan knew a considerable amount about the plans involving Posey, his sources of arms and personnel in the Alabama National Guard, and their schemes for supplying the contras. Then, in June 1984, he was told that Posey had a direct link to the White House. One of his sources reported that he had been introduced by Posey to Robert Owen in a Washington public park, and that Owen had described himself as "the personal representative to the contras of . . . Colonel Oliver North."

It seemed clear enough to the public interest cop that all this activity constituted a violation of a raft of federal statutes, such as the Neutrality Act and the Arms Export Control Act. On the other hand, since he is not a policeman but a private lawyer, he could not fulfill his inclination to drag the lawbreakers into court until he had a plaintiff for a civil suit. The Christic Institute is, however, a nonprofit organization and accepts no fees from those it represents in lawsuits. Such organizations are allowed by law to foment lawsuits, meaning they can come across some instance of wrongdoing, go out and find someone who is suffering thereby, and suggest that they bring suit.

In the course of the battles he had fought on behalf of various good causes in the previous decade, Sheehan had developed some novel legal techniques. One of these was the use of criminal statutes that allow a private citizen to bring suit in federal, as opposed to state, court. There are only two such: the Civil Rights Act, which he had used in a Klan prosecution in North Carolina, and the Racketeer-Influenced and Corrupt Organizations Act, popularly known as RICO.

RICO was originally developed and passed in 1970 as a means of prosecuting the Mafia and other organized criminal conspiracies. Its basic intent is to allow a senior member of a conspiracy, such as a Mafia don, to be charged for crimes committed by underlings in the course of the conspiracy's business, even if the bosses were not necessarily directly involved. Thus the prosecution must prove a pattern of certain specified criminal activities—which include drug smuggling and money laundering—and an ongoing criminal enterprise over a period of years. Although this mechanism was created for the benefit of federal prosecutors, RICO does contain a civil provision, allowing a private citizen to bring suit if he or she can prove they have suffered a business injury as a result of a criminal conspiracy. If Sheehan could prove not only that Hull had been implicated in the La Penca bombing, but that he was associated with others in the contra supply network, then they could all be bagged in a RICO suit. The list of potential defendants, so he later decided, would have to exclude active U.S. government officials. Were they to be included in a suit, then the limitless resources of the Justice Department and the government could be brought to bear on their behalf against him, intimidating, for example, possible witnesses.

Sheehan felt he had his crime. Now all he needed was a victim to represent. His first idea was to find a church group who might have suffered physical injury or property damage from contra attacks in Nicaragua, and he started to look for a suitable candidate. Someone may have heard what he was up to, for word soon came back from contra sources that orders had filtered down to them to stay away at all costs from American churchmen and their property.

For the rest of 1984 and the first half of 1985, Sheehan was busy with the defense of the Catholic sanctuary workers in Texas as well as with a civil suit against the Ku Klux Klan and American Nazi members involved in the murder of leftist activists in Greensboro, North Carolina. It was only when these cases were concluded—successfully, it turned out—that he could turn his attention back to the business of the secret and illegal contra supply network.

While Sheehan was again looking for a client, Tony Avirgan and Martha Honey were now in need of a lawyer. They had published the results of their La Penca investigation in September 1985 and had immediately been stuck with a massive libel suit from an aggrieved John Hull. Sheehan had already heard about Hull, and he realized not only that the two journalists' information dovetailed with his own, but that thanks to Avirgan's injuries at La Penca he now had a victim on whose behalf he could sue. In December, Honey and Avirgan took on the Christic Institute to represent them.

Sheehan and the embattled journalists in San José—not to mention John Mattes—had accumulated a great deal of information about the connection between the secret military and criminal goings-on in Costa Rica and higher authority in Washington—the CIA and Oliver North. But as Sheehan began to piece all this together he received a call that would eventually double his defendants list to include not only Cuban and other Central American desperadoes but immensely powerful former U.S. government officials.

The caller was Paul Hoven, a much-decorated Vietnam helicopter pilot who had settled in Washington to fight for military reform. He and associates in a group called the Project on Military Procurement were working to expose the Pentagon's wanton and slipshod approach to developing and buying weapons. Chastising the military along these lines appeals to true conservatives, and Hoven took pride in his right-wing views (especially when brandishing his Zippo lighter, engraved with the motto "Fuck Communism," at visiting liberals).

Thus ideologically equipped, Hoven had an enormous range of contacts in the murky world of special—i.e., clandestine—operations. Late in 1984 he encountered a denizen of this world, a retired military intelligence officer, who wanted to discuss the corruption and inefficiency with which aid to the gallant Afghan guerrillas was being dispensed by the CIA. The conversation soon turned, however, to something far more out of the ordinary.

Hoven's newfound friend told him that a group of former CIA senior officials, military officers, and Middle Eastern arms dealers had formed what he called a "secret team" to undertake covert operations on a commercial basis. Their activities were massive and wide ranging and, in the case of some members, included political assassinations. They operated independently of the U.S. government, though several of those concerned had previous histories of involvement in government-sanctioned assassination programs, stretching back through the Phoenix program in Vietnam to Kennedy-era attempts to kill Castro. Hoven's friend had stumbled across this group in the course of trying to get some semicovert CIA Central American business for himself, but he had come across their insalubrious tracks years before in Iran, and he knew they were dangerous people.

Conservative though he may be, Hoven was troubled by this news, and he called his friend Danny Sheehan to pass it along and arrange a direct meeting. The three men met in a house outside Washington in February 1985.

The retired spook told Sheehan that in the mid-1970s he had

been assigned as an antiterrorist specialist in the U.S. military mission in Tehran. From that vantage point he had become aware of the existence of what he called an "antiterrorist search-and-destroy project" run by a former CIA agent named Edwin Wilson. Wilson was later to be arrested, tried, and sentenced to fifty-two years in jail for sundry crimes, including arming and advising Muammar Qaddafi. But in Iran, the graying spook informed Sheehan, Wilson had been working under the direct supervision of Theodore Shackley, then second in command at the CIA's (clandestine) operations division, and Shackley's assistant, Thomas Clines.

This "search-and-destroy project," the source told him, had continued as a privately run, non-CIA-authorized program as of 1977, when "outsiders"—President Jimmy Carter and Adm. Stansfield Turner—had taken control of the CIA. It was for Shackley and Clines, the source insisted, that Wilson was working in Libya between 1977 and 1979. He was ostensibly supplying training and supplies for Qaddafi's clandestine operations, and that was the key charge against him when he was later tried in the U.S. But in reality, so Sheehan was now told, Wilson was gathering intelligence on these operations for transmission to a certain Rafael ("Chi Chi") Quintero. Quintero's function was to arrange for the interception of Qaddafi's minions as soon as they left Libya to go about their business, and to murder them. Quintero later testified that he had indeed accepted a down payment for at least one assassination job in the belief that it was a CIA-sponsored "hit." Quintero claimed that he pulled out of the operation when he discovered that the target was in fact on Qaddafi's hit list, not the agency's.

Unfortunately for Wilson, his "cover" activities on behalf of Qaddafi came to the ears of federal law enforcement authorities, who devoted great energy to putting him in jail. Since the alleged Shackley-Clines operation to neutralize terrorists was officially unauthorized, Wilson was unable to invoke it to protect himself.

Shackley and Clines were, however, besmirched enough by their association with Wilson to be forced to resign from the CIA by Stansfield Turner in 1979. They thereupon joined forces with two people whose names were to become well known to Sheehan and, much later, to the press and public: Richard Secord, at the time an active general officer in the U.S. Air Force, and the Iranian-born arms dealer Albert Hakim.

According to the intelligence officer's story, this group began shipping arms, ammunition, and explosives to the remnants of Somoza's National Guard immediately after they escaped from Nicaragua and began to re-form themselves as the contras. Later on, the same cast of characters, employing Quintero among others, delivered lethal supplies to contras in Costa Rica, in part through John Hull. In fact it appeared that this group had been the main suppliers of the contras from 1979 through 1980, and again from 1984 to 1986, during the official cutoff of U.S. assistance.

Sheehan realized he was now getting very close to the background to La Penca. Indeed, he was told that a close associate of Quintero's, a man by the name of John Harper, had actually given a course in Honduras on the construction of bombs identical to the one used at La Penca.

With the help of Paul Hoven's friend, Sheehan now began to probe deep into the world of active and retired intelligence and covert operations specialists, as well as the related communities of drug smugglers and the police agencies that deal with them. What he learned was to become the basis not only of his RICO suit but of a voluminous affidavit he filed with the court in December 1986. This document laid out both the story of Sheehan's own investigation and the history of the people he had earlier identified in his suit as the contra supply network. Although marred by errors of minor detail, the affidavit set forth compelling evidence that men whose names had previously surfaced in histories of America's covert wars had for years been making both narcotics and assassinations an integral part of the way they did business.

The trail that Sheehan followed led back to an era long before the contra war, before even the days of the Shackley-Clines-Wilson operation in Iran. It led in fact to another contra operation, a quarter of a century before, when in the eyes of another administration the major national security "threat" in the hemisphere was Fidel Castro and his successful revolution in Cuba.

Right after Castro's victory in 1959, the CIA had been authorized to conduct a secret program to support right-wing Cuban exiles in an effort to undermine and eventually overthrow the new Cuban government. Early on this operation became allied with Mafia figures, notably Santo Trafficante, the former Cosa Nostra boss in Havana, who had suffered enormous business losses thanks to the Cuban Revolution. The CIA and their prominent underworld recruits agreed that the anti-Castro program should have an especially secret subcomponent: a unit with the express mission of assassinating Castro and other senior figures of the revolutionary regime. They were reportedly known as the "shooter team."

The broad outlines of the CIA's efforts to dispose of President Castro, and indeed the role of notorious gangsters in such efforts, have been general knowledge since 1975, when eight assasination plots conducted by the CIA against Castro were laid out in lurid detail by the Senate Church committee. Their report detailed how the CIA set out to develop a capability to disable foreign leaders or murder them if necessary. This broad directive was known as "Executive Action," or for the cognoscenti, ZR/RIFLE. What intrigued Sheehan were the names he was now hearing as having constituted the Castro assassination teams, for he had already come across several of the same people in his researches into the 1980s-vintage contra war. Rafael Quintero was among them. So was Felix Rodriguez, who also used the nom de guerre Max Gomez. In October 1986 he was exposed as a key figure in the operation dropping weapons and supplies inside Nicaragua, when one of the flights he directed was shot down, resulting in the embarrassing capture of survivor Eugene Hasenfus. It also transpired that Rodriguez had been on close terms with Vice President George Bush.

Even as Rodriguez was coordinating clandestine flights out of Ilopango military air base in El Salvador, he wore Che Guevara's watch. Edwin Wilson, who knew Rodriguez well, has recalled the circumstances of this acquisition. "Felix Rodriguez was a Batista Cuban," he told an interviewer in February 1987, "so he wasn't really liked by the other Cubans. But he was a good soldier. When they needed people down in Bolivia, they put four or five of these guys in Bolivian uniforms down there while they chased down Che Guevara. When they got Che and brought him in and laid him down on the table, well, then Felix came in and was the last guy to talk to Che. Then he got word from the Bolivian general to execute him, so they executed him, and hauled him in a helicopter back to where all the reporters were. He then went to Vietnam. When he got back from Vietnam, I got him a job in Lebanon training people, just to get him a job. He was always in the military thing. He had guns all over the walls of his house. He's not a very smart guy, but he loved war."

Shirley Brill, a onetime girlfriend of Tom Clines and longtime CIA employee, remembers a more lighthearted side to Rodriguez that she got to know during outings in Miami in the late 1970s. He "always carried a concealed weapon," she recalls, and liked to shoot out streetlights for fun. "Then he'd call the police and tell them, 'I'll pay for it tomorrow.'"

Luis Posada Carriles was another name given to Sheehan as a member of the assassination detail established in the early sixties. As is fashionable in such circles, he has used another name: Ramón Medina. According to Eugene Hasenfus, Posada was Felix Rodriguez's deputy in the resupply network that had directly controlled Hasenfus's terminal flight in 1986. Although it does not seem to have perturbed his employers, Posada was a fugitive from justice at the time, wanted in Venezuela for an act of terrorism. He was accused of having put a bomb on board a Cuban airliner in 1976. Seventy-three people died as a result, including the Cuban national fencing team.

Two other names on the sixties list were Rafael and Raoul Villaverde. In the 1970s they had been recruited by Rafael Quintero as the explosives experts for Wilson's planned Libya "hit." In the 1980s, so Sheehan concluded, they had played a key role in the La Penca conspiracy by traveling to Chile and recruiting an old associate, Amac Galil, as the assassin to plant the bomb at Pastora's press conference.

Frank Fiorini, another "shooter team" alumnus, provides an echo of an intermediate scandal. Using the name Frank Sturgis, he was one of the group caught burgling the Watergate offices of the Democratic National Committee in 1972. He was tried and served his term, but he never talked.

In 1961, with the arrival of the Kennedy administration in Washington, the low-profile anti-Castro operation suddenly ballooned into the high-profile and disastrous Bay of Pigs invasion attempt. That, however, was not the end of efforts against Castro. The shooter team continued in existence, part of a general low-intensity warfare program called Operation Mongoose. The program survived the embarrassing discovery in 1963 that some of its personnel had gone in for drug smuggling on the side.

The man overseeing the Miami end of Mongoose and the assassination program from 1962–1965 was a thirty-four-year-old CIA station chief called Theodore Shackley. His deputy was Thomas Clines. They were to be an inseparable team over the years as they roamed the worldwide arena of secret operations, often in tandem. While Shackley, known to his peers as "the Blond Ghost," is a pale, thin, physically inconspicuous individual, peering impassively through thick spectacles, Clines is bluff and burly, far more ready to knock back a beer with the boys and enjoy a good time. His longtime girlfriend recalls how he once entered her in a Dolly Parton look-alike contest packed with CIA employees, which must have been a truly remarkable social event.

As it turned out, Castro and his revolution survived JM/Wave, as the covert destabilization program was code-named, though upwards of twelve thousand operatives were trained in its heyday by the CIA. By the time JM/Wave was disbanded, it had amassed a large navy and dozens of Miami front companies. When some of the assassination program details became public in the post-Watergate investigations, they evoked as much public hilarity as alarm. Sending Castro a poison cigar, one of the CIA's brainstorms, or trying to find a way to make his beard fall off sounded more ridiculous than sinister. Yet Lyndon Johnson reflected after he became president that the Kennedys had been "running a damned Murder Inc. down there in the Caribbean." The team did not fade away, they merely moved on to other wars, where they made new and useful friends.

Following the termination of Mongoose and JM/Wave in 1965 Shackley and Clines were transferred by the CIA to Laos. Shackley was to be the deputy chief of station, with Clines, inevitably, as his deputy. Over the course of the next few years, the covert war in Laos was to serve as the alma mater of virtually every key figure in Oliver North's secret war.

Laos was very much the CIA's own war, where it could operate untrammeled by any massive U.S. military presence. Even before the Americans arrived Laos was a flourishing center of the opium business, and the appearance of the CIA as a major force in this little landlocked country coincided with a major expansion of the trade.

At the time Shackley and Clines arrived in Vientiane there was a three-way struggle going on for control of the local opium business. The CIA station now threw its support behind one of the competing warlords, a certain Vang Pao. Not only did he derive great benefit from the timely provision of air support but, even more usefully, his business competitors were speedily and mysteriously assassinated.

Vang Pao was a leader of the Hmong tribe, and for the rest of the war these unfortunate people provided the CIA with its own army in Laos. In 1964, Hmong youths were organized into teams called "Mobile Strike Forces," after the term "Hunter-Killer Teams" was rejected by the CIA's Far East Division chief William Colby as sounding too unpalatable. It was the contention of Sheehan's informants that part of these operations were financed out of the proceeds of the opium trade.

Meanwhile, the U.S. Military Assistance Command, Vietnam, had set up a Special Operations Group (SOG) with members drawn from all services to carry out unconventional warfare in Southeast Asia. From 1966 to 1968, it was commanded by an old CIA hand, John K. Singlaub, in our own time the best-known of the private aid contra supporters. The SOG was intimately involved in the CIA's secret war in Laos, as directed by Shackley and Clines.

The air wing commander for Laos was an air force lieutenant colonel named Richard Secord. Secord's specialty, then and later, was air transport of the variety that requires secret movements of secret cargoes. His superior at the Special Operations Group was Col. Harry C. ("Heinie") Aderholt.

These names were to feature prominently in the Central American war twenty years later—Secord as the mastermind of the air transport component of the arms shipments to Central America and to Iran, and Aderholt as the head of the Air Commando Association, another funnel of supposed humanitarian assistance to the contras during the congressional ban on military aid. There is even one reported case of Aderholt attempting to enlist old friends from Laos to assist in contra operations. Late in 1986 an Orange County paper reported that according to sources in the local Laotian community, Aderholt was concocting a deal with Vang Pao to supply Laotian pilots for the contra war.

Sheehan was assured that other subsequently significant names had floated through the Special Operations Group roster though not in the context of drug running or assassinations. They included a junior marine lieutenant who served under Singlaub in Laos. His name was Oliver North.

Also reportedly assigned to SOG was a Dwight Owen, brother of The Courier, Robert Owen. He was killed in 1967, although Rob Owen always swore Dwight was working for the State Department at the time he was killed.

Vang Pao's connection with the narcotics business has been a matter for comment by journalists and historians ever since the Vietnam War, as has the integral part played by Air America, the CIA's own airline. At the height of the war this was in fact the largest airline in the world. Old Southeast Asia hands talk of how it was taken for granted that everyone in Air America dealt in one of two currencies, gold or opium. The ubiquity of gold led to an innovation in jewelry design: the Four Seasons bracelet, which consisted of four heavy gold links, far more useful in those parts than cash. Pilots often sported several bracelets on each arm. Opium, however, easily shipped on the customs-free Air America routes, was just as convenient. Among the aircrew who learned their trade in this uncoventional world was Eugene Hasenfus, a practitioner of the humble but necessary specialty of kicking cargoes out the door with parachutes attached.

In 1972 Shackley departed Southeast Asia for a time. He moved back to CIA headquarters at Langley and took over the position of chief of the agency's Latin American Division. From here he supervised one contra operation that worked, the destabilization and overthrow of the democratically elected socialist government of Chile. By the time this operation was triumphantly concluded in September 1973, however, when President Salvador Allende was murdered in a military coup, Shackley had turned his attention eastward again. He was appointed to run the CIA's Far East Division, a plum post.

The Phoenix program was the most notorious initiative undertaken by the CIA in Vietnam, and is indeed the only assassination program to which the agency has ever officially admitted. It involved the murder of tens of thousands of Vietnamese civilians on the grounds that they were part of what the CIA claimed was a Vietcong infrastructure. While some of the victims may indeed have been guilty of belonging to the Vietcong, many others died because they had fallen out with someone influential in the government of South Vietnam, or with an influential rival in the drug trade.

The Phoenix program flourished under Shackley's management during his Saigon tour. According to Ralph McGehee, who worked for Shackley in the Saigon station, "When Ted Shackley took over as chief of station, he notified all personnel that he based promotion recommendations on three criteria: the number of communists neutralized, the number of reports produced, and the number of unilateral recruitments achieved." Shackley's superior, William Colby, testified before Congress in 1971 that in the first two and a half years of the Phoenix program, 20,587 Vietnamese had been killed under its auspices. The Vietnamese estimate was 40,994.

By 1973 the U.S. government had accepted that it was not going to win the war in the sense of destroying the Vietcong. The Paris peace accords had been signed and the American presence in South Vietnam was substantially wound down. But Sheehan was assured that Shackley not only carried on Phoenix-style operations after the gruesome program was officially shut down but financed them through Vang Pao's ill-gotten gains. The chain of command for this program, he was told, did not follow the conventional lines of the CIA hierarchy. The alleged "bursar" who administered this aspect of the black operations finances was a U.S. naval official based in Saigon, Richard Armitage. Another participant in the scheme was reportedly Erich von Marbod, who became comptroller of the Pentagon's Defense Security Assistance Agency while Shackley was in Saigon. Shackley and the genial redhead became fast friends. By 1974 von Marbod ran all military assistance to Vietnam. The following year, with Saigon about to fall, von Marbod had to try and evacuate or destroy the vast amount of materiel he had recently shipped into the country.

According to the Sheehan scenario, not all the Vang Pao opium profits were devoted to financing the murder of Vietnamese. For a year and a half before the fall of Saigon, Shackley and his team foresaw that their secret operations in Southeast Asia would shortly be ending, and they therefore began salting away drug profits. The repository was an Australian bank, the Nugan-Hand.

Fantastic as this may sound, salient features of this part of the story have been corroborated in the sober tones of an Australian police report. Nugan-Hand came under investigation by Australian authorities in 1980 after an Australian partner, Frank Nugan, became dead from a gunshot in what was later ruled a suicide, following which Nugan-Hand went bankrupt. An extensive report presented to Parliament by the Commonwealth–New South Wales Task Force on Drug Trafficking in March 1983 concluded, according to the *Wall Street Journal:*

> Investigations following Mr. Nugan's death and the failure of the bank revealed widespread dealings by Nugan-Hand with international heroin syndicates, and evidence of massive fraud against U.S. and foreign citizens. Many retired high-ranking Pentagon and CIA officials were executives of or consultants to Nugan-Hand.

The report says of Theodore Shackley and his associates Tom Clines and Rafael Quintero that their "background is relevant to a proper understanding of the activities of the Nugan-Hand group and people associated with that group." Shackley's contact with the bank, according to the report, was a certain Michael Hand, "the currently missing former CIA operator who founded, owned and managed the Nugan-Hand group." Hand, according to the report, had worked for the CIA in Laos. The report also states that Edwin Wilson had access to Nugan-Hand money, and that a retired American admiral "was approached to establish a $1.4 million bail fund through Nugan-Hand for international dope couriers caught in the U.S."

By the end of the Vietnam War, therefore, a network born in the anti-Castro operation had been supplemented by alumni of Special Operations and apparently enriched by the happy union of such operations and narcotics. The group now began to shift its activities elsewhere.

In 1975 Richard Armitage was back in Bangkok as what was called a special consultant to the Pentagon on the MIAs—American servicemen lost during the war who could not be accounted for as dead or prisoners. Sheehan was told, however, that Armitage spent very little time retrieving MIAs and a lot of time supervising the repatriation of opium profits to Nugan-Hand and elsewhere. His unofficial duties also supposedly included shifting a large cache of arms that Shackley and Co. had hidden in Thailand, as well as the relocation of thousands of Hmong veterans of the old Shackley secret army.

The curious goings-on in the office of the special consultant on MIAs began to attract comment in the Bangkok embassy. While some of the embassy personnel began to complain that Armitage was not paying the slightest attention to the MIAs, the ambassador, Morton Abramowitz, heard of his connections in the narcotics trade. The State Department began an internal investigation. By 1987 this probe had led to the convening of a grand jury in Oklahoma City, although Armitage had by now become an assistant secretary of defense. Even in 1977, however, the pressure had reportedly been sufficient for him to have to resign the MIA job. He stayed in Bangkok until 1979, opening and running the Far East Trading Company, which, alleges Sheehan, carried on funneling drug money out of Southeast Asia and into Nugan-Hand and elsewhere. It appears that in this period he lodged at the Bangkok home of General Aderholt, Richard Secord's old boss in the SOG air wing.

Much of the rest of the cast had meanwhile moved to Iran, where the shah was spending much of his gigantic oil revenue on buying American military hardware. Edwin Wilson was there, ostensibly running an antiterrorist project, in reality working on an operation to eliminate opponents of the shah. This undertaking was reportedly under the general supervision of Shackley and Clines, who were, so runs Sheehan's thesis, now pursuing what amounted to an autonomous private operation despite the fact that they were still employees of the CIA.

In 1976 Richard Secord turned up in Tehran, posted to run the air force component of the U.S. Military Assistance Advisory Group, the main function of which was to advise the shah to buy lots of expensive American weapons. Weapons sales promoted by Secord involved what one observer calls "some of the biggest bribery in Iran."

The enormous U.S. weapons sales program to Iran was, in addition, marked by a huge disparity between the prices paid by the Iranians and what the U.S. military paid for identical equipment. This, as we shall see, was not the last time the Iranians were to be subject to such official profiteering. Secord's superior and partner in these efforts was Erich von Marbod, who had now become the senior U.S. defense representative to Iran.

Handling bribes, or as he prefers to call it, *baksheesh*, was the speciality of a man whom Secord first met in Iran and who was to become the financial comptroller of Secord's complex business organization. Albert Hakim was a middleman who would receive bribe money from defense contractors to be paid to Iranian officials who were purchasing the weapons. Not all the money would pass out of his control however. As he later testified to the Iran-contra committees, Hakim was trusted by the shah's generals to invest their ill-gotten gains in Switzerland, in accounts untraceable to the true owners of the money.

It was in this period that the network began to set up its own proprietaries, as private companies owned by the CIA are called. Some of these were to become famous when the Iran-contra scandal finally burst on America. They included the Stanford Technology Corp. and Energy Resources. Others, such as CSF Investments Ltd, were specifically Central American in their orientation. This was hardly a coincidence, for in 1978 the network had made a new and fateful connection.

* * *

In 1978 Edwin Wilson was dispatched by his partners to talk business with Anastasio Somoza. The dictator's affairs were going from bad to worse; not only were the Sandinista insurgents growing in strength and popular support, but the church and the middle class were edging to the rails of the sinking ship. Wilson offered Somoza some specialized help. For $650,000 a year he and his partners (Clines et al.) would supply a team of five "countersubversion specialists" ($80,000 a year each, plus expenses) who would take care of Somoza's opponents in a satisfactorily terminal way, as well as supply other kinds of help. One of the specialists was to be Rafael Quintero, who had been plying his old trade since the days of the shooter team; the rest were to be other veteran graduates of that program. In February 1987 Wilson, now incarcerated under maximum security at the federal penitentiary in Marion, Illinois, recalled the occasion for an interviewer.

"I had been contacted by Clines to go down and find Somoza. This was in the Carter administration, and everybody in the agency wants to help Somoza, but they want to do it covertly. So they say, make a money deal with him. What Somoza needed was information. In other words, if you're running a country down there and there are people coming in from every country and you don't have the apparatus to check them out, you need to be able to go through the CIA computer and find out who's who. These [CIA] people were willing to help Somoza behind the scenes. So I went down there to talk to him and made a proposal."

The thifty dictator jibbed at the asking price and haggled to get his countersubversion team for a lower fee, so no business eventuated until the following year. Early in 1979 the Carter administration cut off all military aid to Somoza, at which point further delegations from the old-boy network succeeded in garnering a contract to supply Somoza's embattled forces with weapons, ammunition, aircraft, and other appurtenances of war in total defiance of official U.S. government policy. (Shackley and Clines had been forced out of the CIA in 1979 because of their dealings with Wilson.) The ever-reliable Quintero was the executive officer for this operation. As Wilson remembers it, "Later Clines went back with some other people and they did work out something to get him arms. Once [Somoza] went down the drain, then these same people were in place. They kept coming back to Clines."

From March until July 1979, therefore, our friends helped, along with Israel, to keep the Somoza regime alive and fighting. On July

106

17 the dictator fled the country along with his family and most of the contents of the state treasury. He had not, however, thrown in the towel. One of his first ports of call was a Bahamian resort called North Cay where, according to the indefatigable Sheehan, he met with representatives from the network to plan a comeback. They would supply arms and ammunition that would be used to equip a force drawn from the tattered remnants of the National Guard.

Early in 1981, some new players entered on the scene. The incoming Reagan administration decried the Carterites' weak-kneed attitude toward covert action and toward what they saw as communist advances generally. They were determined to reverse the tide. One of the earliest decisions taken in this regard was to give full (covert) support to the contras.

From 1981 to 1984 the task of supplying, advising, and training the contras fell to the CIA, under the direction of Director William Casey and underlings such as Dewey Clarridge. The effort was too public and controversial to escape either comment or criticism, however, and by early 1984 it seemed that a congressional ban on aid would put the old team back in business, and so it was. The network had come full circle. From secretly supplying Cuban exiles against Castro with the full official approval of the U.S. government, to performing the same service for the Nicaraguan contras.

This time they enjoyed not only the wholehearted endorsement and support of the powerful William Casey, and of the president himself, but the services of an eager young apparatchik, a man who believed in the business of covert anticommunist operations as a holy cause. He was just what the old hands needed.

Chapter Seven
BLUE'S BASTARDS

"He could have gone to the moon and it wouldn't be in the file."
—Lt. Col. John Shotwell, Marine Corps spokesman
December 1986

Oliver North's first assignment with the collection of veteran operatives he would later contract to supply the contra war has been wiped from the record. According to Marine Corps records North was a modestly successful platoon commander in Vietnam from December 1968 through November 1969, a conventional tour of duty. There is no portion of his record that is classified, nothing to hint at the time he logged serving in the secret war in Laos.

Yet on one occasion at least, North has sworn under oath that he took part in secret operations. In 1985 he served as a character witness for a senior NSC staffer, Thomas Reed, in the latter's trial on charges of stock fraud. (Reed was acquitted.) Prior to giving evidence, North listed his duties in Southeast Asia as having included time as "an infantry platoon and company commander in the Special Operations Force, Team Commander." He stated that his tour of duty went beyond November 1969 "through the early part of 1970 and then again in 1971."

Insofar as special operations require bravery, initiative, and a total disregard for the rules, North appears to have been well suited to the role. His ever-present desire to bring himself to the attention of his superiors did not hurt either. Within his unit he was known as Blue, after his radio call sign. The unit was collectively known as Blue's Bastards. On one occasion he led the Bastards on an invasion of North Vietnam. They were stationed just south of the demilitarized zone, or DMZ as it was known, that marked the border between North and South Vietnam. At midnight one night Blue suddenly announced to his men that for unexplained reasons he wanted a prisoner from the North Vietnamese army. Assembling a "killer team" to cross the border, the intrepid lieutenant and his point man knocked out a guard and returned victorious through the minefields, to the delight of his crew. "As for the prisoner, no superior ever asked where we got him," recalled Randy Harrod, one of North's men. "North just told us this was something we had to keep our mouths shut about."

Randy Harrod had other reasons to venerate North. After Harrod had left the Bastards he was court-martialed for the murder of sixteen Vietnamese women and children at Son Thang, a village thirty miles south of Da Nang. The massacre was one of the first war crimes trials in Vietnam, and North flew back to Saigon from the States to testify as a character witness for Harrod.

Although not on a combat assignment, North apparently relished the opportunity for combat. An Oklahoma lawyer, Denzil Garrison, who shared a tent with North during the trial, recalls that when the case dragged, "North hustled down to the dispatcher to volunteer for killer teams heading into the bush on patrol. We'd hear about it at the officers' club. They'd be laughing, 'That damned Ollie North is going out hiding behind trees and slitting throats on his own time.' When we brought it up he'd just shrug it off, but he didn't deny it. We were afraid we'd lose our best character witness before he had a chance to take the stand." Harrod was acquitted.

There can be no doubt that North was an intrepid combat commander. Most of the medals that he sported so conspicuously during his testimony before the Iran-contra committees in 1987 had been profligately distributed by the high command in Vietnam, including decorations passed out by the then government of South Vietnam. But the Silver Star was still hard to come by, and North won his, according to the official citation, while rescuing another platoon that was pinned down by enemy fire. He "assumed the foremost assault position and, seemingly oblivious to the intense machine-gun fire impacting around him, led his men against the hostile position."

North's conspicuous ardor may have impressed his superiors. It did not always gratify those who had to share the risks he sought. "He was a zealot. . . . Some of us wondered, 'If we're pulling out, why are we marching up the hill to kill our men?' " recalls Don Moore, who served as a junior officer under North. "But to Ollie, it was always, 'Let's sweep this ridge, take this hill.' "

In the fall of 1969, North returned to teach at the marine base at Quantico, Virginia. Academic life did not dampen his theatrical inclinations. On occasion he would arrive in front of his counterinsurgency class via a rope suspended from the ceiling. He once jumped onto a classroom desk carrying an automatic rifle and accidentally opened fire on the students. Fortunately the gun was loaded with blanks.

At the beginning of 1970 he was back at the real thing, returning to Vietnam for what he later told his friend Andy Messing, a conservative activist and associate in the contra aid network, were "classified missions." In July 1971, however, he returned to the U.S. to again defend American soldiers who had massacred civilians. This time the venue was William Buckley's television show *Firing Line*, and North and two fellow marines were there to protest press coverage of the infamous and bloody My Lai massacre.

At the time the show was broadcast the Peers Inquiry, the army's internal investigation of the massacre, had amassed twenty thousand pages of testimony on what had happened in March 1968, when Task Force Barker, a unit of the Americal Division, had wiped out a village known on army maps as My Lai 4, together with surrounding hamlets.

At the time North made his appearance, army investigators had concluded that the victims in My Lai 4 alone numbered 347 men, women, and children. One participant recalled how "we were all out there having a good time. It was kind of like being in a shooting gallery." He told of a machine gunner methodically ripping a woman in half at the waist with bullets, and of a baby barely able to crawl being used by a soldier for target practice. "He fired at it with a .45. He missed. We all laughed. He got up three or four feet closer and missed again. We laughed. Then he got up right on top and plugged him."

Terry Reid, who had been a GI present at the massacre, told a journalist in 1971: "I used to think my company was a bad-ass one until I started seeing others. Sometimes you thought it was just my platoon, my company that was committing atrocious acts, and what bad luck it was to get into it. But what we were doing was being done all over."

Such scenes passed North by. After having spent at least twelve months as a combat soldier in Vietnam, he felt able to tell an appreciative William Buckley and the TV audience, "I never witnessed— and I hate to think that anyone would imagine I went into this thing with blinders, and I think I saw a little bit of what went on over there the time I was there—but I never witnessed a single ear being cut off, a single round being fired at a man without a rifle, a single piece of ordnance dropped at, on, or near a village of any type, or a single civilian being maltreated by either South Vietnamese or American personnel."

Sixteen years later, the contra forces that North so strongly supported were apparently holding to the same exemplary standards of conduct he claimed for the soldiers in Vietnam. There is no lack of reports of atrocities in Nicaragua. Interviews in May of 1985 revealed dozens of witnesses and victims of contra atrocities, including a farmer who had been shot in the head as punishment for selling a cow to the Nicaraguan army. His son, whose head was blown away in the same incident, died in his arms. The farmer regained consciousness as the pigs were eating his son's brains. In another village a ten-year-old girl had bullet wounds in her chest and the back of her head. She had been used for target practice. A younger and less fortunate girl in her area had been raped and beheaded. Her head was stuck by the side of the road as a warning to the others not to attend government clinics or schools. In March 1987, despite stout declarations to the contrary, contra units, according to the *New York Times*, were still bayoneting infants.

Oliver Lawrence North's father, also named Oliver, was an army colonel who earned his Silver Star in World War II. His eldest son was born in 1943 while the family was posted in San Antonio. Their itinerant life as a service family ended after the war when Oliver Senior retired and went to work in the family business, a wool-combing mill, in Philmont, New York, a village in the Hudson River valley. Oliver Junior had an idyllic middle-class upbringing, installed with his three siblings at the house on Maple Avenue, even after polyester finished off wool combing in the Hudson valley and his father went to work as a statistics teacher at a local college.

Growing up as a fifties teenager in this backwater, where life was slow, young Oliver was hardly a rebel without a cause. He served as an altar boy at Sacred Heart Church, beyond indeed the call of duty.

111

"Usually, once a kid gets in high school the altar boy [activity] stopped," reported Mr. Gibbons, who lived across the street from the Norths. "But he stayed on longer, until he was a senior."

In 1961 North signed up for classes at the state college in Brockport as an English major. It was a period he would rather forget, it seems, for he subsequently lied about his academic career to give it a bit more polish. In 1985, under oath, he attested that he had gone not to Brockport but to premed at Rochester. At Brockport he earned solid Bs with the odd D in mathematics. He also joined the Marine ROTC. After a summer at Camp Lejeune he would be saluting for life.

He entered Annapolis, class of '68. Oliver North was already looking ahead. Classmates remember him studying South America: "He felt that's where communism was going to make a stand somewhere in the future." He took to driving a 427-horsepower Shelby Cobra painted in Marine Corps green. When injuries from a car accident threatened his nascent military career, North devised a novel rehabilitation program. "He was always jumping off his roof and his garage," remembers Howard Rhodes, a neighbor. Then he took up boxing. In a celebrated match he beat a classmate, James Webb, who was later to become secretary of the navy. Webb always claimed that the boxing coach, who says North was like a son to him, told Webb to go easy on his lighter opponent.

After Vietnam and Quantico, North moved to Okinawa to run a jungle prep school called the Northern Training Area. His official NSC biography cites a stint as the head of the "Special Operations Training Detachment" there. There is no record of such a unit, which means little in a world where covert operations require "deniability." At the school, North rigged a booby trap on his hut that sprayed red dye, and hung a banner that proclaimed, "Lead, Follow, or Get the Hell Out of the Way."

His next posting was to the Naval War College, where the reviews ranged from a "delight" to a "sycophant and chronic name dropper." There is no doubt that peers from his pre–White House days react violently to the mention of Ollie North, either pro or con. One marine who had served alongside him in Vietnam said in March 1987, "There is a part of me that would like to see Ollie twist slowly in the wind." Others among his brother officers had more damaging revelations to make after North became famous in November 1986. They recalled his period of psychiatric treatment in 1974, for example, after he was discovered late one night in a Virginia suburb roaming about naked and brandishing a .45, pronouncing his intention of killing himself. Like other episodes of his career, this has been expunged from the official record. Exactly why he was in such mental distress is unclear; the kinder explanations dwell on the delayed effects of his combat experiences. It is certainly the case that his fervor does dangle over the edge at times. One administration official who worked closely with North on the contra program recalls him suddenly remarking, "It's too bad Reagan is so old. It's good to die with our leaders."

One former marine colleague vividly remembers the reaction of his peers when they heard that North had been seconded to the White House. "We all thought that Ollie was just the worst possible person to be in that job. He is a person of overwhelming ambition and overweening opportunism. He is incapable of questioning an order from a superior, however unwise or foolhardy that order might be."

There were plenty of orders floating around the Reagan National Security Council from the time North joined it as a junior staffer in 1981 that might be considered unwise or foolhardy. One of the early obsessions of the administration was the question of fighting and winning a nuclear war. Thomas Reed, the staffer for whom North went to bat at his 1985 trial, once declared that the policy was that the U.S. should "prevail with pride" in a nuclear conflict. To this end ambitious plans were laid for civil defense in a nuclear emergency. The Federal Emergency Management Agency (FEMA) labored over schemes to evacuate the urban population of the United States. Lieutenant Colonel North, as the NSC liaison with FEMA, worked diligently on one portion of the plan: the suspension of the Constitution and the imposition of martial law. This might also come about in conditions short of nuclear war, for it could be imposed during conditions of violent opposition to a foreign military operation.

In this task, as in so many others he was to undertake before his downfall, North devoted his energies to a scheme that was not originally of his making. No one who knew him or worked with him during his time on the National Security Council ever thought of him as a "rogue elephant" or an "out-of-control cowboy," as the damage-control experts at the White House tried to portray him. Back in the early spring of 1986, before a desperate administration attempted to pin the blame for everything on the lieutenant colonel, a close associate of North's responded to every question about the latter's involvement in the covert contra aid effort by repeating: "Go ask the president. North is a messenger boy. Ask the president."

North himself testified before the Iran-contra committees in July of 1987, "I realized, there's a lot of folks around that think there's a loose cannon on the gun deck of state at the NSC. That wasn't what I heard when I worked there. I've only heard it since I left. People used to walk up to me and tell me what a great job I was doing, and the fact is there were many many people, to include the former assistant to the president for national security affairs, the current national security adviser, the attorney general of the United States of America, the director of Central Intelligence, all of whom knew that to be wrong."

Similarly, it was always common knowledge within relevant portions of the bureaucracy, as one such individual admitted as early as the spring of 1985, that North was only one of a regular planning group on the contra war made up of representatives from the White House, the State Department, and the CIA. North was, of course, the White House representative. The other ranking members were Elliott Abrams, the nervously acerbic assistant secretary of state for Latin American affairs, and Alan Fiers, a CIA bureaucrat who was appointed director of the Central American Task Force at the agency just days after the Boland Amendment became law. This group led the RIG, the Restricted Interagency Group, a triumvirate among the departments.

Even after North made the basis of his defense before the Iran-contra committees the assertion that he was only following orders, the impression still prevailed that he had been functioning as part of something distinct from the U.S. government. Yet, when he took over a leading role in the running of contra operations in the early part of 1984, essential CIA operatives continued functioning just as they always had. North himself remarked, long after the passage of Boland, "The contras couldn't buy a Band-Aid without the CIA." Indeed, North's deputy at the NSC, Vincent Cannistraro, moved to that job from the same position under Duane Clarridge at the CIA.

Part of the confusion was caused by North's irrepressible appetite for self-promotion. In his heyday, journalists in Washington knew him as a ready source of inside information whenever some flamboyant special operation was in the news. It just so happened that these helpful leaks tended to accord a starring role, on background of course, to Lt. Col. Oliver North. A summary that appeared in *U.S. News & World Report* on December 8, 1986, is indicative: "When the U.S. launched its abortive effort to rescue American diplomats held hostage in Iran in 1980, there was North on the Turkish border with a force of marines poised to cover the escape. When American troops invaded Grenada in 1983, it was North in the 'nerve center' of planning. That same year, insiders say, he supervised the mining of Nicaraguan harbors by the CIA. He is credited with helping to plan the capture of Arab terrorists who hijacked the Italian cruise ship *Achille Lauro* and with picking targets for the bombing raid on Libya." One feat for which North likes to take credit that is missing from this roll of honor was the disbanding of the Salvadoran death squads.

The problem with this litany of accomplishments is that North simply was not the boss in many of these operations, including the invasion of Grenada or the bombing of Libya. Away from the journalists, North was in fact a staff officer, anxious to protect his rear on all occasions and do nothing without the approval of those above him. The internal NSC communications released by the Tower Commission and the Iran-contra committees show that North was forever writing memos to his superiors keeping them apprised of what he was up to and apologizing whenever he feared he might have overstepped his authority. As North himself testified, "I sought approval of my superiors for every one of my actions."

Even before North began his artful program of self-exculpation in his congressional testimony, investigators had begun to see the hand of one superior in particular behind North's actions. William J. Casey, director of Central Intelligence and close confidant of the president, had pushed for North to take control of covert operations in Central America.

By the time this realization began to dawn, Casey was in Georgetown University Hospital, with one tube in his stomach and another in his brain, his body rotted by cancer. The spymaster's brain tumor, requiring treatment the day before he was due to testify before an inquisitive Congress, was tragic for the former director but convenient for the CIA and the administration.

The boyish North was adept at collecting mentors and father figures. His Annapolis boxing coach, Emerson Smith, was one of many who were to declare, "Ollie's like a son to me." His high school track coach, Russell Robertson, had felt the same way: "He's like a kid you would like to have for your own." It was common knowledge among his brother officers that North's career in the marines had been nurtured by Lt. Gen. E. C. ("Dutch") Schultz. His move to the NSC was assisted by Navy Secretary John Lehman. During his rise in the White House his filial relationship was with National Security Adviser Robert McFarlane, who said, "North is not a rogue elephant . . . [he is] like a son of mine."

Casey was very much in this tradition. North freely admitted this relationship in his testimony: how he and Casey had conferred several times a week, how the director's White House office was just down the hall from his own, how Casey guided him every step of the way. As North explained to the Iran-contra committees, "Casey was for me a man of immense proportions, an adviser. He never once, that I can recall, disagreed in any way with what I was doing."

Powerful as he was, however, Casey may not have been the most important in North's patriarchal collection. "Ollie was very, very close personally to the president," according to one senior administration official. "Reagan thought of him almost as a son. He briefed him often. Several times he helped write presidential speeches. Everyone who knew anything thought of him as a plenipontentiary for Ronald Reagan."

Until it became impolitic to do otherwise, North was never one to minimize his close relationships with the mighty. He not only told close associates that he briefed the president more than once a week, he gave the same message in addressing public groups, such as a United Methodist Church congregation in Washington in February 1986. He told this gathering that he briefed the president twice a week on terrorism and Central America. North's statements and the recollection of knowledgeable associates conflict with the official records of the president's schedule, which show him meeting with North no more often than once a month.

North's bluntest description of his relationship with his commander in chief came during a meeting with CIA and shooter team alumnus Felix Rodriguez in June 1986. Pointing to a televised congressional session, North exclaimed, "These people want me, but they cannot touch me, because the old man loves my ass."

Oliver North, at the time a major, was assigned to what the National Security Council called its "contra account" in 1982. It was his chance to implement the Reagan Doctrine, which in essence called for the "rollback" of the Soviet threat by taking a stand against their "surrogates," which to the doctrinally pure meant the Sandinistas and the leftist opposition in El Salvador. Once at work, North liked to refer to congressional critics of Reagan's Central American policy as "commie bastards." Assigned to liaise with the Presidential Commission on Central America, in 1982, North referred to himself as "the advance man for the invasion."

North worked out of a bare, cramped office on an upper floor of the Old Executive Office Building, the Victorian architectural extravaganza behind the White House. His dedication to work, arriving before seven and toiling away on his masters' business until late in the evening, has become legendary, leaving little time for his wife and four children parked in Virginia. His immediate staff consisted of two aides and two secretaries, one of whom was Fawn Hall, the twenty-seven-year-old beauty with all-American values whose ultimate ambition was to pursue her modeling career full-time. It was convenient for North that if he wished to communicate with father figure McFarlane, Ms. Hall could simply call up her mother, who was McFarlane's secretary.

Exactly when North became the key figure in the administration's efforts to pursue a Central American policy in defiance of Congress and in secret from the populace at large is unclear. In his congressional testimony he spoke of how he and Casey had discussed the question of, in effect, evading a congressional ban on contra aid "in 1983." It was in the spring of 1983 that North became a member of the RIG, the Restricted Interagency Group. The RIG had been founded in 1981 by Thomas Enders, then assistant secretary of state for inter-American affairs. Enders later forfeited his job by making an enemy of Senator Jesse Helms, who considered him soft on communism in El Salvador. (Enders had been insufficiently considerate toward Maj. Roberto D'Aubuisson, also known as Major Blowtorch, whom Helms considered a "chamber-of-commerce type.")

During Enders's time at the RIG the membership included Dewey Clarridge, CIA point man for Central America, Vice Adm. Arthur S. Moreau, the representative of the Joint Chiefs of Staff (and a candidate for father-figurehood in the North pantheon), and, representing the office of Caspar Weinberger, Nestor Sanchez, an old CIA Latin America hand lately transferred to the Pentagon. After the "liberal" Enders had been packed off to exile as ambassador to Spain, to be succeeded by a more amenable official, the same faces continued to play their central role.

North's first important Central American mission came in the fall of 1983, when he played a part in persuading the Salvadoran military to tone down the activities of their notorious (and supposedly independent) death squads. At the time these squads were murdering an average of eight hundred people a month, which was posing difficulties for the Reagan administration in getting funding for more orthodox Salvadoran military operations. The RIG determined that Vice President Bush should pay a visit to El Salvador to get the numbers down. Of course, the United States was not entirely blameless for the death squads. Their techniques for rolling back communism had been imparted by U.S. advisers back in the 1960s. General Medrano, the godfather of the death squads, proudly displays to visiting journalists a medal given to him by President Lyndon Johnson. According to administration sources, Nicholas Carranza, heavily implicated in death squad activity, was actually on the CIA payroll.

North gave the vice president at least one long briefing in the White House before the party set off. North flew south on *Air Force Two* to provide further advice and consultation. The expedition was a success; death squad activity diminished and U.S. military aid increased along with the aerial bombing of the countryside.

The first time the outside world, or at least the Senate Intelligence Committee, heard of North's rising position in the scheme of things came in 1984, when the CIA mined the Nicaraguan harbors and (belatedly) brought about a congressional uproar.

In early March of that year North sent National Security Adviser Robert McFarlane a top secret "action memo" entitled "Special Activities in Nicaragua" (which was definitely not given to the intelligence committee): "On the night of February 29 [word deleted] emplaced four magnetic mines in the harbor at Corinto, Nicaragua. . . . In accord with prior arrangements, ARDE's 'Barracuda Commandos' took credit for the operation. . . . Our intention is to severely disrupt the flow of shipping essential to Nicaraguan trade during the peak export period." North the strategist goes on to advocate sinking a ship so that "no insurers will cover ships calling in Nicaraguan ports." North recommended that McFarlane approve the operation and brief the president, which McFarlane dutifully did.

In the spring of 1984, therefore, while resentment against the covert war in Nicaragua mounted in Congress (although Boland did not pass until October, Congress was threatening to cut off aid as early as May), North was traveling frequently to the contra camps in Honduras. He spoke regularly with Adolfo Calero, sometimes several times a day. When the uproar over the infamous CIA manual forced the agency to reshuffle those responsible, the key figures, such as Vincent Cannistraro, moved from Langley over to North's office.

As it became clear that despite the entreaties of the administration, Congress was actually going to ban CIA aid to the contras, William Casey directed North to put together an "off-the-shelf, stand-alone entity with no direct ties to the CIA." North accordingly drafted an operational plan to transfer responsibility for arming, training, and supplying the contras from the CIA as an institution to a supposedly private aid network, controlled from the White House. Sometime in March 1984 North drafted a three-page memo that was discussed by senior officials at the NSC and finally read aloud to the president. The commander in chief gave his (verbal) approval to what was clearly an attempt to evade the law.

North lost no time in passing on the good news to those whom this intrigue was meant to benefit. Edgar Chamorro, who at the time was one of the CIA-selected Directorate of the FDN, described to the World Court how North had arrived in Honduras and assured him and his fellow directors of "continued U.S. government support, notwithstanding the refusal of Congress to appropriate more funds." Nor does it appear that North was in any doubt about the legal basis, or lack of it, of what he was up to. As the program moved into high gear he remarked to at least two close associates, "If it weren't for those liberals in Congress, we wouldn't be doing half of what we do illegally."

This system has been subsequently portrayed as something separate from the official machinery of government, and yet it is clear that all the important centers of power in the executive branch were fully briefed. For example, on March 1, 1985, North wrote an eyes-only memo to his mentor and old RIGmate, Vice Adm. Arthur Moreau, that is full of news on the supply and direction of the contra war effort, including dates of weapons shipments, staging areas, and road improvements. North asked Moreau to pass the information on to "the Chairman," Gen. John Vessey, chairman of the Joint Chiefs of Staff. He also noted that "we are in the process of expediting our delivery of items on FMS backlog." FMS is the foreign military sales operation of the Pentagon, which indicates that this section of the Defense Department bureaucracy, so useful for generating both funds and weapons, was well integrated into the contra supply effort.

Whether or not the entire scheme had sprung from the brain of William Casey, it very much fitted into Casey's vision of the proper way to conduct covert operations: with a minimum of restraint from the irksome trappings of democracy and accountability. By the summer of 1984 a system was in place by which the president and his closest advisers could conduct a secret foreign policy, and a secret war. Inevitably, this new order required the services of people who had a great deal of experience in running self-contained covert operations.

Richard Secord had had to resign from the Pentagon under something of a cloud in 1982 as a consequence of his links both with Edwin Wilson, the man accused of supplying the archterrorist Qaddafi, and with Thomas Clines, whose company, EATSCO, was convicted of submitting eight million dollars' worth of false invoices to the Pentagon. In April 1984, however, Secord was once again invested with an important official (and secret) role. According to Pentagon sources, he was appointed to head an antiterrorism task force set up by presidential directive on April 3 and answerable to the National Security Council. Although its primary area of activity was intended to be the Middle East, knowledgeable sources confirm that within the NSC the term "antiterrorist" applied to the contra war as well.

Oliver North subsequently testified that it was William Casey who had "suggested" that he turn to Secord to play a leading role in the secret system being put in place: "Director Casey is the one who suggested General Secord to me as a person who had a background in covert operations, a man of integrity, a West Point graduate . . . a man who, by Director Casey's definition, got things done and who had been poorly treated" when he had retired from the air force.

General Secord had crossed paths with North in the secret war in Laos (where, it has been reported, Secord may have saved North's life, though Secord denies it). They had teamed up again in an overt operation in 1981, lobbying Congress for approval of the sale of AWACs radar surveillance planes to Saudi Arabia. This was in fact North's very first job at the NSC, but Secord was an old hand at the business of big arms sales. Secord does not remember his junior colleague playing a particularly important role in the affair, describing him as a "scheduler type." The sale got approval, after the fierce opposition from the Israelis was quelled by promises of extra U.S. military largesse for their country. For his efforts, Secord received the Distinguished Service Medal, generally awarded for valor in war.

Now they were to work together again. North had come a long

way since 1981, but compared to Secord he was still a callow youth. Secord after all had learned his business in the piratical world of Southeast Asian air operations; he had made his way in the rough-and-tumble of the shah's arms buildup, where serious men played for billion-dollar stakes; he had dealt with characters such as the redoubtable Edwin Wilson and Theodore Shackley, the Blond Ghost himself, and he had not done it by becoming like a son to them. An old acquaintance of the general's, who had watched his career with interest if not approval, had this to say when he heard that Secord had teamed up with North: "Dick is very smart, he has nerves of steel, he knows absolutely how to work the national security bureaucracy and the arms business. He and his people can sniff out people like North, and they know how to use them."

Secord testified that his first meeting with Oliver North to discuss contra aid was in July 1984. North had then introduced him to Adolfo Calero. Later Secord brought along none other than Rafael Quintero to discuss weapons shipments—exactly the business Quintero had been doing with the contras prior to 1981. Calero "had to find quality munitions and arms," Secord told the senators and congressmen. On December 21, 1984, Adolfo Calero deposited $425,000 in the Swiss account of Energy Resources, one of the many Secord/Hakim corporate entities, and the "enterprise," as Secord called it, was off and running. "Calero liked the prices we were coming up with . . . there was nothing spooky about it."

It was in fact the most ambitious and spooky project in many years, even for the seasoned members of the old JM/Wave and Southeast Asian special operations network. It was also profitable. Of the arms deals that were to follow after the initial negotiations, Secord testified that "the intended profits would be shared by myself, [Albert] Hakim, and the arms dealer." After some initially botched arrangements with some Canadian arms dealers, Secord "got Mr. Tom Clines to manage future procurement. . . . I wanted Clines in the loop. I had a lot of trust in him."

With Secord, Quintero, and Clines involved, it should come as no surprise that other old comrades, such as Felix Rodriguez and Luis Posada Carriles, were not far behind. Nor should it have come as a surprise to North that the personnel of the "enterpise" were adept at turning special operations to personal profit, but in the summer of 1984 the lieutenant colonel still had a lot to learn.

Secord later claimed that he waived his profits from the North operation because of a keen desire to return to government service.

He was still peeved at having had to resign from the Pentagon because of his association with Edwin Wilson. His ambition was to become the deputy director of the CIA for (covert) operations. One senator asked, pertinently enough, whether that would not have been something of a demotion in view of his responsibilities in the North operation.

The White House also recruited retired Gen. John Singlaub, North's former superior in Laos, to open fund-raising efforts and organize missions to old friends in Korea, Taiwan, and Israel. Among other services, he was able to arrange to buy quantities of weapons and ammunition captured from the PLO by the Israelis in 1982. Singlaub had another, equally important responsibility, which was to serve as a very public representative of the supposedly private aid that was now to replace the contra support cut off by the dastardly liberals in Congress. Robert Owen, who would act as North's covert ambassador to Central America and to other private groups such as CMA and the Miami Cubans, began working out of North's office in the fall of 1984, though as a "cutout" he was deliberately kept off the government payroll. Deniability was in place, laying a fig leaf of legality over the ongoing U.S. government operation. In reality, of course, many of the same old faces were doing the same jobs both before and after the cutoff. Cannistraro was in the White House; Nestor Sanchez kept a watching brief from the office of the secretary of defense; the head of the CIA contra task force, Alan Fiers, sat on the RIG along with North and the assistant secretary of state for Latin American affairs, Elliott Abrams. William Casey, the guiding light of the whole operation, stayed in daily touch.

Since the RIG and its adjuncts were directing the contra war in Washington, it is small wonder that this tight control extended to Central America. Although President Reagan never ceased to cite the Nicaraguan "freedom fighters" as a spontaneously generated force—"the moral equal of our Founding Fathers"—the contras were throughout this period a wholly owned subsidiary of the U.S. This central truth is made abundantly clear in the internal documents of Oliver North as released by the congressional select committees.

On March 2, 1985, the contra luminaries Adolfo Calero, Alfonso Robelo, and Arturo Cruz issued the San José Declaration, a resounding declaration of lofty goals and undying unity among the "resistance" forces. It concluded with the words "May love for our fatherland overcome selfishness and foreign involvement."

These worthy sentiments appear somewhat ironic in light of a memo North wrote to McFarlane a month later, in which he proudly revealed that "the document was written by Calero, Cruz and North in my hotel room in Miami on Jan 29th and 30th" after the Nicaraguans had been "convinced that this document was necessary to bring unity to the movement."

The former Brockport English major was very proud of his Jeffersonian handiwork and had originally concocted a terrific scenario for unveiling it to the world. The scheme, on which he evidently devoted a good portion of some of those legendary sixteen-hour workdays, was to charter a Caribbean luxury liner called the *Sea Goddess* and stage a contra constitutional convention on board. The ship was to be flanked by U.S. Navy subs and aircraft carriers while contra leaders signed the declaration written in the Miami hotel room in January. There was some debate on whether the declaration should be proclaimed from Grenada (on "soil liberated from communism"), Boston, or Philadelphia. "I think they'd pretty well settled on sailing up the Delaware River to Independence Hall," says someone who worked on the scheme. "Ollie had wanted to do it on Grenada for symbolic reasons, but everyone thought that was too much—it was just too tacky." Former Ambassador Walter Annenberg would foot the $429,000 bill for the charter, they hoped, and Reagan, as North told associates, "thinks it's great." Sad to say, stick-in-the-mud State Department bureaucrats killed the plan and instead of the *Sea Goddess* they got San José.

The full flavor of North's relationship with Calero is amply conveyed in a letter from the colonel addressed to "My Friend" and signed, with North's customary appetite for the theatrical, "Steelhammer." It is undated, but internal evidence suggests that it was written toward the end of 1984 or at the beginning of 1985. The first part consists of intelligence information on Sandinista troop movements (transmission of intelligence to the contras was illegal at the time). There then follows a more cheering note:

And now for the best news of all:

Next week, a sum in access [*sic*] of $20 million will be deposited in the usual account. While this must be husbanded carefully, it should allow us to bridge the gap between now and when the vote is taken and the funds are turned on again.

Steelhammer the strategist provides detailed advice:

> ... The battle plan for the near future should involve getting as
> many as possible out of the border camps and hiding them per-
> haps in the areas I have shown. ... Attacks can be launched with
> great vigor against the Sandinista rear, hitting them hard. ...

Arturo Cruz had been very successfully marketed to wavering
moderates in Washington as the "respectable" contra leader, but as
the memo makes clear, his care and nourishment provided problems:

> ... Lastly, we mave have to very soon assume the cost of what
> the company [CIA] is providing to Arturo. You and I both recog-
> nize his value and limitations. Some in our Congress are aware
> that the company is paying him and have threatened to expose
> the connection. This could be devastating to our forthcoming
> campaign to restore the funding. I will find out how much he is
> getting and let you know, but it seems as though something
> should be set aside for this purpose.
>
> Finally, we ought to look at a maritime capability and something
> on the southern front. I had a very useful meeting with the
> Security Minister of the place down south [Costa Rica]. He has
> agreed to meet with you very discreetly, I well let you know
> when this can be arranged. He is anxious to help, but only if it
> can be done without exposing him or making operations visible
> in his country.

The letter closes with this heartfelt and telling plea:

> Please do *not* in any way make *anyone* aware of the deposit. Too
> much is becoming known by too many people. We need to make
> sure that this new financing does *not* become known. The Con-
> gress must believe that there continues to be an urgent need for
> funding.

The reference to the "southern front" is significant, for all the
information to hand about North's particular responsibilities in the
war suggests that Costa Rica and the southern front were the prime
concern for him and for Project Democracy, as he liked to call his
operation. As General Secord puts it, "the southern front was the sine
qua non. North agreed with that. Casey agreed with that."
True, the main contra force continued to reside in their Hondu-

ran sanctuary in the north, but it appears that their nurture and supply were more a matter of routine, with the Pentagon and the Honduran military doing much of the donkeywork. In the "Dear Friend" letter quoted above, for example, North writes ("on the brighter side") that

—[Honduras] has agreed to approve the arrival of FDN supplies on a blanket approval basis. They are willing to provide end-user certificates for munition orders.

—They are willing to loan the FDN munitions when your supplies get unacceptably low and to sell essential quartermaster supplies.

—The Hondurans will also make available trucks to move FDN supplies from points of arrival all the way to Las Vegas [the main contra base in Honduras].

—[word deleted] is going to meet next week with the [Honduran] Minister of Public Works . . . to arrange for the repair of the road between Las Vegas and Cifuentes. Supposedly they will charge only for the cost of fuel and drivers.

Given the enormous weight of Pentagon resources pouring into Honduras in this period (see chapter 1), it is hardly surprising that North should have been able to devote so much time to the effort to get a suitable (non-Pastora) contra presence off the ground along the southern front, in Costa Rica.

If such a move were successful, so the map seemed to show, then the Sandinistas would be hemmed in. All the evidence, however, suggests that the southern front was considered more than just a desirable development. It may have been the fact that the northern contras had so little to show for all the millions of dollars and tons of arms being poured into Honduras. It may also have had to do with the plan that the Special Forces officer outlined to me in Tegucigalpa in May of 1985, by which the contra force of mercenaries, such as Glibbery, Carr, and the Cubans, would be part of a scheme to provoke a direct military confrontation between Nicaragua and the United States. It was not that long, after all, since North had been describing himself as "the advance man for the invasion."

Whatever the strategic considerations underlying the quest for the southern front, the local U.S. government officials on the ground were left in no doubt about its priority.

* * *

At the end of January 1985, the press carried reports that Lewis Tambs, the forceful U.S. ambassador in Colombia, was being moved to Costa Rica. Due to State Department and congressional quibbles regarding his appointment, Tambs did not move to San José until July. Before he left for his new post he was given his marching orders from the key members of the RIG. As Tambs later stated to the Tower Commission, "Before I went [to Costa Rica] Ollie said when you get down there you should open the southern front. In the subsequent meetings and conversations (of the RIG) that was confirmed by Abrams and [Fiers]. That was sort of our mission."

Once Tambs was installed in San José he called in three key staff members. The CIA station chief, José Fernandez, was one of them. "When Ambassador Tambs arrived in Costa Rica," Fernandez told the commission, "he called together the Deputy Chief of Mission, the Defense Attaché and myself, and said that he had really only one mission in Costa Rica, and that was to form a Nicaraguan resistance southern front." It is hardly likely that the announcement came as any sort of surprise to Fernandez. According to senior administration officials, he had been personally recruited to assist the North-Secord operation by William Casey himself. Casey had told Fernandez to report to him through Clair George, the CIA's deputy director for operations.

A key element of the strategy was the construction of a remote, secure airfield capable of handling large multiengine transports such as C-130s. The strips on John Hull's ranch, though serviceable for smaller planes, could not handle the bigger transports that would be needed in a major buildup.

The idea that the U.S. government should authorize the secret construction of a military air base without authorization from Congress in an avowedly neutral country to provide aid specifically forbidden by Congress in an undeclared war was born at a meeting in Miami on July 1, 1985.

Up until then arms for Costa Rica had been coming down from Florida by way of the Miami Cuban network of Rene Corvo. But the new scheme was a much bigger operation, with regular airdrops to contra bands behind the lines. The meeting took place, as Secord later testified, at a Miami airport hotel, perhaps the Howard Johnson's favored by Brigade 2506 and their friends and associates. The participants on this occasion were very high-powered. They included Adolfo Calero, Enrique Bermudez (the former National Guard colonel who was now the military commander of the FDN), Richard Secord, the old shooter teamster Rafael Quintero, ex–CIA man Tom Clines, and Oliver North.

North was late. He flew down to Miami on a government plane, and the meeting did not get under way until ten o'clock at night. Secord, in his testimony before the select committees, described the conclave, held at a time when it was illegal to aid the contras militarily and illegal to conspire to plot military actions against other countries on U.S. territory, as a "program review."

The proceedings began on a hard note. It seems that North, always so eloquent on the nobility of the "freedom fighters" in public, was well aware of their shortcomings. On this occasion he was angry that the contra leaders were playing fast and loose with U.S. covert aid. According to Secord, North complained that the money was being "wasted . . . squandered" or, "even worse," that the freedom fighters were "lining their own pockets." North was particularly concerned about Calero's brother, Mario, who was shipping supplies out of New Orleans. From what Jack Terrell, the former mercenary, has to say about the rampant corruption he observed in this particular part of the supply operation, North had every reason to feel annoyed.

Once North cooled down, the topic turned to the southern front. As Secord patiently explained to the select committees two years later, the southern front had to be "created and supported. In the past there had been the famous Eden Pastora, but that fell apart." Pastora's faction had of course at that point fallen apart only in the baleful eyes of the CIA and the White House. Commander Zero did not actually give up his fight until May 1986. But he had been abandoned by the CIA after the La Penca bombing in the spring of 1984. By the time of the Miami meeting, the embryo of a new southern front had been hatched on John Hull's farm, paid for by Oliver North and backed up by Fernandez and the CIA hierarchy. Steven Carr, who had been talking to reporters from his San José prison cell for a month by the time of the meeting, had compromised the old Florida–Ilopango–Hull farm route, and a new channel had to be opened. As Secord remembered, "After the meeting, I was asked by North whether I could put together this operation."

The spot selected for the new heavy-duty airfield lay in mountainous jungle terrain just south of the Nicaraguan border on a finger of land jutting out into the Pacific. Known as Santa Elena, it was right next to a plantation that had been owned by Anastasio Somoza, and was ideally placed for its purpose. Though it could take a bulky C-130, the seven-thousand-foot strip was hard to find from the air, let alone the ground, unless you knew exactly what you were looking for. The lush mountains, daunting for small craft because of the consequent turbulence, hid it from view.

The strips were built by the supposedly private enterprise, using a Panamanian shell company called Udall Research Corporation S.A., set up by Secord and run by Secord and North.

Robert Owen had been the location scout for the Santa Elena project. In an August 1985 memo addressed to "BG: FOR YOUR EYES ONLY" (BG was Blood and Guts, one of North's favorite code names), Owen detailed the possibilities. He and José Fernandez had toured the country looking for the right spot. The land chosen was "owned by an American living in New York." Owen had given his imagination free rein in developing an elaborate cover for the operation: "The cover for the operation is a company owned by a few 'crazy' gringos, wanting to lease the land for agricultural experimentation and for running cattle. A company is in the process of being formed. It might be a good idea to have it be a Panamanian company with bearer shares, this way no names appear as owners. The gringos will own two planes registered to the company and duly registered to the country in question. Cattle will be purchased as will some farming equipment and some land plowed."

The amateur covert operator had all the bases covered. "The main house . . . will be vacated and used by the Gringos. It will be possible to use third country nationals, although this was not extensively discussed. The Colonel [an agent in the Costa Rican Civil Guard] will provide a cook, the peons to work the farm, and security." Owen never mentioned "peons" when testifying before Congress on his great concern for "the people" of Central America. The plantation would be "designated a military zone."

Such an important asset required an old and trusted operative to run it. As manager for the project Richard Secord therefore selected the ubiquitous Rafael Quintero. "I had sent Rafael Quintero to consult with the FDN [contra] leaders," Secord testified. Quintero then "negotiated with the local military" in Costa Rica.

Santa Elena apparently fulfilled expectations. As North told NSC director Poindexter in September 1986, "The airfield at Santa Elena has been a vital element in supporting the resistance. . . . The field was initially used for direct resupply efforts (to the contras) (July 1985–February 1986). . . . The field has served as the primary abort base for aircraft damaged by Sandinista anti-aircraft fire." Judging from a firsthand view of the strip, it was a very professional and expensive project. It came complete with contra barracks, and was still restricted territory for outsiders in early 1987, months after the new Costa Rican government of President Arias had discovered its existence.

Under questioning from the Tower Commission, the U.S. government officials involved were quick to run for cover, pointing fingers at each other. Fernandez, the CIA station chief, said Santa Elena "was a matter which I had been monitoring, kind of as an aside, but it was essentially the ambassador's initiative." Ambassador Tambs, according to the commission's report, told investigators he "learned of the airstrip project from a CIA field officer [Fernandez]. The officer informed him that private benefactors were behind the efforts to build the airstrip and Mr. Secord coordinated the flights."

If the men on the spot were in trouble for assisting in this truly massive violation of the ban on contra aid, Assistant Secretary Abrams also had cause to sweat, since his complicity was very clear. The political sensitivity of such a strip was, to say the least, explosive, both for the supposedly neutral government of Costa Rica and the White House. Tambs told the committee: "According to a CIA field officer [Fernandez], Mr. Abrams . . . [was] well informed of this project. On a visit to Costa Rica shortly after he was confirmed to his new position Mr. Abrams raised the subject with the CIA officer: During the course of this conversation [about] Point West [code name for Santa Elena] . . . I became very upset with Assistant Secretary Abrams for bringing out [sic] the question. . . . I thought it should be closely held. . . . I said what is this with the airstrip? Where is this known? He said, well this is known in Washington by—Colonel North told me about it and I assume that [Fiers] knows about it."

Ambassador Tambs was equally blunt in his testimony to the select committees: "It was obvious to me that [Abrams] knew as much about it as I did."

Abrams blustered his way past the Tower Commission and the select committees when brought face-to-face with these embarrassing reminiscenses. He stated that he had no recollection of when or how he had first heard of the infamous strip, and asserted that his "understanding was that nobody ever used the airstrip . . . that it had never quite gotten into operation."

As it so happens, CBS News had a firsthand description of the strip and its location from an American pilot who had flown in and out of there in C-130s. (CBS News did not put the strip's existence on the air, because the pilot reported that most of the freight he had ferried in and out had been drugs. The story thus required exhaustive checking.) If CBS knew about Santa Elena, one would assume Assistant Secretary of State Abrams knew.

In early May of 1987, Tambs, who had had to resign as a result of his involvement with the contra aid project, became irked at the continued efforts of Abrams and others to leave him holding the bag. From his new position as a history professor at Arizona State University he fired a warning shot, in the form of an on-the-record interview with the *New York Times,* at his former superiors. "These guys are trying to save their jobs," he said bluntly. "These guys" were the RIG, "Abrams, the guy across the river [i.e., Fiers at the CIA] and North. There was no doubt in our minds that this was a triumvirate." As Tambs pointed out, the chain of command had been crystal clear: "It was up to the RIG to tell us what the margins were. . . . It was complicated and how were we supposed to know. We didn't have a legal staff at the embassy. If orders came from Washington, I assumed they were legal."

José Fernandez had meanwhile been fired from his post as station chief when his connection with Project Democracy became public. Tambs, forgetting his recent attempts to shift responsibility for Santa Elena onto Fernandez, told the *Times* reporter that it was "absolutely outrageous to fry lower-level officers who were carrying out orders." Although Tambs is still consigned to academic life at the time of this writing, such rumblings of discontent may have helped his old comrade-in-arms Fernandez, who has now been reinstated by the CIA.

As far as his central mission was concerned, however, Tambs was ready to declare victory. By September 1986, he claimed, he and his staff had "succeeded in building a 'southern front' of between 1600 and 2000 men." This claim, as we shall see, is open to doubt.

The importance of Santa Elena, and by extension the southern front, can be gauged from the fact that North and Abrams bullied the president of Costa Rica himself in attempts to keep its existence secret. In August 1986 the Arias government attempted to stop use of the strip. Obstacles were placed on the runway, although local residents later reported hearing C-130s landing and taking off, which leaves the ultimate resolve of the Costa Rican government open to question, or at least its competence in blocking airstrips.

The fracas began when North was tipped off by "our Project Democracy representative in Costa Rica" (this could have been Fernandez, Tambs, or Hull) that the Costa Rican government was about to blow the whistle on Santa Elena. On September 9 North told Poindexter that he had just finished a conference call with Tambs, Abrams, and Fiers, who, as the Tower report summarized, "all agreed that Lt. Col. North would call Costa Rican President Arias to insist that the press conference be stopped. Lt. Col. North said that they agreed he would take a tough line with President Arias, threatening to withhold U.S. assistance."

Since Costa Rica was hopelessly in debt and totally dependent on aid from the United States, this threat left Arias facing the economic collapse of his country. North also reported in writing to Poindexter that Tambs and Abrams had reinforced his message: "Tambs then called Arias from his leave location in West Va., and confirmed what I had said and suggested that Arias talk to Elliott for further confirmation—Arias then got the same word from Elliott. . . . At 0300 Arias called back to advise that there would be no press conference."

North justified this blackmail of a foreign head of state in a memo to his superior, Poindexter. "I recognize that I was well beyond my charter in dealing w/a head of state this way and in making threats/ offers that may be impossible to deliver but under the circumstances—and with Elliott's concurrence—it seemed like the only thing we could do." Poindexter replied: "You did the right thing, but let's try to keep it quiet."

Abrams, true to form, insisted that none of this ever happened, and if it did he had nothing to do with it.

One of the facilities granted by the government to North in his work was a number of portable encryption devices, courtesy of the National Security Agency (which must have required the approval of either Weinberger or Casey, if not both). These allowed North to communicate over ordinary telephone lines in the expectation that he would not be overheard. It is interesting to note how many of the messages still extant deal with the southern front.

On March 24, 1986, for example, Secord contacted North about an upcoming arms shipment to the FDN contras that had been so assiduously nurtured along the Costa Rican border: "[Deleted] should have held discussions with [deleted] by now re L-100 [a type of C-130] drop to Blackie's troops . . . also emphasize we ought to drop something besides 7.62 [ammunition]; e.g., grenades, medical supplies, etc." "Blackie" was El Negro Chamorro, military commander of the FDN troops in the south, whose civilian counterpart, Dr. Lecayo, was reportedly on John Hull's payroll.

Despite all this high-tech backup, El Negro may not have been the most fitting recipient of the drops. A year later his accountant was running around San José with the hot information that his boss had pocketed half of all the NSC money he had received. El Negro was meanwhile in Miami, anxious to spill the beans about corruption by other contra leaders. Miami police had to be called to his house to investigate a sudden flurry of death threats. In August 1987, General Secord succinctly summarized his views on Blackie Chamorro: "I didn't pick him, the agency did. You couldn't get him into the field. He stayed in Costa Rica, doing whatever you do in Costa Rica."

Back in the spring of 1986, however, station chief Hernandez was full of can-do optimism. Calling North after the drop had been carried out, he gives a glimpse of what he hoped to contribute to the overall plan in his role as chief military adviser to the southern contras: ". . . carrying all remaining cached lethal material to join UNO South Force. My objective is the creation of 2,500 man force which can strike northwest . . . to form solid southern force. . . . Realize this may be overly ambitious planning but with your help believe we can pull it off."

Robert Dutton, a retired air force colonel brought into the operation by Secord as an airdrop specialist, later made it clear to the select committees that the drops he arranged for the contras on behalf of Project Democracy were coordinated with Fernandez— i.e., they were concerned with the southern front.

The spring of 1986, with the supply network in place and arms showering down over Nicaragua, was a heady time for Oliver North. According to the Tower report, in May he told Poindexter that "he believed the Contras were readying to launch a major offensive, to capture 'a principal coastal population center' in Nicaragua and proclaim independence." He warned in a memo that if this occurred, "the rest of the world will wait to see what we do—recognize the new territory—and UNO [yet another label for a unified contra movement] as the govt—or evacuate them as in a Bay of Pigs." The report then says he "suggested that the U.S. should be prepared to come to the Contras' aid."

Of course the contras never succeeded in capturing any kind of population center, still less holding it, nor did they ever seem to try. Their strategy was and is hit-and-run raids on farm cooperatives and isolated hamlets, killing anyone whom they suspect of being a government sympathizer or who simply gets in their way.

Even so, North, who has never been accused of having an underdeveloped imagination, may actually have believed in the "major offensive." He was aware, however, of trouble brewing from another direction. As he told Poindexter in mid-May via their favored means of communication, the computer, he was anxious for the CIA to once again resume its (official) management of the contras. He was worried that his work might be exposed and that the president would suffer thereby. "The more money there is (and we will have a considerable amount in a few more days) the more visible the program becomes (airplanes, pilots, weapons, deliveries, etc.) and the more inquisitive will become people like [Senator] Kerry, [Congressman] Barnes, [Senator] Harkin." The latter two of these elected representatives were taking an unhealthy interest in what had happened to more than half of the $27 million appropriated for humanitarian aid by Congress. "While I care not a whit what they say about me, it could well become a political embarrassment for the President. . . ."

North was right to be concerned, for trouble was indeed brewing in Central America, and it was coming from the foot soldiers of the secret army of Project Democracy who had been cast off and left to rot in prison.

Chapter Eight
OBSTRUCTION OF JUSTICE

"We's in too deep now to turn back."
—Robert Owen to Oliver North
April 7, 1986

W hen Assistant U.S. Attorney Jeffrey Feldman stood over the helpless Steven Carr in the San José jail and announced that he was after "the guns, the drugs, and John Hull," it seems that he was aiming to do just that. The aggressive prosecutor who had bullied the mercenary into signing a statement without a lawyer present was determined to indict the members of the illegal arms ring. But, despite what Carr told him, he had failed to appreciate that he was meddling in the affairs of powerful forces.

Feldman had intended to confront John Hull himself, but the U.S. embassy put a stop to that. As Feldman later informed his boss, in a memo stamped "SENSITIVE":

> [Hull] told me that he had been advised not to talk to us without counsel. He denied that he had received this advice from people at the U.S. Embassy.
> Approximately thirty minutes after Hull called me, Kirk Kotula, the U.S. Consul General in San Jose, informed me that

134

he had advised Hull the day before not to speak with us without counsel. Kotula said that he gave Hull this advice after Hull had asked him why the agents and myself were in Costa Rica.

Easy as it had been to avoid Feldman, Hull was nonetheless in something of a panic. He called Oliver North direct and warned that if Feldman continued his investigation out of Miami, the whole operation was "in jeopardy."

North, meanwhile, was getting the same worrying news from his faithful courier and watchdog, Robert Owen, who kept himself fully up to date on Feldman's movements:

> The investigative team was headed by Jeffrey Feldman, Assistant U.S. Attorney, Southern District of Florida. He had with him a special agent from Panama and two from Miami. They are Kevin Currier and George Kiszynski, who is with the Anti-Terrorist Task Force. In the past, he has followed and been assigned to watch Felipe Vidal.
>
> According to [deleted—probably CIA station chief Fernandez] Feldman looks to be wanting to build a career on this case. He even showed [deleted] and the ambassador a diagram with your name on the top, mine underneath and John's [Hull] underneath mine. . . . Feldman stated they were looking at the "big picture" and not only looking at a possible violation of the neutrality act, but at possible unauthorized use of government funds.
>
> They went several times to the prison to question the five in jail. They tried to talk with John, but he was advised not to talk with them unless he had a lawyer present. John arrived in the US on Saturday, so they will probably try to track him down.

Owen attached to this memo letters written by Glibbery and Carr to John Hull. Among them was a statement from Carr retracting everything he had said to date about the Hull operation (though as noted, Carr later told CBS News that he signed the statement for a box of food). "Attached are several letters John has received from the people in jail," Owen told North. "There is also a notarized statement by one Steven Carr, who has done most of the talking. In it he states Martha Honey and Tony Avirgan told him what to say. These two 'reporters' are nothing more than disinformation experts, and they are after me and you. If and when I am contacted by the FBI I will not answer any questions without an attorney present. Even then, I will not answer any questions. It is the only way I can see to stem the tide. Perhaps it is time I retire from this line of work and focus on another part of the world and against another group of Godless communists."

Owen was nervous, for himself and for the cause. Not only was Feldman on their trail, but UNO, the umbrella organization that had grown out of the San José Declaration and that was supposed to unify the various contra bands, was falling apart. Two of the directors, Alfonso Robelo and Arturo Cruz, were threatening to resign if promised reforms were not made. The problem was rampant corruption among the FDN, Calero's group. "If some changes are not made, they both see no reason to continue." A full-blown investigation by the U.S. attorney's office in Miami would surely bring down the house of cards. "I do not want to do anything that will end up causing you problems," Owen told North, "but that time has already probably come and gone, and as some would say, 'We's in too deep now to turn back.' No question I am hot property, as even people on the Hill are asking questions about me. I want to see this through, but not at the cost of jeopardizing it, as I am the only one out on a limb without a genuine safety net or fallback position."

North did not need Owen to tell him about the FBI end of the investigation. He was receiving copies of all FBI files regarding their monitoring of the contra network throughout, possibly from the antiterrorist specialist George Kiszynski, who reportedly owns property near Hull's ranch in northern Costa Rica.

That people on the Hill were getting interested was in part the result of the efforts of John Mattes, the Miami public defender who had stumbled into the rats' nest of Project Democracy through his efforts on behalf of Jesus Garcia. At the beginning of 1986 Mattes, irked and depressed at the attitude of the authorities toward his finding, had complained to his sister, Sarah Mattes-Ritz, who lived in Massachusetts and was an active constituent of the freshman senator from that state, John Kerry. She in turn called Kerry's office.

Kerry, a former leading light of Vietnam Veterans Against the War, assigned his staff to follow up on the story. It was the first attempt by any senator or congressman to probe a secret network that had been actively running a war for almost two years.

The Kerry staffers Dick McCall, Ron Rosenblith, and Jonathan Winer were intrigued by Mattes's extraordinary story of Jesus Garcia's role in the illegal arms shipment, as well as his account of the plot to bomb the America embassy in Costa Rica as a pretext for U.S. forces to attack Nicaragua.

Since Kerry was a member of the Foreign Relations Committee, they had legitimate grounds for demanding answers from the CIA and the Justice Department. The CIA did go so far as to admit that a flight had left Fort Lauderdale, Florida, for Ilopango military base in El Salvador on March 6, 1985 (the one that carried Steven Carr). But instead of the six tons of arms collected and loaded by Garcia, Carr, Rene Corvo, and others, the plane, according to the agency, had been full of nonlethal, humanitarian aid, such as web gear. By the CIA's account there were no guns. The Justice Department was even more evasive. Asked why the investigation they had undertaken under Mattes's prodding had been dropped, the department responded with a statement that they had found no evidence requiring a criminal investigation.

The Senate staffers' questions did at least have an effect on the Miami U.S. attorney's office. The threat to put John Mattes in front of a grand jury suddenly softened to an offer to assist him in any way possible. It was, in fact, the impetus of the Kerry office inquiries that had stimulated Feldman and the Miami bureau of the FBI into buying their airplane tickets for Costa Rica.

Kerry was only a freshman senator, and a liberal at that, so his interest was for the moment more irritating than threatening. A full-fledged official investigation by a U.S. attorney's office could be quite another matter, unless it were quickly derailed. That, thanks to the helpful attitude at the upper reaches of the Justice Department, is exactly what happened.

North conferred with his superior, Admiral Poindexter, who then contacted the attorney general himself, Ed Meese. According to senior administration officials, Meese assured Poindexter that he would "get on top of the situation" and make sure that the investigation did not destroy the contra operation. (Meese offered his services once again in November 1986, when he ordered the FBI and customs to "suspend" their investigation of Southern Air Transport after the Hagenfus plane was shot down in Nicaragua. "The investigation was indeed suspended," wrote North on November 14 (see chapter 12).

Meese was as good as his word, putting in a call forthwith to Leon Kellner, the U.S. attorney in Miami and Feldman's boss.

According to a source inside Kellner's office, Feldman was full of prosecutorial zeal as of early May 1986. He assured his boss that he had enough evidence to indict several members of the arms network on gunrunning and violations of the Neutrality Act.

In early May the Justice Department in Washington told the Kerry staff that there was nothing to investigate. The illegal arms network was "much ado about nothing." It appears that John Hull was being kept fully abreast of progress on the cover-up. On May 12 Hull wrote to two FBI agents working with Feldman on the contra arms investigation. The gist of the letter was that senior Washington officials had made assurances to Hull that there was "insufficient evidence" to charge Hull with any crime.

As late as May 14, 1986, however, the Miami prosecutors were still ready to do their duty. That was the day Feldman wrote a memo with the pregnant conclusion, "We have sufficient evidence to begin a grand jury investigation . . . [which] would ultimately reveal criminal activities including gunrunning and neutrality violations." Leon Kellner added, in a handwritten note, "I concur that we have sufficient evidence to ask for a grand jury."

A week later Meese and his deputy, Lowell Jensen, turned on the heavy pressure on Kellner. Whatever they said, it worked.

Kellner instructed his deputy to stall the investigation, to proceed very slowly. According to the source within his office, he told a staff meeting: "Individuals in Washington are upset. . . . I'm under a lot of pressure from Washington. Don't you know there's a vote coming up?"

The vote referred to was the impending decision by Congress, set for June 25, on whether to grant the contras $100 million in aid. Revelations from a U.S. attorney's office, of all places, would have soured the atmosphere, not to mention opening up the White House to criminal prosecution.

No grand jury was convened. Jeffrey Feldman's offending memo was rewritten. It now meekly concluded: "At present it would be premature to take this matter to a grand jury. . . . A grand jury investigation at this point would represent a fishing expedition."

Thanks to the attorney general's helpful intervention, a potentially disastrous development had been turned right around. When the revised version of Mr. Feldman's memo (obviously rewritten in haste; though still dated May 14, it refers to events two weeks later) reached the Justice Department on June 3 it was promptly passed along to Republican members of the Senate Foreign Relations Committee. Senator Kerry, all this while, had been demanding that the committee open a full-fledged investigation of the illegal network and the foot-dragging by the Justice Department. The memo was waved before the committee as a reason to postpone hearings.

In Costa Rica meanwhile there were other legal developments that could *not* be influenced by a phone call from the attorney general of the United States. John Hull's libel suit against Tony Avirgan and Martha Honey for their report on La Penca was due to be heard in May. Hull appears to have brought the suit in the confident expectation that the defense would not be able to get anyone to testify for them, but it was becoming clear that his confidence had been misplaced.

In April 1986, the doors of La Reforma prison in San José had swung open and all but one of the mercenaries arrested a year before on John Hull's ranch were released on bond. Steven Carr was the only one left inside. Peter Glibbery was amazed to discover that John Hull had paid his bond, even though Glibbery had resisted Hull's efforts to sign any statement withdrawing his allegations.

When the Englishman, pale and thin after his prison ordeal, walked out past the guard towers into the burning sun, he found two cars waiting for him. One belonged to John Hull; the other contained Tony Avirgan and Martha Honey. The journalists had called both Glibbery and Carr as witnesses in the upcoming trial.

Glibbery hesitated. If he chose Hull, he would be whisked to the ranch and sheltered, with the expectation that a quiet departure from Costa Rica could be arranged in exchange for his silence. A simple signature at the bottom of a sheet of paper prepared by Hull's lawyer stating that Glibbery had lied repeatedly in the hopes of gaining his release would appease his host, and Glibbery could gracefully disappear. On the other hand, there was the unpleasant possibility that Hull's fury had reached the point where a free Peter Glibbery, even back in Birmingham, England, would be too much of a risk. Glibbery believed that Hull could easily have him killed.

Climbing into the back of Tony Avirgan's car was equally dangerous. If Glibbery took the witness stand and said what he knew under oath, the mercenary would have crossed the point of no return. His circle of friends would narrow to a few journalists and the staff of one senator. He would be used and then discarded. In the end they were in no position to guarantee his life.

Standing there in the hot sun, the prison gates at his back, Glibbery had to decide which was the lesser of two evils. Finally he made up his mind, and sauntered toward the journalists' car. His mind had been made up by an innate belief that, somehow, if he told the truth, if he could just make people understand how he was just a pawn in a White House operation, just a "grunt," he would be all right. It was a mixture of blind faith and an inexplicable innocence he had managed to carry with him through all the vicissitudes of Northern Ireland, South Africa, and the contra war.

Safe, for the moment, inside the car, Glibbery was relieved. He was at the mercy of others regardless of which way he turned. At least this way he would get to say his piece, savoring, for the moment, a delicious revenge.

His new friends had little choice but to install Glibbery in their home, a typical San José town house with cool tile and stone floors and just enough room for the journalists and their children. They had to rearrange their lives to accommodate a man who could not walk out on the street alone. Tony Avirgan's mother took over the cooking, baby-sitting, and general chores. The journalists concentrated on preparing for a trial that would bankrupt them if they lost. (Hull was asking for $500,000 in damages plus $500,000 in costs.) It was a prelude to the much bigger confrontation they faced with Hull and the secret network behind him in the suit Danny Sheehan was preparing in Washington.

While Glibbery made himself useful with the housework, Carr was still sitting in his fetid cell, livid that he had been left behind. He called the consul general, Kirk Kotula, who tried to calm him down with promises of a new passport and a vague offer to help Carr make his way to the French foreign legion. "As soon as you get out," said Kotula, "come down to the embassy and we'll talk." Carr felt reassured by the embassy man, with his professional phone manner that seemed to level with the prisoner. Kotula said, "Well, you're there because of politics, and you're not going to get out until the politicians say you're going to get out."

In reality of course there were lots of good reasons why the politicians and the diplomats too would want to keep Carr just where he was. Ambassador Tambs was fully aware just how much damage Carr could do to the North operation. Carr had ferried weapons down from Florida and had killed civilians at the battle at La Esperanza inside Nicaragua.

Finally, shortly after Carr had mentioned to the embassy that the Senate Foreign Relations Committee (in the form of a Kerry staffer) had expressed an interest in his testifying on Capitol Hill, an embassy official named John Jones turned up to say that Carr's "boss,"

John Hull, was on the case and he would soon be released—after thirteen months in jail. Jones reiterated that Carr should head for the embassy "to talk things over" when he was set free.

It was in fact Carr's family who eventually bailed him out a week before the libel case was due in court. He kept the appointment at the embassy and found Jones with another diplomat, Jim Nagel, and two marine guards.

"It took me an hour and a half to figure out what they were trying to say," recalled Carr later. "I went in and said, 'Well, what do we do now? I'm subpoenaed to go to court Thursday and Friday.' They said, 'No, you're just requested.' I whipped out the subpoena and said, 'Well, if I go to court and I tell the truth, then I open myself up to more charges. If I don't show up, then I'm violating the law.' They said, 'Yes, that's true also.' 'Well, what am I supposed to decide? You know John Hull's lying, and he wants me to decide for him.' "

At that, Jones picked up the phone and said to Carr, "You want to speak to John? John's not mad at you anymore."

Carr was unnerved by the cozy relationship between Jones and Hull. "It was like long-lost friends or something; it wasn't, 'Can I speak with Mr. Hull?' John Hull is never right on top of the phone, so he was waiting for the call. Right then I said, 'I'm being set up or something.' "

One message that Carr got loud and clear was that the embassy was anxious for Carr to jump bail and get out of Costa Rica. Their refrain was, " 'It's decision time,' and the decision was on leaving. They did not want me in court, period." Rather than returning his papers, Jones and Nagel handed Carr a temporary document not suitable for travel. By withholding his passport they had control over his movements.

Carr asked for "some time to think." He left his address as the Hotel Johnson. "Of course I didn't stay there because I didn't trust those guys. I didn't trust any of them. They had been lying to me for thirteen months. They weren't suddenly turning over a new leaf." Instead, he headed straight for the Avirgan house, where he dropped his bags. Glibbery was pleased to see his old cellmate, and the journalists were delighted they had another witness. Carr proceeded to make contact with an old girlfriend in San José and, in what may have been a foolhardy move, passed up the kind of protection that Glibbery was getting and moved in with her.

John Davies and Claude Chaffard, two of the other mercenaries released at the same time as Glibbery, had meanwhile vanished into safe houses in San José. They had never discussed their activities on John Hull's ranch and had no intention of doing so. The fifth man, the former Florida policeman Robert Thompson, returned to the Hull ménage. He accepted the rancher's hospitality and would be the only witness for the rancher in the courtroom. He and Hull had rehearsed their story, which was that Carr and Glibbery had been paid by the Avirgans to lie.

The obscure court case would later gain notoriety as it belatedly dawned on the press and Congress that the notion of a war conducted from the White House "basement" was not a mad delusion of conspiracy theorists. It was a curious and select collection of observers and witnesses who began to emerge from the crowded airport customs hall a few days before the trial opened.

Danny Sheehan appeared with his sidekick Bill Davis, a deceptively mild-mannered Jesuit priest. Father Davis is both stubborn and fearless, two excellent qualities for doing battle in Central America.

They were joined by Jack Terrell, the mercenary. Terrell, the good old boy with thinning gray hair and steely blue eyes, a line of droll humor and war stories better suited to a *Soldier of Fortune* convention, parked himself in the Avirgans' living room to wait his turn in the witness box. He cultivated an air of mystery, and appraised each newcomer to the house like a poker player judging his opponent's hand. His slow drawl and cautious speech came with knowing looks, as if to say, "You don't really know who I am." He was right. Terrell knew a great deal about covert operations, so much that one might conclude that he was working for some rival agency determined to sting the CIA—a DIA man perhaps, or an agent of some CIA clique at odds with the way Casey and the White House were running the war. He had old and curious ties to the Korea lobby, shadowy figures who had briefly come into the limelight in the seventies Koreagate scandal. Whether that old tie had any bearings on his activities in Central America was unclear. Certainly there were a lot of old Korea hands floating around this particular war: General Singlaub; Joint Chiefs Chairman John Vessey, who had been Singlaub's commander in Korea and now received memos from Oliver North; and Don Gregg, former Seoul CIA station chief, who was now Vice President Bush's national security aide.

Terrell had his own agenda, and meted out only as much information as was required. Peter Glibbery watched him from across the room, not sure whether this fellow mercenary was, perhaps, a plant

142

from the other side. He was not, and indeed occasionally let drop uncannily prophetic statements about the future of the scandal that had brought everyone to San José on a hot week in May 1986. "It's a cancer, it's like Watergate," he said then. "It's not going to go away. There is great potential here for a Contragate." It came in a cool manner, as though he knew exactly what was to come, raising again the question of exactly who he was.

Sitting off in the corner was Jonathan Winer, from the staff of Senator Kerry, a trim little figure who, in his neatly pressed suit and beard, wore the heavy scent of Washington officialdom, distinctly out of place in Central America. His gravity betrayed his inexperience, but it was at least reassuring to have tangible evidence that somebody in Washington was paying attention.

The final member of this motley party was John Mattes, the gregarious public defender from Miami, who had come to tell the story of his client Jesus Garcia on the stand. He had traded his suit and tie for a tee shirt and jeans, and seemed perfectly at home with the mercenaries. He listened eagerly to the conversations and stored every anecdote, absorbing the atmosphere of intrigue that permeated San José.

The sleepy capital was deceptively ordinary on the surface. A trip to some of the local bars, packed with spooks, mercenaries, and contra commandantes, told a different story. There were smugglers of every hue: from those moving cocaine, to dealers selling U.S.-supplied contra weapons to anyone with the right price in their pockets, to those hustling emeralds and pre-Columbian art. There were also, at this time, some characters taking a very direct interest in the affairs of Avirgan, Honey, their lawyers, and their witnesses. By April, Richard Secord had become sufficiently worried about what Sheehan was finding out to have hired a former CIA "technical services" expert named Glenn Robinette to spy on Avirgan and Honey. In the course of his researches, Robinette came to San José and distributed, so he later testified, seven thousand dollars to informants in the hope of picking up dirt on the couple and their associates.

Meanwhile Martha Honey tended to her guests while nerving herself for this possibly ruinous suit against her and Tony. Though as efficient as always, she was worried, particularly that one or more of her witnesses would not make it as far as the courthouse. Steven Carr, as noted, had slipped off to his girlfriend's house. Whereas Glibbery was responsible, Carr was less predictable. At least he had promised to show up, and he had a powerful motive—to expose the man who had left him to rot in prison. Even Eden Pastora, who had just given up the contra business for good and requested political asylum in Costa Rica, was going to testify.

It turned out that Honey had been right to be worried. Two days before the trial was due to begin, Steven Carr disappeared. The Avirgans frantically called the court to see whether they had any word of the missing witness. The court officials said yes, Carr had been picked up from the sidewalk in front of the journalists' home by a U.S. embassy car. He had, they surmised, perhaps gone to John Hull's ranch.

Jonathan Winer switched on his tape recorder and his most official congressional manner and phoned the embassy. He reached Jim Nagel, who feigned ignorance and claimed he had not seen Carr since the day before. Offhandedly, he suggested that Carr was with Hull, or had skipped the country to join the foreign legion. More calls to the embassy yielded nothing. When I went to the embassy the following day to demand answers to the same questions, I was handed a press package with some useful facts on the annual rainfall of Costa Rica. I demanded an official confirmation by noon the following day that the embassy had no knowledge whatsoever of Carr's whereabouts, and an official explanation of how they had determined that Carr's entire story was a "fantasy." The response was that they were unable to discuss "intelligence operations."

The trial would go on without Steven Carr, but the fate of the missing witness created enough tension to keep everyone else on edge.

On Thursday, May 22, 1986, the court convened in downtown San José. Jack Terrell was late. Frantic runners were dispatched to the Holiday Inn to see if he too had disappeared. He was simply lingering over a late breakfast.

The courtroom was tiny and desperately hot. Security was heavy. Roughly two dozen observers watched the proceedings, among them a maimed victim of La Penca in a wheelchair. On one side sat the Avirgans and a small coterie of supporters. John Hull sat on the other, flanked by employees and associates. The rancher, in a neat lightweight suit, appeared cool and businesslike.

In his original papers filed with the court, Hull had offered the argument that "my unselfish and humanitarian attitudes toward the welfare of Nicaraguan refugees exiled from their country by a totalitarian regime is publicly known." He stated that because of this, "I have become the target of totally false accusations" and "I present this suit with the end of demonstrating the absolute falsehood of the affirmations of the parties named." He had brought the libel suit on the assumption he would win, for the entire national security apparatus on the southern front was potentially at stake here. However, Hull submitted no evidence other than a copy of the *La Penca Report*, in which the Avirgans named Hull as a possible accomplice in the attempted assassination of Eden Pastora. Hull called only one witness—mercenary Robert Thompson—and declined to take the stand on his own behalf. Tony Avirgan and Martha Honey thought that Hull had based his case on the belief that they would not be able to get any witnesses to testify publicly in court.

Throughout the proceedings, Hull had a young blond man by his side. His name was Wesley Smith, a Mormon, who explained that he was there to translate for Hull (who is fluent in Spanish). Over a friendly coffee at a local café he confided to me that he had come down to Hull's ranch from the United States to instruct the rancher on how to use a computer.

Smith was a foot soldier in Oliver North's network and a veteran of the administration's propaganda battles over human rights abuses in Nicaragua. When human rights organizations such as Americas Watch and Amnesty International issued stinging reports detailing contra abuses against civilians, including rape, mutilation, torture, and kidnapping, the State Department struck back with a report authored by Wesley Smith. Smith, billed as a "Mormon student," accused the Sandinistas of countless atrocities on the basis of evidence taken from hundreds of witnesses.

In a Washington press conference to introduce the report, it emerged that Smith had not conducted hundreds of interviews as claimed, for he had been ill and confined to his Managua hotel room for all but a couple of days during his visit. He finally admitted to having relied on precisely one source for his accusations. Nonetheless, the State Department had flogged this fabricated report for all it was worth. Robert Owen later testified that he had commissioned the report, using his shell company, I.D.E.A. Inc.

Equally interestingly, Smith was a close associate and good friend of Carl ("Spitz") Channell, a key (and richly rewarded) component of Oliver North's contra funding organization.

145

When the proceedings opened, Peter Glibbery took the stand. The pallor of his English complexion stood out in the courtroom full of sunbaked faces, and he was gaunt after a year in jail. He spoke in a calm, matter-of-fact way about training contras for John Hull. He laid out how he had been sent by Tom Posey of Civilian Military Assistance to meet Hull in Miami and how Hull had paid for part of his ticket with an American Express Gold Card, hard evidence of violations of the Neutrality Act. Glibbery told once again of the conversations in which Hull's "friend on the NSC" had come up. Hull was sitting three feet away from the witness stand but Glibbery, perhaps because of his British military training, was not one to be intimidated. He would occasionally adjust his horn-rimmed spectacles and carry on, never once glancing at Hull. The judge—there is no jury in Costa Rican libel cases—listened closely.

When John Mattes took the stand, Hull had met his match. The Miami public defender could not be dismissed as a jailbird or a man "who would do anything for pay," as Hull liked to categorize his accusers. Here was an upstanding lawyer with a practiced courtroom manner. His booming voice silenced the room, keeping everyone rapt as he told of the investigation of a covert network of which John Hull was just one part. He told the story of Jesus Garcia helping to collect arms for the March '85 shipment from Fort Lauderdale to John Hull. He talked of the plot to blow up the American embassy. By the time he stepped down, the plaintiff was looking like a lot more than just a much-maligned rancher.

Hull was livid, and when the court adjourned for lunch he gathered his cronies for a strategy session in a restaurant across the street. I was asked to come along. The rancher ordered one of his men to call the embassy about Mattes, and to contact Leon Kellner, the U.S. attorney in Miami, to say that Mattes was misrepresenting himself as a prosecutor. Mattes had done no such thing, but the interpreter assigned to the court had mistranslated his title, and Mattes, not knowing Spanish, had no idea there had been a mistake.

As we were returning to court, Hull and Smith enlisted me in some anti-Mattes machinations. They asked me to approach Mattes and find out in the course of friendly conversation where he was staying in San José. They would then get his passport number from the hotel and arrange to have the public defender detained in Costa Rica. I respectfully declined the mission and suggested that Hull and Smith speak to Mattes themselves. During the afternoon session I passed a note to Mattes suggesting that he watch his back. The lawyer prudently changed hotels that evening and caught the first plane back to Miami in the morning.

Thanks to Hull's complaint Mattes was eventually dressed down by Theodore Sackowitz, the head of the public defender's office in Miami. Sackowitz had been contacted by Kellner, who told him that he had received a cable from the American embassy in Costa Rica complaining that Mattes had misrepresented himself at the trial. "I remember wondering at the time what the hell the State Department was cabling [Mr. Kellner] for," said Sackowitz later. Had he known of the close connection between Hull, North, Tambs, and Fernandez he might perhaps have been able to understand things a little more clearly.

Terrell was as effective as Mattes on the stand, delivering his bombshell testimony with a cool diffidence, volunteering nothing and forcing the lawyers to extract every piece of information. He gradually divulged how he had sat with Hull in meetings, discussing how to open the southern front with cash from the White House. He detailed the meeting at Adolfo Calero's house where he had plotted with Hull, Calero, Owen, and others to make another attempt to kill Pastora after the failure of La Penca. He made it clear that Robert Thompson, Hull's only witness, was a mercenary rather than a journalist as claimed. He mentioned in passing that during a visit to La Reforma prison Thompson had complained about some of his duties at the ranch, specifically the task of guarding a large consignment of cocaine.

Thompson did not do so well as a witness. He insisted that he had never stayed at Hull's ranch and had only met the plaintiff, on a formal basis, in the course of his journalistic endeavors. The Avirgans' theatrical lawyer, Oto Castro, asked why, to general hilarity in the courtroom, Mr. Thompson was wearing Mr. Hull's jacket. Thompson was not pleased, and when he ran into Terrell in a back hallway he threatened to kill him if they ever met again in the United States.

The court also heard testimony from Eden Pastora himself, the now-retired Commandante Zero, who spoke from a secure room out of the public eye. He described his erstwhile relationship with Hull and Hull's withdrawal of support. Then came the testimony of Carlos Rojas Chinchilla, the middle-class *tico* who had become caught up in the web of intrigue surrounding Hull's ranch thanks to his chance meeting with David in the Rendezvous Bar.

At the end of the first day, Hull remained confident. He confided to me that it was all a KGB conspiracy and he would soon be back at the ranch, victorious, ready for another alligator hunt.

At the end of the second day Judge Jorge Chacon ruled that the defendants' investigation of Hull's role in La Penca was valid. Hull had lost.

It was a blow, not only to the rancher's cover and ego, but to the North network as a whole. Damning testimony, taken under oath, was now on the record. Six days after the judgment, Danny Sheehan filed suit in Miami against Hull, not to mention Secord, Hakim, Shackley, and the rest of the alleged conspiracy, charging RICO violations in connection with the attempt to kill Pastora.

In San José, however, celebrations within the camp of the victorious journalists were marred by the disappearance without a trace of Steven Carr. The embassy's refusal to comment, even to a Senate investigator, was less than reassuring. Carr's last signed statement was the one prepared by Hull saying that everything Carr had ever said about his involvement in illegal activities was a lie. Extracted in exchange for the box of food while he had been in jail, it was now a useful document for Hull. With Carr safely out of the way the rancher could brandish it freely.

The mystery of Carr's disappearance was eventually solved. He had been spirited out of the country by embassy officials, a flagrant violation of Costa Rican law. (The requirement of his bail was that he must remain in the country.) Actually, the operation as reportedly executed by John Jones and Jim Nagel was so inept it hardly deserves the word *spirited.* They had furnished him with identity papers invalid for travel; they had misdirected him on how to cross the border into Panama; they had failed (despite promises) to alert anyone on the other side he was coming. Finally, after an exhausting five days of Kafkaesque misadventures, Carr found refuge—back in jail. He had once been convicted for forging his mother's checks and had broken probation by joining Oliver North's war. When he arrived in Miami he turned himself over to a baffled U.S. Customs Service official as a probation violator, got himself transferred back to Naples, Florida, and went to bed in the Collier County lockup.

Carr was delighted to be back in a small-town jail to serve his six months with bland American food and television sets. There were no parasites, no beans, and no one, at least in the immediate vicinity, who wanted him dead or permanently out of the way. Before they said their goodbyes the embassy staff, according to Carr, had threatened that if he ever talked about the way he left Costa Rica they would see to it that he landed in a federal prison with the key thrown away, or just kill him.

Carr was back in his hometown, with his mother and blind sister nearby and one of the best lawyers Naples, Florida, has to offer. Jerry Berry thought he had a routine case of probation violation. He had not the vaguest idea of the mess his client was in, at the center, as he was, of a White House covert operation in danger of public exposure. His suspicions were aroused when Carr was visited by a staffer from Senator Kerry's office. The Kerry investigators were attempting to keep Carr's location a secret. As it turned out, he was not hard to find; there are not that many jails in Naples.

When I arrived with a CBS News team after he had been there a month, Carr, with the embassy's threats still ringing in his ears, was afraid to talk. It took five hours at a corner table in the local Justice Department building's snack bar to convince Jerry Berry that Carr *had* to say something. It was his only insurance policy. We had just returned from a somewhat tense two-day visit to Hull's ranch. We had also spent several days with Peter Glibbery, hacking through the jungle to find what remained of the overgrown and burned-out contra camps, the evidence that the mercenaries' story was true. Carr finally gave in, anxious to hear news of Glibbery. His lawyer consented only after hearing, at length, what it was that Carr was involved in. Finally, when he was handed a recent AP wire story detailing a covert aid network run out of the White House with verbal approval from the president, it sank in that his client was a key witness to something very important.

Carr looked wan and had several days' growth of beard when he shuffled in wearing orange prison pajamas. He asked for cigarettes and cracked jokes about Hull's ranch. Mindful of the specific embassy warning, he refused to talk on camera about how he had left Costa Rica. On the other hand, he was anxious to put on the record that he had received threats on his life from several quarters, including not only the embassy but John Hull and the Miami contras. These last were angry that he had temporarily disrupted their arms pipeline through El Salvador. He was frightened for his family, particularly his mother and blind sister. He knew all about the mortar round left on Jesus Garcia's doorstep, and firmly believed that his particular enemies would have no scruples about a blind girl.

The person who scared Carr the most was Felipe Vidal, the CIA operative whom he referred to as "Hull's pet bulldog" and who was not only reputed to be a hit man in Miami but mingled with NSC emissaries and State Department officials. Carr vividly recalled that Vidal had once told him he did "John Hull's dirty work." Carr suspected that he himself might qualify as dirty work to be done before long.

There were some topics that this amiable orange-clad youth (he was still only twenty-six) did not care to discuss. One of them was the meeting he had attended at the Howard Johnson's in Miami to plot the bombing of the U.S. embassy in Costa Rica. Jesus Garcia had placed him at the meeting, and Carr had subsequently written to Garcia stating that he "would never kill Americans." When asked about it, Carr became mute. He would not lie on camera, but instead preserved several seconds of a meaningful silence.

His other difficulties came with any mention of drugs. Carr had seen at least part of a shipment of cocaine—three kilos, worth about forty thousand dollars on the glutted Miami market at the time—at Paco Chanes's house when he and Jesus Garcia came to collect arms for the Fort Lauderdale flight.

Carr also knew that one contra commander, who had fought alongside Eden Pastora, had lost his head in a very literal way after threatening to disclose details of drug dealing among the contras in Costa Rica. The head of Hugo Spadefora was found stuffed inside a U.S. mailbag in Costa Rica, and his body just the other side of the border in his native Panama. Not long before, Peter Glibbery had taken a telephone message from Spadefora for Hull at the latter's residence in San José. "Tell John Hull," Spadefora had said, "that I am on the second chapter of my book."

Carr also remembered what Peter Glibbery had said about Hull's phone call from his "friend at the NSC" in March of 1985. It seemed that the subject of the call had been drugs. Hull had had to go into town from the ranch to take the call. When he returned he mentioned that the friend had asked whether he, Hull, was involved in drug trafficking, because the FBI was investigating him on that account. "For God's sake, John, tell us if you are, because we can do something about it," Hull had quoted the friend as saying, volunteering his services to squelch the investigation. Hull later denied the call ever took place. Oliver North said he could not recall. But it was North who was routinely perusing FBI reports on investigations of his own covert network.

It was this sort of knowledge, albeit limited, that terrified Carr. It is an axiom in south Florida as well as Central America that crossing drug dealers can produce nasty results. Short life spans were common in that world and, as he remarked to one visitor, Carr was anxious to see his thirtieth birthday.

Chapter Nine
THE COCAINE CONNECTION

"Ask about cocaine."
—A banner unfurled by a spectator at the Iran-contra hearings
July 1987

The elegantly dressed man sitting in the beautifully manicured garden was talking about the everyday facts of life of
his business. "There seems to be a big to-do about the CIA
having connections with drugs," he explained patiently. "It
might be news now, but it's something that has been quite
prevalent for quite some time. Outside of the United States,
drug dealers are very powerful people. They have the ability to put governments in power or topple them, if they do it subtly.
They have cash. The CIA deals primarily with items outside of the
U.S. If they want to deal in foreign countries' policies and politics,
they are going to run up against, or run with, the drug dealers. It
can't be done any other way . . . if the end result is for the benefit
of everyone, it usually works. You know, whether the players are the
contras today or the Tupamaros or whatever, as far as I've been able
to see, that's the way it's always been."

Ramón Milian-Rodriguez can safely be described as an expert in
his subject. Until his indictment in 1983 he was one of the world's
busiest money launderers, running $200 million a month through his

Panama-based operation. Milian-Rodriguez's most famous clients were Pablo Escobar and Jorge Ochoa, who together made up the Colombian cocaine cartel that controls 40 percent of the world market. At the height of his career the accountant ran six distribution centers in major U.S. cities to expedite the movement and hiding of drug cash. In order to keep his business running in Panama, Milian-Rodriguez paid Panamanian leader Gen. Manuel Antonio Noriega $4 million a month. That paid for the privilege of continuing to do drug business.

Milian-Rodriguez was convicted in December 1985 on no less than sixty counts of racketeering and laundering narcotics money, a record that earned him a starring role in a *Forbes* magazine cover story on fashionable havens for loose cash. "Your background," boomed the judge at his trial, "was almost the American dream." He was sentenced to thirty-five years and fined $6,495,000, which at the time was the largest fine in U.S. history. He was thirty-four at the time. The federal agents who arrested him found $5.4 million in cash on hand, and Vice President Bush rushed to Miami to pose with the stacks of bills as a public relations coup for the war on drugs.

In the spring of 1987 the trim and elegant Cuban, his suntan and wardrobe seemingly unaffected by incarceration, was serving his time at a "country club" prison of the kind reserved for high-class or well-connected offenders, which is why he was able to receive us beside a garden beautifully manicured by the inmates. He himself had already risen to be chief orderly in the hospital.

It was the first time that anyone had come to ask him about his dealings with the CIA and the contras, despite the fact that one exhibit at his trial had been a spreadsheet of financial accounts with one column, totaling over three and a half million dollars, boldly labeled "CIA."

The connection between the CIA, Oliver North's network, and the drug trade floated just below the surface throughout the public investigations of the Iran-contra scandal. Whenever the subject was raised in open hearings administration witnesses treated it with open derision. North himself, in a prepared statement read to the Iran-contra committees, stated, "Some said . . . that I condoned drug trafficking to generate funds for the contras. . . . These and many other stories are patently untrue."

Others knew better, and one of them was Ramon Milian-Rodriguez. Just about the time North was making his affecting pitch to the congressional select committees investigating the Iran-contra affair and to the TV audience, Milian-Rodriguez was also addressing a group of senators. They were members of the subcommittee set up by the Foreign Relations Committee in order to probe unwholesome allegations of a CIA-contra-narcotics link.

Unlike North, Milian-Rodriguez did not have a TV audience to play to, since the senators had decided that his information was rather too explosive to be shared with the American people. He had been subpoenaed to testify how he and his clients in the cocaine cartel had been solicited to help the contras, and how they had wholeheartedly responded with cash and services. Nicaragua had first crossed his ledgers back in the mid-1970s, when he had arranged for the covert delivery of "$30 to $40 million," as he recalled, from the CIA to Anastasio Somoza. But his connection with the agency had begun long before that. When he graduated from Santa Clara Business School his mentor was Manuel Artime, one of the grand old men of the Miami Cuban community. Artime had been political head of Brigade 2506 at the time of the Bay of Pigs (selected for the post by Watergate conspirator E. Howard Hunt). Artime had arranged for his bright young protégé to take instruction in the finer points of money laundering from old associates at the CIA. Young Milian-Rodriguez's apprenticeship in the business was to arrange $200,000 individual payments for the Cuban burglars jailed for their part in the Watergate break-in. "They were real men," Milian notes approvingly; "they didn't talk, like Haldeman and Ehrlichman."

Good relations with government are as important for the cocaine trade as for any other billion-dollar business, and the accountant continued to make himself useful in this regard. Indeed, in 1981 he was actually invited to the presidential inauguration in recognition of the $180,000 in campaign contributions from his clients (the cocaine cartel) that he had channeled to the victorious camp in thousand-dollar lots.—"Reagan was our kind of candidate."

Given these kinds of credentials and associations it is hardly surprising that Milian and his clients should have been called on to do their bit for the contras. In an interview in June 1987, Milian casually disclosed what may be the most shocking revelation in the entire Iran-contra affair. He said he had laundered a $10 million contribution from the Colombian cocaine cartel to the "freedom fighters," at the behest of a CIA veteran and key figure in the White House contra supply network. Milian repeated his story under oath to the members of the Senate Foreign Relation Subcommittee on Terrorism and Narcotics in July. The hearing room in the Capitol was surrounded by heavy security; the session was closed to the public and the press. Senate staffers were warned not to leak the explosive information.

Ten million dollars in cash was disbursed, the accountant told the senators, through an established network of couriers in Miami, Guatemala, Costa Rica, and Honduras. The first payments were made, Milian testified, in late 1982 and continued through 1985. The accounting spreadsheet, seized with approximately five hundred documents when Milian was arrested in 1983, lists a $3,690,000 expenditure, in a column marked "CIA." This November 1982 entry, said Milian, represented a portion of the cartel's contra aid program.

Such largesse did not come unsolicited, according to the accountant. Payments were made at the request of an old friend and CIA veteran, who along with Milian was a longtime associate of Bay of Pigs leader Manuel Artime. The old friend, Milian told the Senate subcommittee, was Felix Rodriguez, the shooter team alumnus who wore Che Guevara's watch and counted George Bush among his friends. From the cartel's point of view, the $10 million outlay was petty cash. It bought, according to Milian, influence and "goodwill." It was in line with the "conservative politics" of cartel members, he explained, who considered the contra forces substandard (in contrast to the cartel's own crack mercenary force) but fighting for the right cause. Milian named contra leader Adolfo Calero, among others, as one of the recipients of the cash transfers. The allocation of the money "drops" was the responsibility of Felix Rodriguez. "Felix would call me with instructions on where to send the money."

When Felix Rodriguez took the stand behind closed doors in August 1987, he told the committee that he was indeed an old friend of Ramón Milian. Rodriguez claimed he had never solicited drug money. Yet the drug accountant's intimate involvement with a U.S. government–approved contra supplier raised serious doubts about Felix Rodriguez's testimony, as did the veteran CIA man's former business partners.

In late 1984, Milian said, Felix Rodriguez called the accountant for another favor. His expertise was needed to launder cash from a dozen or so Miami companies to the contras. It was about that time that Felix Rodriguez's former business partner, Gerard Latchinian (they were both directors of the Giro Aviation Corp.), was arrested by the FBI for smuggling $10.3 million worth of cocaine into the U.S. to finance a coup against the president of Honduras, Roberto Suazo Cordova. Latchinian has always stoutly maintained that the cocaine deal was part of a CIA operation. The insalubrious associations publicly revealed by the Latchinian case certainly never seemed to trouble Felix Rodriguez's high-powered friends like George Bush or Oliver North.

One of the companies on which Felix Rodriguez asked Ramón Milian-Rodriguez to "look favorably" was called Ocean Hunter, which was later to provide part of the grounds for Steven Carr's well-justified pessimism about reaching his thirtieth birthday.

For Milian, the amounts involved in the Ocean Hunter–contra transactions were negligible compared with his $2.5-billion-a-year money-laundering operation. The Ocean Hunter account required moving only about $200,000 a month—"cash money . . . to a designated courier, I'd say never less than fifty thousand dollars" in one drop. But $200,000 a month to the contras from one company alone was by no means a negligible amount for the war effort.

One of Ocean Hunter's partners was Paco Chanes, the man from whose house Steven Carr had picked up a large assortment of arms, and where he had seen three kilos of cocaine. Carr had glimpsed only three kilos, but Jesus Garcia, who was with him at the time, knew that was only a part of an enormous shipment of 350 kilos just arrived from Costa Rica.

Officially, at least, Chanes was in the shrimp business. Ocean Hunter shipped blast-frozen shrimp from Costa Rica to Florida. The company made no pretensions to corporate respectability. Headquarters was a hole-in-the-wall upstairs office in a run-down Miami shopping center, with "Ocean Hunter" scrawled on a scrap of lined paper Scotch-taped to the glass door. Inside were a handful of well-built Cubans and a grizzled "cracker" American sporting a baseball cap and a well-chewed cigar. There was no shrimp in sight save for a sticker that read "Prueba Mr. Shrimp" (The Proof Mr. Shrimp) underneath a picture of a hamburger. It transpired that Mr. Shrimp was the name of another of the many companies listed in the name either of Chanes or of one of his partners—companies that seemed to come and go as fast as the filing of annual reports with the state of Florida. Aquarius America and NCP Trading, for example, were now defunct, leaving a trail of curious addresses including an old-people's home and a berth in a warehouse building where the landlord complained of unpaid bills and men who came and went with suitcases full of cash. (According to Ramón Milian-Rodriguez, Ocean Hunter had originally been set up as a vehicle for buying shrimp from boats operating out of Fidel Castro's Cuba, thus breaking the U.S. trade embargo. A nicely ironic touch.)

The atmosphere in the Ocean Hunter office was decidedly cool to uninvited outsiders, as I discovered when I paid a visit with a CBS News team in June 1986. Simple questions such as "What do you do here?" were received in stony silence. Apart from the hamburger poster the only clue to the business was a detailed map of Costa Rica pinned to the wall. The corporate records listed a certain Luis Rodriguez as president. He also refused to say what the company did. As it happens, this Rodriguez had, according to Panamanian records, been a business partner of Ramón Milian-Rodriguez back in 1979 in two companies called Ahoremusa Holdings S.A. and Akaba Investments S.A. Sources in the U.S. Customs Service describe Luis as a major cocaine trafficker. Santiago Rosell of Miami was described in the records as a director. Rosell, a lawyer, initially claimed he had never heard of Ocean Hunter, then subsequently conceded that he might have drawn up the corporate papers.

It is hardly surprising that the corporate officers were somewhat reticent about their enterprise. As Jesus Garcia, who knew a lot about Chanes and his associates, put it, "It was just a front. What they wanted to import was cocaine." Shrimp boats, it should be noted, are especially suited for smuggling drugs, since if the containers are opened for an inspection the shrimp will unfreeze. If the inspectors find nothing, they have ruined a legitimate shipment and might be liable for damages. According to Garcia, the company had excellent protection in other ways: "The CIA have a lot of front companies, for moving money, arms, supplies, people. Ocean Hunter was established as a front." Several U.S. government and contra sources confirmed that claim.

The cocaine glimpsed at Chanes's house by Carr and Garcia when they went to pick up the arms was, according to Garcia, part of a shipment that had come in along with a load of bad shrimp. "Paco Chanes had a cocaine shipment ten feet away from Oliver North's arms shipment."

When John Mattes persuaded the FBI to investigate the arms shipment in January 1986, bureau agents took a statement from Garcia. Mattes was present and recalls how, when Garcia named Francisco Chanes as the man from whose house he had collected arms, the agents spontaneously remarked, "We're investigating him for drugs."

This investigation must have started no later than 1983, which is when those loyal FBI informants Joe and Hilda Coutin told their bureau contacts about Chanes's envoy Rene Corvo. Coutin, it may be recalled, had become suspicious as to what Corvo was doing with the money he had been given by the Cuban Legion to go fight communism in Costa Rica. They had dispatched a couple of investigators, who had reported that Corvo was not only squandering the funds on loose women and Bavarian beer, but was also heavily into the drug trade.

Garcia remembers very clearly telling the agents that "the arms shipment was for the contras, that it was taken to Fort Lauderdale and, with permission, left the country. Realizing that the FBI was being used to cover this up, I brought out that ten feet away from the arms there was a cocaine shipment. Just to make sure that they understood that, my wife wrote a letter to FBI internal affairs, and told them about it, told them that the FBI was covering things up in my case, and that I had told them about the arms shipment and the cocaine shipment."

Coincidentally enough, Jack Terrell encountered the same Chanes drugs and bad-shrimp shipment that Garcia and Carr had bumped into. Terrell remembers how Chanes tried to saddle him with the shrimp as a kind of charitable contribution to Civilian Military Assistance, the Alabama mercenaries.

Mattes explains the FBI's reluctance to pursue the investigation in straightforward terms. "The drug-smuggling charges are intertwined with the gunrunning. The same individuals. So when you have information in FBI reports that these individuals are shipping large amounts of guns through south Florida, you've got to ask the FBI, well, what the hell were you doing with the information?" The answer, in Mattes's view, is clear enough. "If they looked into the cocaine charges, they'd be looking into the network. Too much was at stake for them to try and proceed."

Mattes saw Ocean Hunter wedged in the center of the network. "It certainly had connections right into Costa Rica. It had connections here in Miami and, more importantly, it had cash. When cash is paid for large-scale flights, chartering planes out of Fort Lauderdale airport, paying for pilots, paying for fuel, that cash didn't come out of the blue sky, it came out of somebody's back pocket."

Actually, that last statement is not strictly accurate. In August 1985 the State Department began to dispense $27 million authorized by Congress for the purposes of strictly "humanitarian aid" to the contra fighting forces in the form of bandages, food and clothing for refugees, saline drips for soldiers wounded on the field of battle, and other good causes. A special department, the Nicaraguan Humanitarian Assistance Office, was set up at the State Department to cast about for worthy recipients for the taxpayers' money. Several accounts were established to receive periodic infusions of cash, which was then to be handed over to responsible contra leaders, or to so-called brokers under their control.

If there were any responsible contra leaders, they fell down on the job. As a subsequent General Accounting Office audit and an investigation by a House subcommittee revealed, no less than $17 million out of the $27 million promptly and simply disappeared. A check through the bank records turned up countless illegible signatures for receipt of cash. Even when the recipient was identifiable, it was hard to feel confident that the money had been spent the way Congress intended. In the space of ten days, in January 1986, a broker called Supermercado (Spanish for "Supermarket") received $740,000, allegedly for food purchaces. Bank records for April 15, 1986, show one Supermercado transaction noted as follows: Payee: "illegible"; Endorser: "illegible"; Location: "illegible"; Amount: $100,000. On April 28 the performance was repeated; this time the amount was $175,000.

Large sums found their way to a Cayman Islands bank called BAC, Banco de America Central. BAC was established by wealthy Nicaraguan sugar interests in conjunction with Wells Fargo Bank as a safe haven for wealthy Nicaraguans stashing funds prior to the downfall of Somoza, in anticipation of the Sandinista takeover. By the time Somoza took off in 1979, $28 million worth of Nicaraguan capital had fled into BAC. By 1985 the exiles' bank had, unsurprisingly, become the contras' bank.

Among other choice recipients of humanitarian aid through the Miami brokers' accounts were Mylers Fashions, which received $3,437 by wire, and Thelma Lecayo, relation of Glibbery's jungle camp acquaintance and fellow Hull subordinate, who collared almost half a million dollars.

Even amidst this indiscriminate largesse, however, it is startling to find that one of the coveted humanitarian accounts went to Paco Chanes. The actual recipient, as recorded by the Nicaraguan Humanitarian Assistance Office, was a Costa Rican shrimp firm called Frigorificos de Puntarenas. It requires no great investigative feat to discover Frigorificos is the Costa Rican sister firm of Ocean Hunter.

The NHAO account, established at the Consolidated Bank in Miami, had three signatories, Chanes himself, Luis Rodriguez, and a Costa Rican partner, Moises Dagoberto Nunez. "Dago" Nunez is a Cuban American and a friend of John Hull's. Between January and May of 1986 this trio received no less than $231,587 of U.S. taxpayers' money. Some of the money was in turn paid out to accounts in Israel and South Korea (Israel Discount Bank and Korean Exchange Bank) at a time when the two countries were reportedly supplying arms to the contras.

Puntarenas, the home of Frigorificos, is a Pacific coast port town a few hours' drive from San José. It is a peaceful place, where scratchy Latin music wafts from seedy bars and dogs vie with drunks for a shady spot to sleep on the sidewalk. The company occupies a modest stretch of wharf surrounded by shanties full of incessantly crowing roosters. It is on the other side of town from the overrated promenade where guides like to steer the tourists. Dago Nunez commutes between there and his San José office in his Mercedes. Our reception when we paid a call on Frigorificos was fully equal to the mute hostility we had encountered at Ocean Hunter in Miami.

Under the system set up by the State Department, each account had an overseer in the NHAO office. By some strange coincidence the Frigorificos account drew none other than Robert Owen as its watchdog. Owen had received a fifty-thousand-dollar contract from NHAO, which one colleague described as "a payoff" for his work for Oliver North. Owen, as his reports to the home office show, was in close touch with the leading lights of Frigorificos, Dago Nunez and Paco Chanes. That the State Department was giving a humanitarian account to an obscure shrimp company was peculiar in the first place. But to reward a crew who had first come to the attention of the FBI in 1983 as cocaine traffickers smacks of criminal conspiracy. At the very least it is clear that Owen had some nonhumanitarian intentions regarding the funds he was guarding.

When Owen reportedly picked up a fraudulent receipt for fifteen thousand dollars' worth of uniforms and boots from the Creaciones Fancy store in San José, the money that was being diverted came from the Frigorificos account. Franklin Reed, a member of a Costa Rican contra faction called Kisan South, later claimed that this money was then used by the infamous Felipe Vidal to buy guns with which to lure fighters away from Eden Pastora. Ambassador Robert Duemling, the old State Department stager inserted by George Shultz to run the NHAO, later said he had received a detailed explanation of the diversion, but offered no further explanation. The FBI opened an investigation.

The NHAO had actually been ordered to check the credentials of the people getting the money both with the FBI and with the Drug Enforcement Administration. According to a well-informed State Department source, Robert Owen was advised, at the very latest by February 1986, that he was consorting with drug traffickers. The information on that occasion came from an unofficial source, not the FBI or DEA, but it is highly unlikely that the FBI would hide their reports from Washington for no apparent gain. On the other hand, it is easy to see why Owen might not have been overly anxious to take the matter further.

Nunez, according to Eden Pastora and his aide Carol Prado, had been instrumental in bringing Miami Cuban fighters and suppliers into the southern front. They said Nunez worked closely with Felipe Vidal and, like Vidal, was a CIA operative. He had, according to Pastora and his aide, sat in on high-level contra meetings in Costa Rica, not the usual pastime for a simple shrimp exporter. His partner Paco Chanes had, as we already know, done yeoman service supplying weapons shipments that ended up on Hull's farm. Like Chanes, Nunez's name was all over a stable of fly-by-night companies in Miami: Lindsay Cleaners Inc. on West Flagler in Miami, dissolved 1977; Industrias Nacionales de Peten on Northwest Eleventh Street, dissolved 1977; 11–44 Development Corp. on North River Drive, dissolved 1976; Transatlantic Distributors Inc., with the same address as Lindsay Cleaners, dissolved 1977; Aquarius Seafood Inc. on Northwest Sixty-sixth Street, dissolved 1982; NCP Trading (same address), dissolved 1981.

When Joe Coutin alerted the FBI in 1983 to the results of his inquiries into Rene Corvo's activities in Costa Rica, he had also had plenty to say about Dago Nunez. "There were some illegalities, something wrong was going on," as Coutin recalled. "With the shrimp, they were shipping cocaine. It seems that the Cuban group was just a front to cover for the drug business. There was a large group of people like Frank Chanes [Paco], Rene Corvo, Felipe Vidal; another one who participated in helping Rene Corvo's group was Frank Castro, who has a record of being previously convicted on drug charges. I told George Kiszynski from the Federal Bureau of Investigation and I told Destado Diaz [of the Miami Police Department]. They started investigating." Coutin says he was told by the FBI agent that they "were going to start issuing subpoenas to all these people involved." No action was taken. "They were covering up for the CIA," concludes Coutin. "They only wanted to know how much information we got."

Agent Kiszynski certainly took note of allegations of drug running, and by early 1985 at the latest the news had reached Oliver North. That was when a Hollywood producer named Lawrence Spivey saw FBI memos from Kiszynski detailing the progress of the Miami contra-drug investigations sitting on North's desk. Spivey had been granted an audience with North because he was working on a screenplay about Tom Posey of CMA.

Senator John Kerry's office got wind of the Ocean Hunter/Frigorificos operation in early 1986, while the principals were receiving U.S. government checks. Kerry took the case to FBI headquarters in Washington in April 1986. He was still waiting for a response a year later.

The senator expresses proper indignation at the implications of all this. As he sees it, the covert network "became a channel for further exploitation of the American people by violation of the narcotics laws, and it became a channel for the perversion of our own judicial process and enforcement process. We shouldn't be involved with these kinds of people in so-called humanitarian efforts or in any official or unofficial actions of the United States government." However, despite these laudable sentiments, Senator Kerry refuses to comment on the allegation that Ocean Hunter is or was a CIA proprietary.

When Kerry's staff asked the State Department whether anyone had checked out Ocean Hunter and Frigorificos before handing them a humanitarian account, the staff was told, as Kerry himself recalls, that State "had checked that out prior to the contractual arrangement being entered into."

That, according to a State Department source who had worked closely with the Nicaraguan Humanitarian Assistance Office, is not exactly what happened. The source recalls how a team from the NHAO had sought to go check out Frigorificos in Costa Rica, but had been prevented by the direct intervention of Ambassador Tambs. Ambassador Duemling later said that the offending companies had never at any point been checked out with the FBI or DEA.

In April 1987 Greg Lagana, a spokesman and aide for Assistant Secretary of State Elliott Abrams, claimed that the NHAO grant to Chanes et al. arose out of confusion born of setting up a distribution agency overnight. If they were in bed with shady characters, it was because the FBI and DEA had not warned them, while the CIA had vouched for the companies. Even as he spoke, Ocean Hunter and Frigorificos were still up and running. The FBI was still claiming to have an ongoing investigation. The State Department had been reminded by the General Accounting Office back in July 1986 that the DEA was actively investigating Ocean Hunter, although in early 1987 the DEA was proclaiming ignorance of any such investigation.

Despite such official denials, by 1987 the DEA was very well informed indeed about the shrimp business. In November 1986 senior officials of the DEA in Washington were visited by two bounty hunters who saw Ocean Hunter as a lucrative target and wanted to take it on.

Fred Valis and Dan Hanks looked like what they purported to be: drug dealers in the music business. Their L.A. apartment was a sea of gold records and black leather. They pursued a specialized sideline in the narcotics trade. Their practice was to infiltrate cocaine rings on both coasts, orchestrate a bust by the DEA, and take a percentage of the haul. "We're given hundred-dollar sequentially numbered bills in cash from the DEA, and we sign a form that doesn't even have our name on it. We get paid for the amount of drugs seized. So if we can nail a thirty-kilo shipment, you know, we're talking about a quick thirty grand plus however many bodies are involved in arrests."

The bounty hunters had first gotten wind of Ocean Hunter in September 1986, when they were briefed on the more interesting aspects of the operation by a journalist who asked whether they might be able to dig for more information.

Valis and Hanks had also been given details by a Virginia drug dealer of a Coast Guard radar operator who was selling details of AWACS schedules to cocaine smugglers in Miami. (The smugglers, exhibiting a touching faith in military technology, believed that the AWACS, an airborne radar, could enable the authorities to track incoming flights and shipments.) The bounty hunters found reason to believe that there might be a connection with the shrimp operation. They took their information to Hayden Gregory, counsel to the House Judiciary Subcommittee on Crime, chaired by Congressman William Hughes. According to Valis, Gregory "knew the names we were talking about, and was real interested in fishing for what we had. So we told him we had a lead that we thought we could follow into Miami for a guy who was trading radar schedules for kilos of cocaine, and that perhaps if we could bust him, we could get the whole operation."

Gregory arranged a meeting at DEA headquarters at Fourteenth and I in downtown Washington. "We met there with a whole bunch of people who never gave us names, just titles," remembers Valis, "the assistant to the administrator of the DEA, the head of Latin American Affairs, the agent in charge of Costa Rica, the head of the cocaine division." There were others in attendance who remained totally anonymous. "There were a couple of thugs there also; they purported themselves to be local agents, but when they went to lead us out of the office, they didn't know their way out."

The atmosphere was formal. "It was sort of like the Paris peace talks. We sat on this side of the table and they sat on that side. They were treating it like an inquisition. They wanted to find out who the source was to try to trace it back. And they were very much interested in finding out if we were telling them everything we knew."

It slowly dawned on the eager bounty hunters that there was a curious lack of enthusiasm for the project around the table. As Hanks puts it, "It just surprised me that they weren't willing to invest a bit of money. I mean, Reagan had come out recently and said that they have a billion-dollar budget, or something to that effect [for the war on drugs]. And they can't raise three thousand dollars to send us down to Miami to check something which might be a leak not only on a CIA operation, not only on a major drug smuggler, but also on somebody who's selling national security secrets?"

Valis and Hanks had gone into the meeting thinking that their lead was too good for the DEA, supposedly in the midst of a drug war, to pass up. "What we [had been] told was that someone was smuggling in a ton of cocaine a week into Miami, and that it was coming into two warehouses down in Miami, Ocean Hunter and Mr. Shrimp. That is what we were told by our informant. And that those narcotics were turned over to people in Miami and marketed, and that the money was returned back to Mr. Shrimp and Ocean Hunter, and guns were purchased with it and traveled back to Costa Rica. It's apparently been going on since 1983."

Seasoned as they were in the drug business, Valis and Hanks were impressed by the reputed size of the operation. "Can you envision how much a ton of cocaine is?" says Hanks. "It's like filling up this living room to the ceiling with cocaine. You know, you've got to have an awfully big straw to do that much cocaine." (Though

Ocean Hunter was almost certainly importing cocaine on a very large scale, sources well versed in Miami cocaine market conditions say that Valis and Hanks had been given an exaggerated impression of the quantity the company was bringing in.)

While the DEA officials at the high-powered Washington meeting might have appeared uninterested, they certainly seemed well informed. "We brought up the names of the owners of Ocean Hunter and Mr. Shrimp, [and] they acted like these were long-lost buddies, that they'd known about these guys for years." The DEA men, say Valis and Hanks, identified the shrimpers with "this group that was a Cuban revolutionary anti-Castro group, the 2506 group. Then they said all coke dealers that are Cuban are former members of this political group, the anti-Castro group. So we did some checking around with some CIA people that we know. And they said that the CIA has been very tight for years with that particular group, they've worked with them. In fact they trained them prior to the Bay of Pigs."

The DEA, concluded the bounty hunters, knew precisely what was going on. "They knew they were dealing cocaine. They said, 'That's under investigation.'" The investigation, if there was one, was languishing. "We got the impression that they had a lot of information but were sitting on it. In fact, while we were sitting there, there was a big map behind them of Central America. And there's a pin on the map at Puntarenas, a little pin on the map."

By the time they left DEA headquarters, says Hanks, he had concluded that they had been talking about a CIA operation. "I don't think everyone in the DEA is clean on it," adds Valis. "I think somebody at the top who directs who gets investigated and who does not get investigated has to be dirty, because field agents are as gung ho as you can get, they want to make points. That's how they keep their scores up. Every field office that I have ever been in, they actually have a scoreboard of what they've busted every month. It's like a sales office; they've got to make better points than the office in San Diego or the office in San Francisco. So for them not to go after something, they have to be directed not to go after it. It's like a guy selling vacuum cleaners. He's going to go out and make that next sale, unless the boss says, 'I don't want you to sell a vacuum cleaner to this guy over here.' And that's what we think happened." Adds Hanks, thinking sadly of the catch that got away, "We're not talking about one vacuum cleaner here, we're talking about a whole building of vacuum cleaners. Why sell door-to-door when you can scoop them all up in one shot?"

By February 1987, while the DEA was still diligently steering clear of Ocean Hunter and its sister companies, the United States Customs Service had leapt into the fray. Miami customs officials let it be known that they were initiating an investigation into Ocean Hunter for large-scale cocaine trafficking. They decided (somewhat belatedly) to start taking a look at the clients who had been serviced by superaccountant Ramón Milian-Rodriguez, who had been sentenced in 1985 and indicted as long ago as 1983. One of them, according to the documents seized at the time of Milian's arrest, was Luis Rodriguez, president of Ocean Hunter. Another was Danny Vasquez, owner of Florida Air Transport, the carrier of choice for Paco Chanes when he dispatched the six tons of arms along with Steven Carr and Rene Corvo to Costa Rica. The pilot for the flight to Ilopango had been Vasquez's son.

In the summer of 1987 the customs inquiry did at least appear to be proceeding. The investigators had established, for example, that Ocean Hunter owned a freighter, used on at least one occasion in late 1983 to ferry cocaine from Limón, on the Atlantic coast of Costa Rica, to Miami. It still remained to be seen whether this agency would, unlike the FBI and DEA, choose valor over discretion and indict the principal. Asked what would happen if Miami customs should receive a call from Washington, one plucky agent replied, "I don't like interference."

It would be surprising if John Hull's name did not pop up in connection with a contra-related Costa Rican business, and sure enough the rancher appears to have been taking a distinct interest in shrimp at around this time. In December 1985, Steven Carr and Peter Glibbery received one of their periodic visits from John Denby, an American farmer from Illinois who, like Hull, farmed in northern Costa Rica. Indeed it was Denby who had participated in the prank where the boys at the ranch stole Pastora's jeep and tacked Illinois plates on it.

Denby was something of a mystery, for although he was an associate of Hull's, and well briefed on his covert operations, he made a point of visiting the jailed mercenaries for a gossip. On this particular occasion Denby brought the latest information about John Hull and Robert Owen. According to both Carr and Glibbery, he confided that the two men were putting humanitarian assistance money to good use by going into the shrimp business. "The war's been canceled," joked Denby, "due to lack of interest."

A direct question to Hull on this curious association drew a curt reply: "I'm not in the shrimp business." Yet earlier, while admiring the magnificent smoke rings spewing from the volcano across his pastures, Hull had mentioned his Cuban-American friend Dago Nunez. He described him as an embittered veteran of the Bay of Pigs sympathetic to the contra cause. Later, when asked directly about Nunez, Hull became vague: "I've met him in town. I met him socially. Seems like a very nice fellow. I've been out to Puntarenas, where he has a shrimp business."

Somehow, with Robert Owen running the shrimp account for the State Department, and falsifying that account in order to buy weapons, it is less than likely that Hull's links with Nunez were purely social. Whether the rancher was closely involved in shrimp matters or not, his connection with the narcotics trade appears to have been close, massive, and profitable. Just how massive only became clear when a powerful druglord, and the men who worked for him, began to describe the part they had played in Oliver North's operation.

Chapter Ten
GUNS FOR DRUGS

"Nice group the Boys chose."

—Robert Owen
February 10, 1986

The current holder of the record for the fastest time in a powerboat between New York and Miami is a Colombian-American named George Morales. Morales achieved this honor in 1985, when he raced a catamaran with four 635-horsepower engines from one city to the other in nineteen hours and thirty-four minutes. The feat earned him the substantial prize of half a million dollars.

Powerboat racing is so expensive that even that amount of money would not have financed Morales's sporting activities, which included an unbeaten three-year spell as Miami's offshore powerboat champion. What made it all possible was the elegant thirty-seven-year-old's line of business, the importation and sale of very large quantities of cocaine. Both business and pleasure came to a halt on June 13, 1986, when Morales was jailed and eventually sentenced to sixteen years in prison.

Morales was very good at his business. He owned his own airline, Aviation Activities Corp., and kept its impressive fleet of planes right next to Hangar One at Opa-locka Airport, outside Miami. He had a stable of pilots, men with years of experience flying dangerous missions and dodging radar. Also on the payroll were presidents and generals throughout the Caribbean and Central America. His was a one-man Caribbean Basin Initiative. His enterprise kept complete dossiers on south Florida's best and brightest DEA agents, and law enforcement officials of easy virtue abroad and at home could depend on him for generous bribes.

This was the man who had gone into partnership with the ruling Duvalier family in Haiti to promote the island republic as a major transshipment point for cocaine on its way north to the U.S. Prior to Baby Doc's departure in 1986, Morales had presented the porcine president with what became his best-loved toy, a high-speed Cigarette boat.

Asked whether Morales was the Dan Rather of the cocaine trade, one of his colleagues replied, "More like the Walter Cronkite." He certainly lived in a style befitting his status. In a 1986 report one DEA agent described the domestic trappings of Mr. and Mrs. Morales and their two children in glowing terms. "There were at least seven or eight vehicles that were valued at more than $30,000 each. I observed five or six maids, servants and hangers-on; also observed a very elaborate security system including closed circuit tv and electronic gates . . ."

In the spring of 1984 there appeared a troublesome threat to this American dream. Morales was indicted for conspiracy to import and distribute cocaine. It was this awkward development that made him particularly receptive to the proposal he received from the group of contras and a CIA man who turned up at his Opa-locka office soon after the bad news.

As Morales recalls it, the delegation proposed a fair trade. They would see to it that his indictment was "taken care of," that is, slowed down if not dropped altogether. In return, he would donate $250,000 every three months to the "cause," train pilots, and put his planes at the disposal of the war. The contra pilots would, however, be at his disposal for the occasional run from Colombia to Costa Rica and points north.

Morales was no stranger to the contra movement. Prior to his indictment he had mixed with contra leaders and activists in Miami. He had bought and leased safe houses for the contras in Miami, as well as generously sharing his expertise in offshore banking transactions.

The CIA man who came to see him that spring day, according

169

to Morales, was Octaviano Cesar. Cesar was a well-heeled Nicaraguan exile based in Costa Rica who later took the position of "director of international relations" for a contra faction called the Southern Opposition Block.

Morales attests that Cesar became his regular CIA contact, regularly stopping off to see him as the patrician Nicaraguan shuttled between Costa Rica and Washington. He assured the drug dealer that "high-level Washington people" would keep him out of jail. Specifically, Morales remembers Cesar telling him that "he had spoken with Vice President Bush about my situation," that is, about clearing up his indictment on drug charges. "The indictment was dying away. It was the sort of situation where the DEA got into bed with the CIA just to the point where I was in the middle. The CIA knew I was working with them full-time. The CIA knew what was going on. They needed the support."

Since accusations of CIA affiliation are easy to throw around, Morales's description of Cesar requires exhaustive checking. No less than eight separate sources, ranging from senior contras to high-level administration officials in Washington, attested to the fact that Cesar was an operative of the Central Intelligence Agency.

As the relationship blossomed, says Morales, he donated a total of $3 million in cash, as well as additional services in the form of pilots, houses, and planes. The money flowed to the contras through offshore banks, sometimes delivered in "boxes, suitcases, bags" stuffed with hundreds of thousands of dollars in cash.

In October 1984 Cesar actually accompanied Morales on a trip to the Bahamas to pick up a donation—$400,000 in cash from a local bank.

Asked about this trip in an interview early in 1987, Cesar suffered a slight memory lapse. He admitted knowing Morales, as well as soliciting aid from the wealthy boat racer. He even remembered going to the drug dealer's Opa-locka office and boarding a plane to the Bahamas with Morales, but as Cesar tried to maintain his composure at the awkward questions, his recollections somehow missed the trip to the bank. Cesar's hands began to shake violently as he stumbled through his version of the Bahamas jaunt. "We took one of those old taxis they have there. We went to a place where supposedly they have excellent hamburgers. . . . We had a couple of beers, we had a hamburger, and then we came back."

It subsequently transpired that no investigator interested in the subject had to rely solely on Morales's version of the trip. The U.S.

Customs Service discovered that the dutiful Cesar had actually noted the $400,000 on a signed customs declaration form dated October 13, 1984. Throughout the interview CIA man Cesar stoutly maintained that he had had absolutely no knowledge that Morales was an indicted drug dealer.

Morales was not particularly fussy about which contra factions benefited from his contra aid program, though the southern front received the lion's share. Eden Pastora admits having received at least one Morales suitcase, though he insists that once he discovered the source of the funds he cut ties posthaste. Morales recalls that Adolfo ("Popo") Chamorro, Pastora's deputy and supply officer and Cesar's cousin, arranged the money transfer. Chamorro was at the time in the process of being lured away from Pastora by Oliver North. According to Pastora, Popo was well enough connected to have asked for and received a personal interview with Robert McFarlane to confirm North's bona fides. By 1987 Chamorro was to be found running a small business in Miami, across the street from Ocean Hunter. He claimed never to have heard of George Morales, but once again customs records dispute his claim. Chamorro was listed on the flight manifest of at least one trip to the Bahamas with Morales, and he had also signed the purchase papers for a Morales plane.

It is worth pointing out that whenever the stench of the contra-drug scandal became too strong to be dismissed out of hand in Washington, Pastora was served up as a convenient scapegoat. As CIA Central American Task Force chief Alan Fiers was at pains to point out to the Iran-contra committees: "there was a lot of cocaine trafficking around Eden Pastora. . . . None around FDN, none around UNO."

One of the many problems with such glib assertions is that while Octaviano Cesar and Popo Chamorro were at one point allied with Pastora, they later split with him—with the CIA's blessing—and functioned happily in the FDN/UNO camp. This change of allegiance does not seem to have discommoded their relationship with Morales.

By August of 1984, according to Morales, he was doing a brisk business with the fledgling FDN contra group in the south. The hub of the operation was John Hull's ranch.

The arrangement was convenient for all concerned. Morales's pilots would ferry guns down to Hull in support of the North operation, and bring substantial quantities of narcotics back on the return trip. Hull not only got his guns, he got paid too. Morales remembers paying the rancher $300,000 per flight, a small percentage of the value of the cargo.

Gary Betzner, one of Morales's pilots, talked to us about two runs he made to the ranch. "I took two loads—small aircraft loads—of weapons to John Hull's ranch in Costa Rica and returned to Florida with approximately a thousand kilos of cocaine, five hundred each trip."

As Betzner reminisced about his trips down south, he, like Morales, was languishing in MCC, the Metropolitan Correctional Center in Miami, popularly known in select circles as the Miami Country Club. (With its manicured lawns and condo architecture MCC looks like as good a place to serve time as any.) Betzner was serving fifteen years on a drug charge unrelated to his contra missions. As he put it, "I was fairly tried, fairly convicted, and fairly sentenced." He was known around MCC for a dramatic escape attempt that involved a helicopter landing in the flower beds to collect him. Unfortunately, federal agents had infiltrated the scheme and were on board.

Betzner had been a veteran drug pilot, and an Arkansas crop duster before that, when Morales pulled him out of retirement to make the flights to Hull's ranch in August 1984. It was not the first time that this seasoned professional had seen and taken part in an operation combining drug smuggling and covert activities. In 1983, prior to the mining of the Nicaraguan harbors (planned by Oliver North and Dewey Clarridge when they sat together on the Restricted Interagency Group), the pilot says he picked up a DC-3 that had been confiscated from another drug dealer at Boca Chica Naval Air Station in Key West. It was loaded with six ship mines. He offloaded the mines at Ilopango, the big Salvadoran military base outside of San Salvador. The mines were picked up, according to Betzner, by "military people there with camouflage uniforms" who rolled up "in a military truck. At the time I was there, about three o'clock in the morning, there was a Panamanian C-130 loading up crates. We got fueled up and we got out of there about an hour before sunup."

As Betzner tells it, the mine delivery was part of a package deal. After leaving Ilopango he and his copilot, Richard Healey, went on to Río Hacha on the north coast of Colombia, where they picked up "six thousand pounds of pot." The marijuana run was sanctioned as a payment for delivering the mines. The exercise, says Betzner, yielded him $200,000.

A few months later, when Morales approached him about what sounded like a similar kind of operation, he was ready to sign on. The elegant Colombian gave him a brief overview of the situation. "He gave me a rundown on what was going on, that he was working with the contras and it was sanctioned by the CIA . . . and it went all the way from George Bush down." Unsurprisingly, this assertion receives a strenuous denial from the office of the vice president.

According to Betzner, the question of his remuneration was handled in a very gentlemanly fashion. He asked, "How much will I be paid?".

"Well, whatever you want, you know, whatever the going rate is," replied Morales.

"Okay, I'll take what I think it's worth, and then we'll go from there."

"Fair enough."

The going rate turned out to be quite handsome, paid in the form of cocaine. "I took twenty kilos each trip. It came to about $350,000 a trip. John Hull's strip is a little short, you know, I thought it was kind of dangerous with the load I went down there with."

The soft-spoken pilot's nickname was "Hippie," although he looked nothing of the sort. "I have five names, five passports, and whatever I had in my pocket is who I was, and that person was legitimate. He had a business, he had insurance, he was like a real person. That was just the paperwork that I needed to be able to move freely in the world."

Apart from the shortness of Hull's strip, Betzner recalls the trips to the ranch as smooth sailing, with both landings and takeoffs at both ends in broad daylight. On one trip he picked up a load of weapons at the Fort Lauderdale airport. "There were some C-4 explosives, M60 machine guns. It was stacked all the way to the ceiling." He estimated the load at roughly twenty-five hundred pounds. "I was way overloaded when I left Fort Lauderdale."

He established radio contact "about fifty or sixty miles out en route to the ranch. I was given a frequency to call." The call sign was a whistle. The answer from the ground was, "Everything's okay. C'mon home." Betzner managed to land his Cessna Titan on what the pilot remembered as a "thirty-three hundred-foot strip." Eden Pastora's pilots had also flown Titans in and out of Hull's strip, ferrying weapons and men.

When he landed, "people that were hired by John Hull or working for him would load the aircraft. In both cases, John Hull was there." Hull, according to Betzner, "physically saw the weapons coming in" and "physically saw the bags" of cocaine loaded for the return trip to Florida. "The cocaine was there when we off-loaded the weapons, because they had the fuel on the same truck with the coke. They had the fuel in barrels, and a big pump, and I fueled the aircraft myself." Betzner took care to supervise the loading himself: "I loaded the heavy bags forward and the boxes aft. One blond-headed kid was there, a couple of Costa Ricans . . . John Hull had on a baseball cap." The pilot's conversations with the rancher were strictly small talk. "I told him I was from Arkansas. He said he was from Indiana and asked me how I liked his place. I had some coffee."

Betzner's understanding of what he dubbed "the guns-for-drugs program" was that the cocaine would be converted into cash for more weapons. "I understood right away that it wasn't the private guns that went down that were that important; it was what was coming back. That could buy much larger and better and more sophisticated weapons, and it was unaccounted-for cash."

The veteran drug pilot explained the breakdown of the proceeds from the operation. "Say five hundred kilos of cocaine at that time was worth about twenty thousand dollars a key wholesale. That's ten million. So let's say you paid the Colombian connection five thousand dollars a key for it. So that's two-point-five million dollars that went to them. That leaves seven and a half million dollars. Now my part and the aircraft and George [Morales] was probably another million, million and a half. That leaves six million, then the people who sell it will have to make some money off of it, so they probably came out clearing four million off that load."

Betzner says that on the second trip, he flew into a different strip at the back of Hull's ranch. It was called Los Llanos and was an improvement on the hair-raisingly short runway he had landed on the first time. He described it as being near a sawmill and tall radio towers. The strip, as my CBS News colleagues and I discovered when we went to look for it in early 1987, is no longer in frequent use (though clearly marked on aviation maps). It is indeed next to a sawmill. A powerful Voice of America relay station, complete with very tall radio towers and surrounded by thick barbed wire and armed guards, is on a nearby dirt road. (When we visited the strip, Costa Rican security police followed our vehicle and questioned us.) According to Betzner and other sources the sawmill (the same one where Peter Glibbery found the claymore mines) had a logging truck

with a false compartment, used to store cocaine awaiting transshipment.

Once the cocaine was loaded at Los Llanos, Betzner set a course
for Opa-locka airport, outside of Miami, where Morales based his air
fleet. "I called the tower, gave them my number, landed, taxied up
to Aviation Activities, east of Hangar One there. Parked the aircraft
on the ramp, right in front of the office. Shut it down, opened the
door, got my bag and my stuff and got out of the aircraft. I jumped
off the wing, and George was standing there, his hands in his pockets,
talking to these guys, just real casual."

Betzner identified the men with Morales as DEA agents.
Morales later clarified their role. They were, he said, on his payroll.
Betzner recalled that "one guy said, 'Have a nice trip?' and I said,
'Yeah, fine, no problems,' and I walked straight past George and
didn't even say hello or goodbye." He drove away, free as a bird, in
his Honda.

There is absolutely no doubt in Betzner's mind that Morales,
above and beyond the bought-off DEA agents, had the full and potent protection of the CIA. "George Morales is a very, very careful
man. There would be no way in the world that he would ever risk
a three-hundred-thousand-dollar airplane and his friend—myself—
and his own life, his own business, and everything to be so foolish as
to [have me] fly into Opa-locka airport with five hundred kilos of
cocaine right in the middle of a drug war when there's an agent on
every corner. There's security on the airport and he's being watched
all the time—taxi right up in front of his place and unload? I mean,
that's ridiculous."

At one point Betzner sat down with paper and pencil to try to
calculate how much the contras had garnered from such drug flights.
He arrived at a total of "around forty million. Probably more than
that. I mean, why get into the business if you're just going to make
a few million dollars? You can buy a few helicopters [for that, but]
it won't feed a big army very long."

Sitting on the verandah of his *finca* in June 1986, Hull stoutly
denied any involvement of any kind at any time with drugs or arms
shipments. He stated, "We're not involved in drugs; we're not involved in arms movements." He insisted his employees kept careful
logs on the "five or six" operable airstrips he controls. "I keep them
not for me but for the Costa Rican narcotics people." George Morales
found this assertion amusing since, as he confided, a top official of the

Costa Rican narcotics force was one of the many such officials on his payroll.

Pat Korten, spokesman for the U.S. Department of Justice, admitted in March 1987 that John Hull had been under suspicion "for years" for cocaine trafficking, but that federal agencies, including the FBI, simply had not been able to amass enough evidence for a criminal prosecution.

By the time Korten made this statement Morales, Betzner, and others had of course produced abundant evidence of Hull's connections with the guns-for-drugs program. But, as with the case of Ocean Hunter, the authorities displayed a curious reluctance to accept such testimony. Instead, law enforcement officials in both Washington and Miami routinely dismissed Morales and Betzner as convicted criminals spinning tales in the hopes of a lighter sentence. By July 1987 Leon Kellner, the U.S. attorney in Miami, turned to dissembling in order to discredit Morales—much to the annoyance of the Senate Foreign Relations Committee, which was about to put Morales in the witness chair. He told at least one reporter that George Morales had failed a lie-detector test. In fact, Morales had never taken, much less failed, any such test. Superficially at least, these explanations and excuses sounded convincing, which is why various journalists who took a cursory perusal of the Morales/Betzner charges accepted them. The theory, however, does not hold up under close examination. By the time they began to talk, both men had already been tried, convicted, and sentenced on separate charges entirely unrelated to their contra-related activities. There was no possibility of shorter sentences. Indeed, since they were confessing to a whole series of offenses for which they had never been indicted, they ran the risk of increased sentences for new charges.

The best they could hope for was immunity from prosecution for the contra drug runs they were now disclosing. After George Morales told his story on CBS News in April 1987, he waited patiently for Congress to call him to testify. When the DEA found out that Morales would be testifying under oath, one of their agents made him an offer, a shorter sentence for an agreement not to take his story to Capitol Hill. One of Morales's battery of lawyers was also present. When Jack Blum, the chief drug investigator for the Senate Foreign Relations Committee, got wind of the attempt to shut Morales up, he was livid. Blum shored up the drug dealer's resolve to appear before the Senate and forgo the DEA offer. Morales testified without immunity.

None of the professional cocaine traffickers were particularly anxious to broadcast the story of their involvement with the contra supply effort, and it took months of patient persuasion and digging by myself and my colleagues from CBS News before they began to open up. They felt under no such obligation to reporters who later rolled up at the jail and brusquely demanded to hear the facts. Such reporters, unfortunately, were then all the more ready to accept the carefully prepared excuses and explanations furnished by law enforcement officials—not to mention John Hull, who routinely and adamantly stated, "I have no contact with the drug business. I have never let a drug plane land or be refueled on any airport here, at any time."

Eden Pastora takes a different view. "I knew [from pilots] that much of what went through his airstrips was related to narcotics trafficking." The flight plan of the movements through the strips, as Pastora describes them, are illustrative enough: "Colombia–Costa Rica, Costa Rica–Miami."

Hull claims that he was in fact an active partisan in the war against drugs. "I wrote a letter to the DEA in the U.S. embassy, requesting that they come out and help us set up a better surveillance system, a better security system in this zone against any drug traffic that might come about."

This was peculiar, as the team of DEA men in Costa Rica, Robert Nievas and Sandy Gonzales, seemed to be efficient fellows who would have liked nothing better than an invitation to better police the myriad of strips that peppered northern Costa Rica. It was also curious that Hull should ask for such service in the light of his repeated assertions that there was no drug trafficking whatsoever in his neighborhood. It must be said that the local DEA men did not share this view. When I talked to them in San José in 1986 they said that the San Carlos Valley was a "problem" and that that part of Costa Rica had become a major transshipment point for cocaine. They had been instructed by the head office in Washington that they were not permitted to discuss the subject of contra drug trafficking. The only office cleared to do that was Washington. When questioned in Washington, the DEA responded that contra drug trafficking did not exist.

Scandalous though the use of Hull's strips for drugs and arms may seem, there was another airfield in Costa Rica reportedly being used for drug trafficking, one that puts Oliver North and his associates in even closer conjunction with the narcotics business. The secret airfield at Santa Elena authorized by North and Secord, promoted by Ambassador Tambs, scouted by Station Chief Fernandez and Robert Owen, and managed by Rafael Quintero was also, according to several sources, a transshipment point for cocaine.

Geraldo Duran, whom George Morales describes as one of his top pilots, reportedly used Santa Elena for drug runs. Duran is a Costa Rican who has performed double duty for the contras and Morales. He had been hired for the contra effort by Alfonso Robelo, who was later selected for contra stardom by the Restricted Interagency Group as a director of UNO, the United Nicaraguan Opposition. Duran worked for various contra factions in the south, including Pastora and El Negro Chamorro, known as "Blackie" in North's internal memos. At one point he served a brief jail term in Costa Rica when apprehended with a 421-pound cocaine shipment bound for the Bahamas. Duran, incidentally, is or was a friend of John Hull's. In typically brazen style, the rancher successfully passed off this notorious drug runner in 1987 to a well-known U.S. investigative journalist as "a friend." In July 1987 the Senate Foreign Relations Subcommittee on Narcotics and Terrorism released copies of gas receipts to confirm several trips taken by Hull and Duran to Colombia in 1983.

The use of Santa Elena as a drugstrip was also confirmed by an American pilot who is not nor ever has been behind bars. "Tosh," as he is known, said in June of 1986 that he had made at least two cocaine runs through Santa Elena. His claim is all the more interesting because at the time he made it, the very existence of Santa Elena was a tightly guarded secret, unknown to the press or Congress.

According to George Morales, the purpose of U.S. government involvement in the drug trafficking was very simple: "They needed the financial support for the contras and it was one more way for them to obtain that financial support. The word came down from Washington, from the top, that no matter what has to be done in order to get money to supply the contras has got to be done." The bait for him, he says, was CIA protection, "the protection of the U.S. government, from the CIA, otherwise, you know, we wouldn't be able to do anything." Apart from this attractive commercial inducement, Morales claims higher motives. He considered his mission one of patriotic duty. "To fight for freedom, it doesn't matter what we have to do in order to obtain the money to fight against the communists." According to his calculations, he and his peers made a notable contribution to funding the cause on the southern front: "I would say that seventy to eighty percent of the money went to the south."

178

Morales claims that the drug money performed an additional and less lofty purpose by being used to fill in the gaps when legitimate funds disappeared into Miami real estate or offshore bank accounts at the expense of the troops. "Some of the money got stolen before it ever got out of here [Miami]. They had to come up with some idea, some sort of way, to reimburse that money and also to supply more to the contras." By late 1985, says Morales, echoing the private sentiments of Robert Owen, the contra war had become a "business." He lamented that the fight for freedom had gone by the wayside: "They were just fighting for profit. It was not necessary to prove how you spent the money. No questions asked. No receipts." Asked whether the CIA could have been involved in the drug trafficking without White House knowledge, Morales replied, "I doubt it very much, that's not what we were told."

In a memo to Oliver North dated February 10, 1986, Robert Owen brought up the drug issue: "No doubt you know the DC-4 Foley got was used at one time to run drugs, and part of the group had criminal records. Nice group the Boys chose." Owen later told the congressional select committees that Foley worked for Summit Aviation, the Delaware company with long-standing CIA ties that had outfitted the planes that crashed on the Santa Clara raid inside Nicaragua in September 1984. The "Boys," as Owen testified, were the CIA. That particular DC-4, Owen elaborated to the select committees, was used to ferry humanitarian assistance supplies. He said that the "group that provided that plane had been recommended to NHAO by the CIA." In the memo cited above, Owen wrote, "The company is also one that Mario [Calero] has been using in the past, only they had a quick name change. Incompetence reigns."

In 1987 another veteran drug pilot passed through the "Miami Country Club" prison before being shuttled off to more obscure Florida jails, less accessible to the press. Michael Tolliver was serving a two-year drug sentence on charges, as with Betzner and Morales, unrelated to CIA–White House–contra affairs. His account of his role in the guns-for-drugs program suggests an even greater level of institutional government agency complicity than that observed by his colleagues.

"Mickey" Tolliver was the Nick Nolte of the drug pilot set. Fair, with blue eyes and a quick wit, he reveled in living on the edge. Tolliver was the renegade in a family of aviators and achievers. His father had been in the U.S. Air Force and had instilled a love of flying in all his sons. His twin brother did aerospace research at Stanford

Research Institute. Another brother was a prosperous lawyer. Tolliver preferred the danger, fast women, and huge sums of cash that went with a career as a top-of-the-line drug pilot. After graduating from Auburn University he had moved to Washington to pursue a career in communications. He quickly tired of the tedium of a local TV station and turned to flying. By 1987 he had chalked up seventeen years of experience carrying unconventional freight, largely guns and drugs.

In August 1985 Tolliver had received a call from his colleague Barry Seal, well known in the trade for his ties to the CIA. Seal asked him if he would be available for some "interesting flying." Tolliver asked whom he would be working for. "He said, well, he wouldn't actually say it was for the U.S. government, but all the innuendos were there. I knew the guy and I knew he was involved with the government. Everybody knew it, everybody in the [drug-smuggling] community." Seal told him that not only would the flying be interesting, the pay would be good too. He told Tolliver to go to Miami and call a particular number. The interesting flying, thought Tolliver, could be "anything from Campbell's soup to dead babies, but knowing Seal, it involved drugs." He had no idea however that he was stepping into the middle of the secret contra supply network, and that his control agents would include, according to Tolliver, at least one high-level operative in the North–Secord–CIA operation: Rafael Quintero.

Tolliver duly went to Miami and called the number. An anonymous voice at the other end told him, "We'd like you to go down to Tegucigalpa, Honduras, to talk to our people down there."

Tolliver asked, "Our people? Who's they?"

"Everything will be explained to you when you get there," replied the voice. "You'll meet a guy there named Wayne Westover. Just go out to Opa-locka [airport], Hangar One, and someone will be waiting for you and they'll take you down there, no problems."

The pilot says he made his way to the airport at seven the following morning. He was greeted by what he describes as "this little Latin gentleman," who ushered Tolliver to a Beechcraft Baron. "So we flew to Tegoose [as the cognoscenti call Tegucigalpa] and I should have figured something right there, somebody was doing something because there was no customs, no immigration, no nothing. We just walked right outside the terminal, got in a car, and went to the Maya Hotel."

Tolliver was accustomed to doing business with people whose

identities and job descriptions were never fully explained. "That's the way things work in our business; you meet people you never met before and they'll have suitcases full of money. It's a big equalizer, you know. A guy comes up to you, says, 'Hi, my name is John Doe and I don't know you but here's half a million dollars, and I want you to—' You know, fine, let's go."

Once at the Maya, center of intrigue for much of the region, the pilot remembers that Wayne Westover was introduced as "our liaison man from northern Honduras, but he's here now to tell you what to do." Actually, Westover's role appears to have been limited to introducing Tolliver to another "liaison," with the unlikely name of José Ferrer. Ferrer explained the mission, which would be flying military supplies. Tolliver was game, so long as the aircraft was in good condition and the crew was up to standard. He was told that he would be with experienced crew and that the pay would be good. For the next stage of the proceedings, he was told to go home and wait for a call from a "Mr. Hernandez."

It took a month for "Hernandez" to get in touch. He turned out to be a handsome, tough, middle-aged Cuban. "He started talking about specifics, dollars and cents, what the merchandise was: guns, ammunition, things like that, for the contras." Hernandez then threw in a sweetener that was bound to interest a narcotics professional like Tolliver. "As an extra added bonus, we could either freelance on our way back, meaning we could bring back our own cargo, or we could bring back their cargo, without ever having to worry about interception, arrest, or anything like this. Everything would be taken care of." The cargo under discussion, as Tolliver was given to believe, was drugs.

According to Tolliver, his new employers were flexible on the kinds of drugs he could carry if he wanted to arrange his own load. "Whatever you wanted," is the way he recalls it, "marijuana, cocaine. It was my understanding that they would make sure we wouldn't get caught. They were providing not only the cargo but the landing areas, crews, everything" for drug runs. As it happened, it was they rather than Tolliver who provided the drugs for the first trip from Honduras.

Tolliver professes ignorance as to who benefited financially from the trafficking. "That's not my end of the business. Never has been. Believe it or not, the entire business is compartmentalized. I'm like a teamster, I'm in transportation. You've got people who are in loading; you've got people who are in off-loading; you've got people who are in distribution; people that are in sales. It's like an IBM situation."

In December of 1985 Tolliver says Hernandez introduced him to Rafael Quintero, the veteran CIA agent who had long worked under the aegis of Theodore Shackley and Tom Clines, and whom Gen. Richard Secord referred to in testimony as "my man." The meeting took place at the Sheraton River House in Miami.

Tolliver proceeded on the assumption that Quintero was CIA. "If he wasn't, he was very heavily connected with someone, either that or he had a direct line to the Lord. They were talking about where they wanted to land down there and the protection we'd have and don't worry, everything's taken care of. The pay was seventy-five thousand dollars." That was less than Tolliver's usual rate for a drug flight but, as he piously remarks, "there's the inherent God-and-country deal. I gave them a GI discount."

The conversation then turned to technical details. Hernandez and Quintero reportedly explained to their new recruit that " 'our initial shipment is going to be fifteen to thirty thousand pounds.' I said, 'Well you're going to have to go with a DC-6 or something of that generation, or a multiple-engine jet.' " The pair said that they thought the strips wouldn't be able to handle a jet, "so I said, 'We'll go with a nice six.' They said, 'Okay, we'll take care of it.' That was the panacea for everything. They were always doling out two thousand dollars here, three thousand there, five thousand for my expense money—my expenses were high."

The following month Tolliver says Quintero summoned him all the way to Ecuador to give him a message he refused to transmit over the telephone (a phone allergy shared by nearly everyone in this business.) Quintero's urgent communication was that Tolliver should not talk to Barry Seal anymore. This was just a month before Seal, a professional informant, was murdered in New Orleans on the orders of the Colombian cocaine cartel.

Finally, in March of 1986, the flight was set to go. Tolliver, armed with ten thousand dollars in expense money and a phony I.D. card that read "Pacific Air," made his way to Butler Aviation at the Miami airport. A Latin crew was waiting, as was his aircraft, a DC-6 loaded with twenty-eight thousand pounds of "guns, ammunition, things like that." The plane, painted an elegant silver with a distinctive red stripe, had been obtained from a man Tolliver remembered only as "Mike," who he had heard had subsequently suffered the embarrassment of a drug indictment in Detroit.

The destination outbound was Aguacate air base, the contra supply base in Honduras established by the CIA. As Tolliver remarked, "Once again, you haven't got to be Sherlock Holmes to figure out that it's not being run by the little old lady from Pasadena. There are numerous tents and hutments and everybody's running around in camouflage uniforms." Security was tight at the base. Uninvited guests were not welcome. Tolliver spotted one American, whom he described as "aloof, tall, slender, blond." Unsurprisingly, there were no customs agents. Contra troops unloaded the plane while Tolliver was bundled off to Tegoose for a three-day furlough at the Holiday Inn.

When the slightly bleary pilot strapped himself back into the lumbering DC-6, the plane was once again fully loaded. This time the cargo was "twenty-five thousand [pounds] and change pot. The piece of paper they gave me said twenty-five, I think, three-sixty." That is to say, he was carrying 25,360 pounds of marijuana. Tolliver described the return trip this way in an interview with Jane Wallace of CBS News:

"We take off from Tegucigalpa, Honduras, and we leave."
"To?"
"South Florida."
"Where in south Florida?"
"We landed at Homestead."
"Homestead?"
"Air Force Base."
"You brought twenty-five thousand pounds of pot and landed at Homestead Air Force Base?"
"That's correct."

Clearance was no problem. As Tolliver recalled, "I was given a discrete transponder code to squawk about two hours south of Miami. I received my instructions from the ground, from air traffic control for traffic separation. I told them we were a nonscheduled military flight into Homestead Air Force Base." By this time it was the middle of the night. "We landed about one-thirty, two o'clock in the morning, and a little blue truck came out and met us. [It] had a little white sign on it that said 'Follow Me' with flashing lights. We followed it." (Homestead does indeed have such a little blue truck.)

"I was a little taken aback, to be honest with you. I was somewhat concerned about it. I figured it was a setup, or it was a DEA bust or a sting or something like that." Yet nothing happened. "The little guy in the truck puts us in the pickup truck and takes us out. I got in a taxicab." He says he was paid his seventy-five thousand dollars.

As he relates it, Tolliver's second effort on behalf of God and country did not involve the U.S. Air Force, but the story has some revealing features. With a memory for figures common in his business, he recalls how he was dispatched to pick up a DC-3 loaded with forty-five hundred pounds of weapons and ammunition in Port-au-Prince, Haiti, in July 1986 (*after* the Duvaliers had fled the country). He flew the load to Aguacate, as before, where it was unloaded. He then flew on to Colombia, where he picked up four thousand pounds of pot and between four and five hundred kilos of cocaine. His next port of call was the Bahamas, where he watched Bahamian police unload the cargo.

Tolliver was paid his seventy-five thousand dollars and did not devote too much time to speculating about his strange experience. "Every time something happens, I become more and more inured to it. No more surprises, there can't be any more surprises." He assumed that this operation had to have been sanctioned at a very high level indeed. "My best guess would be that it would have to be someone in the top four, three slots of the CIA as I know their organization. It has to be someone that high up, because who else can you get that's going to pick up a phone and say, 'Let this happen'?" He neither knew nor wanted to know what happened to the twelve tons of marijuana . . . "as long as I got paid. I mean, I'm not callous, I'm just, you know, basically a whore." He certainly did not believe that his mission was unique. "I'd say that I am one of the very few people who'll stand up and say, 'Yes, I did it.' You have myriads of people who have done the same thing, and they won't say it. So twenty-five thousand [pounds of marijuana] is the tip of the iceberg."

In late April 1987, after CBS News's *West 57th* had run the story of Morales, Betzner, and Tolliver, the U.S. Customs Service claimed that it and the CIA had begun to investigate "whether drugs were smuggled into the United States by traffickers who had learned that routine customs inspections were suspended for the officially sanctioned flights" by the CIA to and from Central America. The *Boston Globe,* one of a limited number of major news organizations to pursue the CIA–contra–drug story, quoted customs officials to the effect that "between 50 and 100 flights that had been arranged by the CIA took off from or landed at U.S. airports during the past two years without undergoing inspection. . . . The system provided for the CIA to notify the Customs Service that a certain flight was about to leave from or land at a U.S. airport. As one customs official put it, '. . . our inspectors took that to mean hands off everything. And they stopped checking everything, personal belongings as well as cargo. . . . It was an invitation for problems.' " (No one seems to have asked what the "officially sanctioned flights" were actually meant to be for at a time when Congress had barred CIA aid to the contras.)

Having conceded that much, however, the customs officials were not about to proceed to the logical conclusion. Instead, the focus was shifted away from a possible active role by the CIA in these carryings-on and directed at wily traffickers who "bluffed their way past our inspectors." Thus one official admitted that Tolliver's account of his epic trip to Homestead "has credibility. We think he did land at Homestead." But, he added, Tolliver must have been a "free-lancer. Unless you believe that the CIA is involved in drug trafficking, which I do not, then the only reasonable explanation is that he knew from his contacts there was an inspection-avoidance system in place there and bluffed his way through it."

That hardly constitutes a "reasonable explanation." Homestead Air Force Base is well enough defended to make it impossible for a DC-6 to turn up out of the blue. Furthermore, had Tolliver tried to "bluff" the air force and customs personnel on the ground when he landed in the middle of the night, he would have had an interesting time trying to explain the presence of twelve tons of marijuana. Someone had to unload that cargo, and it is hardly a speedy job off-loading and warehousing 25,360 pounds of pot.

As it turned out, the clue to the involvement of the CIA and indeed the State Department in this operation was to be found in the aircraft Tolliver had used, the distinctive red-striped DC-6.

John Mattes, Jesus Garcia's public defender, happened to be a friend of a man who worked at a Miami newsstand. The man's hobby, close to an obsession, was taking photographs of every plane that passed through the Miami airport. He had a particular interest in the planes that haunted Corrosion Corner, the collection of aircraft companies, such as Southern Air Transport, known for undertaking covert missions for the CIA.

Mattes passed his valuable contact along to Ty West, a tenacious investigator who was working on the story with me at CBS News, in March 1987. After West had checked with Tolliver for distinctive markings, the photographer was able to supply a whole batch of excellent pictures of the relevant plane. West then began methodically to plow through the documents at the Miami airport to reconstruct the history of this particular DC-6.

The plane was traced to a company called Vortex. We had heard of Vortex a year before, when an administration source had told us that the company was being used to ship arms to the contras in violation of the congressional ban.

While West was puzzling over the Vortex connection, Steve Stecklow of Knight-Ridder Newspapers was checking through State Department records on their humanitarian assistance accounts. Vortex, Stecklow noted, had received a contract on February 25, 1986, for $96,961 from the Nicaraguan Humanitarian Assistance Office to ship supplies to the contras. According to the contract documents, the Vortex vice president who had signed for the contract was a Mike Palmer.

Palmer's career had been very much in the grand tradition of the contra supply effort. He had spent three months in jail in Colombia in the spring of 1985 after he was caught trying to pick up a planeload of marijuana. Four months after Palmer signed the State Department contract he was in trouble again, indicted in Detroit for conspiracy and drug possession as part of a major marijuana-smuggling ring between 1977 and June of 1986. As usual, Ambassador Duemling, director of the NHAO, was the last to know what was going on: "I don't know anything about this and I'm not in any position to comment." Vortex was dissolved in 1986, at a time the contra supply effort was much in the news, only to be reborn as Vortex International.

West concluded that Palmer, the man indicted in Detroit, must be the same "Mike" that Tolliver had named as the supplier of the plane for the Aguacate trip. Thus the State Department had been issuing checks to Vortex in February 1986, just one month before Tolliver says he flew tons of guns and drugs between Florida and Central America in a Vortex plane obtained from an indicted drug smuggler. (The success of Vortex in feeding off the NHAO trough while apparently airfreighting narcotics was paralleled by another State Department contractor, Dioxa, which received a thirty-eight-thousand-dollar contract and whose boss was subsequently indicted on charges relating to half a *ton* of cocaine.)

Excited by this discovery, our CBS News team flew down to Miami and convinced the chief of airport operations to let us shoot pictures of Tolliver's plane. The date was April 1, 1987, just after we had put in requests to the White House, CIA, and State Department for official comment on the allegations made by Tolliver. In the twelve hours before we got there the red stripe down the side of the DC-6 had been painted blue. A new tail number was barely dry, while the outlines of the old identifying number showed through the hasty paint job. The spanking-new facade was apparently not considered enough of a disguise, for the plane had been moved to the back of the hangar, as far away as possible from public view. The plane had also just been reregistered to a new front company, though, in a slip not untypical of covert operations, the new firm had the same address as the old. And the dauntless photographer-newsdealer had meanwhile chronicled the makeover of the plane, including the removal of the tail number.

At about the same time that the painters were busy on the Tolliver plane, Vortex and its indicted executive were in the midst of an interagency squabble. A Vortex plane on its way back from Central America, with Palmer at the controls, was stopped for inspection by customs. Palmer told the customs agents that he was flying for the State Department. The customs agents then ran Palmer through their computer, which raised the red flag of his Detroit indictment and extensive drug connections. They therefore detained plane and pilot for further investigation. An exasperated CIA official then called customs to claim the plane and Palmer, and to demand that customs stop meddling in their business. Customs raised the drug question with the CIA, but were firmly told to let the matter drop.

Yet even though the CIA had openly admitted to customs that the indicted drug smuggler was their man, customs officials continued to insist, at least in public, that the drug shipments were the work of "freelancers" rather than operations sanctioned by the agency: "What happened was, that these people, these freelancers, took advantage of our [inspection-free CIA] program. That's bad enough and it happens to be true."

Just as the Customs Service refuses to acknowledge the role of the CIA and the related White House covert operations network in drenching America in cocaine and other narcotics, Congress and most major news organizations are reluctant to face facts. Perhaps the truth is so shocking that it produces a collective refusal to accept it.

Inside selective portions of the administration, on the other hand, it has been possible to find sources who acknowledge reality. One source who was closely involved in the whole illegal contra supply effort admitted candidly that senior officials in the operation in all concerned agencies and departments were well aware of the drug connection, and indeed considered it to be "business as usual."

The source even suggested that one high-level staffer at the NSC may have had the job of liaising with drug dealers, in order to tap funds for the contra effort. George Morales said he had met twice with an NSC staffer who was soliciting "half a million dollars." The drug dealer declined to oblige, as he was content with his CIA channel and felt the official intended to line his own pockets.

While the story is indeed shocking, it is not without precedent. The flow of heroin from Southeast Asia onto the American market mushroomed during the glory days of the "secret war" in Laos in the early seventies. The anti-Castro CIA team in Florida were already drawing attention to their drug-smuggling activities by 1963. There is evidence of covert cooperation with the drug trade at least as far back as the early 1950s. It may have been that then, as now, those who sanctioned the unwholesome alliance believed, like George Morales, that "it doesn't matter what we have to do in order to obtain the money to fight the communists."

Of course, at the time he was doing well by doing good, Morales, like the rest of the normally well-informed population of Metropolitan Correctional Center, did not know that his partners in Washington had not only been trading drugs for money, they had also been selling arms. This program was as great a secret as the narcotics connection, and with good reason. The American people had been taught to think that if there was anything more unwholesome than drug dealers, it was terrorists.

Chapter Eleven
GUNS FOR HOSTAGES

"Americans will never make concessions to terrorists—to do so would only invite more terrorism—once we head down that path there would be no end to it, no end to the suffering of innocent people, no end to the bloody ransom all civilized people must pay."

—Ronald Reagan
June 18, 1985

"It's going to be fine . . . as soon as everyone knows that . . . the ayatollah is helping us with the contras."
—Lt. Col. Oliver North to Asst. Sec. of Def. Richard Armitage
November 1986

Up until November 1986 the notion that the U.S. government would be selling arms to the Ayatollah Khomeini to raise money for the contras was as unthinkable to most people as the idea that the government had gone into the narcotics business on the contras' behalf.

The Iranian regime had been firmly emplaced in the American mind as an implacable terrorist enemy since the emotional days of the hostage crisis in 1980. The menacing features of the ayatollah, endlessly beamed across the country along with the message that America was being held hostage, had a dramatic and lasting psychological effect. Most immediately, it destroyed the presidency of Jimmy Carter and did more than anything else to put Ronald Reagan in the White House.

Once the awful news broke that Reagan had sanctioned arms sales to Tehran in 1985 and 1986 Reagan did his best to find acceptable excuses. The initial coverup, launched in Reagan's November 1986 address to the nation—"We did not, repeat, did not trade weapons or anything else for hostages nor will we"—was succeeded by stumbling pseudostrategic rationales about bolstering moderate factions in Iran. Those were succeeded in turn by references to presidential anguish brought on by the thought of "Americans in chains."

Throughout, a majority of the American people thought that the president was not telling the truth, and they were right. Ronald Reagan began selling arms to the Iranians at the same time as he began supporting the contras—almost immediately after he took office. The same group of people were involved in planning and executing both of these secret operations as they germinated and flourished from 1981 to 1986.

The first presidential finding to send $19 million to the tattered remnants of Somoza's National Guard was signed by the president within six weeks of his inauguration. A few months later, on July 18, 1981, a CL-44 transport plane strayed across the Turkish border into Soviet airspace, where it crashed after being intercepted by Soviet fighters. The plane was carrying American-made tank parts and ammunition from Israel to Iran.

Early the following year the BBC produced two copiously researched documentaries on the flow of arms from Israel to Iran being carried out with American encouragement. (I happened to view the first of these broadcasts in the plush Tel Aviv offices of two Israeli arms dealers heavily involved in the trade. One of them was the local representative of a very prominent American defense contractor. Their approving comments on the BBC story left no doubt as to the accuracy of the account.) In May 1982 the columnists Evans and Novak reported that the then secretary of state, Alexander Haig, seemed anxious to reinstate a military cooperation agreement with Israel, suspended after the Israeli annexation of the Golan Heights, as a *reward* for Israel's arms shipments to Iran. In October 1982 Moshe Arens, then Israel's ambassador to the U.S., stated in an interview with the *Boston Globe* that Israel had been shipping arms to Iran "in coordination with the U.S. government . . . at almost the highest of levels." This report swiftly elicited official denials from Washington; as Arens reported to the *Globe:* "I caught a little flak from the State Department." The ambassador nevertheless stuck by his story.

The obvious question, considering the potential political dangers of being caught dealing with the hated mullahs, is why Washington was so eager for the business. The answer may lie in what could be the most terrible secret of the Reagan administration.

In October 1980 the presidential election was only a month

away. The foreign policy issue that dominated all others, symbolizing the supposed "weakness" of America under Carter, was the continued incarceration of the hostages. Carter had already tried one desperate measure to rid himself of the problem: the disastrous rescue mission that had literally crashed in flames in the Iranian desert. If, however, Carter were to bring the hostages home in time for the election, an "October surprise," then he might ride to victory on the ensuing national jubilation. That was the specter haunting the Reagan campaign.

With the election just weeks away, the Reagan staff got wind of what the October surprise was going to be. Iraq had invaded Iran in September, with the encouragement of the White House, and Tehran was in desperate need of spare parts and equipment for its armed forces, which had been equipped by the shah almost exclusively with American arms. Carter was prepared to hand over the supplies in return for the hostages.

William J. Casey, who was Reagan's campaign manager, found out about this potentially dangerous development from a spy in the National Security Council staff, a naval intelligence officer codenamed Navy Blue. Reagan's top aides were terrified that Carter might yet snatch victory from the jaws of defeat. That they were aware of what was going on is clear from documents released by the FBI under the Freedom of Information Act in 1987. The documents, 90 percent of which were censored before release, detail the FBI's 1984 investigation into the infamous theft of the Carter briefing book for the debate between the candidates on October 27, 1980. The report contains an account of a meeting of the Reagan high command in a Wexford, West Virginia, garage to rehearse their candidate for the confrontation with Carter. Question 7 on the "Reagan Debate Practice Tape #2" is listed as, "Would the candidate sell military spare parts to Iran in exchange for the hostages?"

The senior Reagan staff took several steps to make sure Carter did not get a nice surprise in October.

First, they leaked news of the impending deal to the press, taking care to disguise their tracks. The first report surfaced on Chicago's WLS-TV's local news broadcast on October 15, and by October 17 the *Washington Post* was referring to rumors of a "secret deal that would see the hostages released in exchange for the American-made military spare parts Iran needs to continue its fight against Iraq." The report issued in May 1984 by a subcommittee headed by Congressman Donald Albosta inquiring into the theft of Carter's debate papers reported that the leak to the TV station had come from "a highly placed member of the U.S. intelligence community."

In the days leading up to the election, news of Carter's bargain with the devil continued to seep into the *Post*. A story from Paris that appeared on election day itself quoted French officials as privately expressing "shock over what they believe is U.S. acceptance of the 'blackmail' of the swap of the American hostages for U.S. spare parts for American weapons." The same edition quoted remarks made by Senator Barry Goldwater the previous weekend that two air force C-5 transports were being loaded with spare parts for Iran.

William Casey, Ed Meese and James Baker 3d later admitted to the Albosta subcommittee that retired Adm. Robert Garrick, a senior aide to Casey in the campaign, had run a network of serving and retired military officers to watch U.S. bases for any signs of military activity connected with the hostages. The voluminous FBI report, however, suggests that Casey was also running a similar network made up of retired and active CIA and FBI agents.

Despite the diligent efforts of the FBI Freedom of Information censors to gut the report of all substance before release, it is clear that the bureau investigators made Casey's secret team, and its knowledge of a possible arms-for-hostages deal, the central focus of their probe.

Putting a spoke in such a deal might be excused, just, as within the limits of fair politics. But there is considerable evidence to suggest that in their determination to win the White House by any means, Reagan and his associates went much, much further. It is very possible that they made their own deal, one that ensured that the hostages were not released in time to help Carter. There is strong evidence that they assured the Iranians that if the hostages remained in Tehran, a Reagan administration would be much more forthcoming in terms of arms supplies.

Abolhassan Bani-Sadr, who was president of Iran during this stage of the hostage crisis and now lives in exile outside Paris, has confirmed that there was indeed an agreement between his government and the Carter White House to exchange weapons for hostages, and that two powerful lieutenants of Khomeini, Hashemi Rafsanjani and Mohammed Beheshti, stopped the deal—with Khomeini's knowledge and consent. He further confirms that Rafsanjani and Beheshti sent an envoy on a secret visit to Washington in the early weeks of October 1980. This intermediary met in Washington's L'Enfant Plaza Hotel with two prominent Reaganites: Richard V.

Allen, the campaign's chief foreign policy adviser and subsequently Reagan's first national security adviser, and Lawrence Silberman, a die-hard conservative and friend of Reagan's. The meeting was arranged by Robert McFarlane, who was at the time a senior staff aide to Republican senator and Reagan campaign adviser John Tower.

All three U.S. officials, Allen, Silberman, and McFarlane, concede that the meeting took place, and that the Iranians offered a timely hostage release in return for military supplies and intelligence. However, Allen, who was later dismissed from the NSC job after a cash bribe from a Japanese journalist was found in his safe (by Oliver North!), says piously that the offer was straightforwardly rejected and that he suggested that the Iranians deal only with the White House on hostage issues. McFarlane has stated that "an individual claiming to be Iranian approached me and was referred to the Reagan campaign staff. He was judged to be a fraud and dismissed." If McFarlane ever did think Rafsanjani, the envoy's sponsor, a fraud, he had obviously revised his assessment by May 1986, when he went to Tehran to negotiate on arms. By that time Rafsanjani had become Speaker of the Iranian Parliament and the Reagan administration's favorite "moderate."

That Allen may have been a little less upstanding in his reception of the Iranian envoys is indicated by what Barbara Honneger, a former Reagan campaign staffer, was told by one of her colleagues at a party at Reagan campaign headquarters later on in October 1980. Honneger served as a researcher on the campaign staff and later as a policy analyst at the White House. She says she was in the Reagan headquarters in Arlington, Virginia, on October 24 or 25, 1980, when an excited staffer exclaimed, "We don't have to worry about an October surprise. Dick cut a deal." "Dick" was Richard Allen.

Bani-Sadr has stated that he received further confirmation that a deal had been struck. After Reagan took office the then Iranian president received intelligence reports from the Iranian military that arms shipments had been assured by the incoming U.S. administration.

(According to Mansur Rafizadeh, the former U.S. station chief of SAVAK, the shah's secret police, and a self-proclaimed CIA agent besides, the CIA gave a helping hand to the Reagan operation: ". . . some CIA agents, such as Sadegh Ghotbzadeh [then Iranian foreign minister], were briefed by agency officers to persuade Khomeini not to release his prisoners until Ronald Reagan was sworn in. The CIA, consistently hostile to Carter, told Khomeini not to bother giving Carter any credit when he would no longer have any power [i.e., between the election in November and Reagan's inauguration in January 1981]. Thus the CIA . . . sentenced the American hostages to seventy-six more days of imprisonment." Later on, states Rafizadeh, the CIA collected a list of anti-Khomeini activists in touch with exile opposition movements and handed it over to the Tehran regime. Those unlucky enough to be on the list suffered predictably unpleasant consequences.)

The Iranians were as good as their word, retaining the hostages until the precise moment Carter left office. They did, however, retain one, just to make sure that Reagan was true to his end of the deal and supplied the arms. Richard Allen has since let slip, on the November 7, 1986, *MacNeil-Lehrer Newshour,* that when the president heard, on the day of his inauguration, that one of the hostages— journalist Cynthia Dwyer—had been kept behind, he indignantly exclaimed that this person had better be sent home fast "or the deal is off." No one asked, "What deal?"

Arms shipments to Iran (laundered through the ever-cooperative Israelis) continued at least up through 1982. There is no evidence of any business in 1983, which may have been because the original deal was for a specific quantity of weapons that had all been delivered by the end of 1982, or because relations significantly worsened between Iran and the White House in 1983. In that year Iranian-backed terrorists blew up not only the CIA Middle East headquarters and senior personnel in Beirut (along with the U.S. embassy in Beirut) but also 241 marines conveniently herded into their barracks on the edge of the Lebanese capital.

In 1984, however, the relationship was certainly beginning to burgeon again. The impetus was the traditional one of hostages, or rather one hostage. On March 16, 1984, William Buckley, officially described at the time as a diplomat attached to the U.S. embassy, was kidnapped off a Beirut street by elements of Hezbollah, a fundamentalist Shiite group with strong links to the Khomeini regime.

Buckley was no ordinary diplomat. He was the CIA station chief in Beirut, and an official with some specialized responsibilities and connections. As Oliver North later testified, Buckley was "an expert on terrorism" involved in a very "sensitive" job before he left Washington for Beirut. North stated that in the course of his antiterrorist work he had developed a "personal" relationship with CIA Director William Casey. Other sources report that Buckley was an old associate of Theodore Shackley, who, it may be recalled, had reportedly had a hand with Edwin Wilson in running a program for eliminating hostile terrorists. Indeed, Buckley had had to approve CIA assassinations undertaken by the Shackley organizations.

Losing Buckley to Hezbollah was bad enough, but anguish in Washington turned to consternation when it was learned that Buckley was being tortured to reveal his copious fund of secrets. It did not take long before familiar figures from the Shackley-Clines secret network began to get involved in this new crisis. On April 2, 1984, less than three weeks after Buckley's disappearance, President Reagan signed National Security Decision Directive 138. This authorized the creation of a new counterterrorism task force charged with planning the rescue of hostages held by Iran (as well as "neutralizing" terrorist threats from Iran, Libya, and Nicaragua). The new group was reportedly to be headed by retired Gen. Richard Secord. Though Secord denies any association with the task force, Pentagon sources confirm it, adding that the directive was drafted by Oliver North.

By November 1985, Theodore Shackley had entered the fray on behalf of his old associate Buckley. On November 22 the Blond Ghost reported to the CIA that he had just met in Hamburg with Gen. Manucher Hashemi, the former head of SAVAK's counterintelligence division. Hashemi had introduced him to Manuchehr Ghorbanifar, who, as Shackley speedily informed the CIA, was another SAVAK alumnus with "fantastic" contacts in Iran.

The basic topic of this meeting—following some high-minded sentiments about "moderates," the desirability of a "meaningful dialogue with Washington," and "destiny"—was to discuss arms shipments, specifically American TOW antitank missiles. Shackley, in his cabled report on the meeting to the CIA, said that Ghorbanifar "further suggested the possibility of a cash ransom paid to Iran for the four Americans kidnapped in Lebanon, including Buckley, who, he said after making telephone calls, was still alive. The transaction could be disguised by using Ghorbanifar as a middleman." Shackley reported that Ghorbanifar needed a response by December 8, 1984. As Shackley told the Tower Commission, the State Department replied later that month, in effect, "Thank you but we will work this problem out via other channels."

No one was paying much attention to the State Department. What Shackley didn't tell the CIA in his cable, at least not in the cable that was produced for the Tower report, was that there were two others meeting in the Hamburg Atlantic Hotel Kempinski at that time. One of them was a British arms dealer named Leslie Aspin. The other was Oliver North.

According to Aspin, he was asked to get hold of five thousand TOW missiles for Iran. He agreed, and was then flown by a U.S. Air Force plane to Frankfurt to be introduced to none other than William Casey. On December 6, 1984, Aspin was given a letter by the Iranian ambassador in Bonn that confirmed the deal.

Leslie Aspin and his brother and partner, Michael, were keen for their own reasons to sell the Iranians a French missile called the ACL-Strim and arranged a demonstration for the customers at the Strim factory outside Paris. To the Aspins' disappointment, the Iranians were uninterested in the Strims; it was American TOWs they wanted. Michael Aspin did not think much of their choice: "Honestly, they were old crap missiles, most of them had trouble getting out of the end of the barrel." Nevertheless he set to work, and eventually located a possible source of supply. He was, however, becoming nervous that he was being set up for a "sting," his suspicions being particularly aroused because of the unprecedentedly overt involvement of the U.S. government. "This one was too easy," he told the *London Observer* later.

Leslie Aspin set his brother's mind at rest by arranging a meeting with North in London in February 1985 at the Churchill Hotel in Portman Square. The professional arms trader concluded that the go-getting marine's energy and enthusiasm were not matched by his competence. "A few sparks flew," said Aspin later. "North didn't know what the hell he was on about."

So, while Oliver North's interest in arms sales to Iran in late 1984 and early 1985 was a matter for comment and derision in British arms-dealing circles at the time, these negotiations received no mention in either the Tower report or the Iran-contra hearings. An ABC News report on the night before North began his testimony to the Iran-contra committees specifically discussed the 1984 arms sales efforts and their direct connection with Buckley's confession, but no senator or congressman saw fit to raise the topic. The even more dangerous question of why the Reagan administration had been selling arms long before there were any American hostages in Beirut was likewise passed over in silence.

The attempt to get arms to Iran via Aspin ran into the sand. Instead, by the middle of 1985, there was a return to the tried and tested arms route to Iran: the Israelis. Once again, it appears that Theodore Shackley was one of the prime movers.

In May 1985, as he later told the Tower Commission, Shackley had lunch with Michael Ledeen, a successful practitioner of the burgeoning industry of terrorism consultancy and a man with contacts in many murky places, including the Italian intelligence community. He was well connected with Israel and was at that time a consultant to the NSC on terrorism. The two men discussed Shackley's Hamburg meeting the previous November, and the possibility of getting back into business with Ghorbanifar, a man who, according to North, "was widely believed to be an Israeli agent."

By August, key portions of the Washington bureaucracy—that is to say the NSC and the CIA—had cobbled together the requisite strategic rationales for doing military business with Iran. In reality, the major spur for all the activity appears to have been the well-being, or lack of it, of the captive Buckley. The Israelis were once again the middlemen of choice, and the ubiquitous Ledeen was ferrying to and fro between the U.S. and Israel as a fixer.

The presidential rhetoric, meanwhile, was maintaining its usual distance from reality. In a speech to the American Bar Association on July 8, Reagan denounced Iran as part of a "confederation of terrorist states . . . a new, international version of Murder Incorporated." He added, "Let me make it plain to the assassins in Beirut and their accomplices that America will never make concessions to terrorists."

In the midst of all this high-powered diplomacy, Oliver North was working away on a bizarre scheme of his own. On June 7 the industrious marine submitted an "action memorandum" to his boss, Robert McFarlane. It included a plan for the private ransoming of two hostages, including Buckley, for $2 million. The operation, as he told McFarlane, would take "considerable time (contacts inside Lebanon, financial transactions, and rental of yacht/safehouse)." For manpower, North wanted McFarlane to ask the attorney general to detail two officers of the Drug Enforcement Administration (which is controlled by the Justice Department) to work with the NSC.

It is worth reviewing the actual background to this proposal, as it furnishes an instructive example of North's fitness for a central role in U.S. foreign policy. It all began with a man named Kevin Kattke. Kattke was not a seasoned covert operator, an old hand from Southeast Asia days, or anything of the kind. His employment and base of operations was the building maintainance office at Macy's Department Store, Hempstead, Long Island. When his duties at Macy's allowed, Kattke liked to take vacations in the Caribbean, particularly Jamaica. In the midst of his pleasant but humdrum existence, Kattke nurtured ambitions for a career in espionage. Thus, in the course of his Jamaican excursions he made a point of buying drinks for the local constabulary and then transmitting items of "intelligence" to the local U.S. embassy. Just prior to the invasion of Grenada in October 1983 Kattke made a potent high-level connection. He contacted the National Security Council, claiming, according to a subsequent FBI report, to represent a "Grenedian [*sic*] student group who were contemplating an overthrow of the communist-leaning government of Greneda." The official to whom he spoke was then-Maj. Oliver North. The two were made for each other. North referred to him as a "rogue CIA agent," while Kattke returned the compliment by referring to North as "the compass."

Kattke's web of contacts were not limited to the Caribbean. Back on Long Island he had a Lebanese friend who sold insurance for Equitable Life. At a meeting in a Brooklyn saloon in the late spring of 1985 the insurance salesman confided to the building maintenance man that the man holding the hostages in Beirut happened to be his cousin. For a mere three-hundred-thousand-dollar down payment his cousin would disclose the prisoners' location.

It was this vital intelligence, quickly relayed to "the compass," that prompted North's rescue plan, which McFarlane approved. The down payment was raised with a phone call to millionaire Ross Perot, whose interest in such affairs dated from a successful operation to extract two of his employees from a Tehran jail during the Iranian revolution. The DEA men were duly dispatched (to the bemused irritation of their superiors), their knapsacks bulging with Mr. Perot's money. As so often happens in the world of covert operations, the mission went awry. The insurance salesman's cousin was happy to accept the three hundred thousand dollars but signally failed to produce any clue to the hostages' whereabouts.

(This was not Kattke's only impact on high policy. In early February 1986 Kattke was monitoring events in Haiti, where the dictatorial regime of Baby Doc Duvalier was crumbling. Prowling around the presidential palace late one evening, Kattke noticed that the lights were out on the upper floors. He immediately called the NSC to report that Duvalier had fled. Shortly afterwards, a contact emerged to say that Duvalier was playing Ping-Pong in the basement. By then it was two A.M., which Kattke thought was an inconsiderate hour to be calling Washington, so he kept the intelligence update to himself. Thus White House spokesman Larry Speakes went on record with the statement that the Haitian leader had left, a week before Duvalier actually did so.)

Such farcical interventions aside, by the end of August 1985 the arms pipeline to Iran was up and running. On August 30 Israel shipped 100 TOWs and on September 14 an additional 408 missiles. Some of them were "old crap," as Michael Aspin would say, and were returned by the customers. The Israelis made a profit of $3 million on the deal. In late August or early September, according to an account by Ledeen, North was told to prepare "contingency plans for extracting hostages—hostage or hostages—from Lebanon." The State Department issued North a fake passport in the name of William P. Goode, and the NSC opened up a secret communications channel to North code-named Blank Check. Robert McFarlane was later asked by the Senate select committee's chief counsel, Arthur Liman: "Were you asked to play God and ask for one hostage?" "Yes," replied McFarlane, "and I asked for Mr. Buckley."

By September 12 North thought that the prize was at hand. On that day he told Charles Allen, the CIA national intelligence officer for counterterrorism, that William Buckley "might be released in the next few hours or days." It was not to be. Instead of the anxiously awaited Mr. Buckley it was the avuncular figure of the Reverend Benjamin Weir who emerged from captivity.

There are conflicting accounts of where Buckley actually was during this period, although there is a consensus that he was having a gruesome time of it. David Jacobsen, a fellow American hostage who was eventually released in November 1986, has said that he was held in the same place in Beirut as Buckley, who was being tortured by his captors in the next room. Buckley, said Jacobsen after his release, had probably died on or about June 3, 1985. This version of events was supported by another released hostage, Father Lawrence Jenco. On October 4, 1985, Islamic Jihad announced that they had executed Buckley in retaliation for the Israeli bombing of Tunis, which occurred on October 1.

According to a "senior Iranian diplomat close to President Ali Khamenei" quoted in the *London Observer,* however, Buckley did not die in Lebanon, but in Iran: "Shortly after his kidnapping in a Beirut street by members of the Emad Moghniya family, Buckley was transferred to the headquarters of the Iranian Revolutionary

Guards, the Pasdaran, in Ba'albeck in the Bekaa Valley." (This leaves open the question of who the tortured victim was in the room next to Jacobsen's.) "In August 1985"—i.e., just before North was getting ready to go to Lebanon and the first TOW missiles were sent off— Buckley, "drugged and bandaged and passed off as a Revolutionary Guard . . . was flown from the military base of Riyagh, in the Bekaa, to Damascus, from where he was immediately put on a plane to Tehran." Buckley was held in a safe house "in Freshteh Street, in the wealthy northern suburbs. Later he was moved to a prison at the military base of Saleh Abad, near the holy city of Qum, where he died of a heart attack while under torture" in late 1985.

However and wherever Buckley met his end, the fact remains that North and his masters in Washington thought the CIA man still alive in September 1985, when they dispatched 508 TOW missiles in the hope of getting him back. Even when, by early October, the administration accepted the fact that he was dead and that he had been in the hands of the Iranians (the Syrians confirmed both facts to U.N. Ambassador Vernon Walters at that time), Buckley remained of vital concern to Washington, for he had left a potent testament, a videotaped recitation of everything he knew.

Buckley had had a lot to say to his brutal captors. "A tortured confession of some four hundred pages was extracted from him," North later told the Iran-contra committees. He claimed to have personally viewed a tape of Buckley's ordeal. The White House was well aware, therefore, of just how dangerous Buckley's testament might be if it became public. It has been suggested that they were anxious to have the Iranians keep it to themselves because it compromised American intelligence networks in the Middle East. There may be some truth to this; it had, after all, been highly embarrassing in the Watergate era when it emerged that King Hussein of Jordan was on the CIA payroll.

Nevertheless, judging by the obsessive concern in the White House and CIA—not to mention by Mr. Shackley—over the question of the confession, it appears that Buckley had told some stories that they wanted very, very much to remain secret.

The Iranians therefore now held a strong card to play with the White House, as potentially devastating indeed as their knowledge of just how and why the original hostages had been held for long enough to get Reagan elected. At the end of 1985, for example, Ghorbanifar called Ledeen to relay a message for Reagan from the Iranian prime minister. As Ledeen told the Tower Commission, the message said, ". . . we have been very patient with you people. We have behaved honorably with you people. We have done everything that we said we would have done, and now you are cheating us and making fun of us and so forth, and would you please do what you said you were going to do." Ledeen characterized the message as "bizarre," which was a reasonable conclusion in view of the fact that only one hostage, Benjamin Weir, had been produced and that Buckley had died at the hands of the Iranians. But it is not so bizarre if there were other ingredients in the deal, if the Iranians had "done everything" they had promised to keep the Buckley confession from being released.

In the ensuing months, as the arms continued to flow to Iran without any commensurate release of hostages, the operation became increasingly intertwined with the parallel illegal arms flow to the contras. Quite apart from the vexed question of diversion of funds from the Iranian arms profits to Central America, there was the fact that the same people were handling both operations. They were in fact the same core of operatives who coordinated the arms shipments to the contras, the same clique of covert veterans who had served time in Laos. While Shackley's role had been to launch the arms-for-hostages notion, retired General Secord took over vital operational tasks, such as procuring aircraft to ferry the weapons, early in 1986. Albert Hakim, their longtime partner, looked after the financial end, using the same Swiss accounts as were already being used to fund contra arms purchases and pay the contra leadership.

As with the contra operation, the CIA was involved in the Iran arms shipments, even though they were absolutely illegal until President Reagan signed a presidential finding in January 1986. Dewey Clarridge, the hero of the Nicaraguan harbor mining and the CIA assassination manual, was one of those called in to help. Clarridge told the Tower Commission that his first involvement came in November 1985, when North asked him for help in getting a plane to ship Hawk missiles to Iran. After trying and failing to get overflight clearances for an Israeli El Al 747, the CIA's air branch suggested the use of a proprietary. "The proprietary," Clarridge told the Tower Commission, "was told to await a call." Clarridge assumed the caller would be Secord, who was known for the purposes of this operation as "Copp." North later reported to his superiors, "Dewey has arranged for a proprietary to work for Secord (Copp). Copp will charter two 707s in the name of LAKE [*sic*] Resources (our Swiss Co.) and have them p/u [pick up] the cargo and deliver it. . . . [T]he cargo will be xfered [transferred] to the three Israeli chartered DC-8/55s for the flight to T[abriz]. Though I am sure Copp suspects, he does not know that the 707s belong to a proprietary. Clarridge deserves a medal—so does Copp." As it turned out, the Israelis were short a plane for the delivery to Tabriz (in Iran), so North dipped into his Central American operation for a solution. "One of our Lake Resources A/C [aircraft] which was . . . to p/u [pick up] a load of ammo for UNO [the contras]" was to be used. "He will have the a/c [aircraft] and put into service nlt [not later than] noon Sat. . . ." Someone was doing a lucrative business in paint jobs for North's outfit. Nevertheless, North was despondent about shifting assets from the contra front: "So help me I have never seen anything so screwed up in my life. Will meet w/Calero tonight to advise that the ammo will be several days late in arriving. Too bad, this was to be our first direct flight to the resistance field . . . inside Nicaragua. The ammo was already palletized with parachutes attached. Maybe we can do it on Weds or Thurs. More as it becomes available. One hell of an operation."

After depriving the contras of their ammunition, it turned out that the wrong weapons got sent to Iran, which may have inspired the outraged references to "cheating" in the message Ledeen passed on to Reagan. The Iranians were urgently in need of the improved version of the Hawk in order to deal with high-flying Iraqi incursions, but the Israelis blithely dispatched tired old early-model Hawks, which the Iranians already had and which they knew were insufficient to meet the threat. They eventually sent them back.

It appears to have been this piece of sharp practice that caused the White House to shift their management policy. From now on the Israeli role would be diminished and North, the man who a professional arms dealer had determined "didn't know what the hell he was on about," was to take an even more leading role in the arms business.

So, undaunted, the White House team forged ahead, backed up when necessary by the CIA and Defense Department. As part of what North had grandiosely christened Operation Recovery, it was now decided the Iranians should be given intelligence information that would help them in their war with Iraq. It was eventually handed over by Secord, who had been officially denied a security clearance by the CIA bureaucracy. North also helped prepare the finding signed by Reagan on January 17, 1986, that made the operation technically legal. The hope and expectation for 1986 was that the Iranians would be given the intelligence and upgraded Hawks, as well as no less than thirty-three hundred TOW missiles.

Deputy CIA Director John McMahon, the Cassandra of the national security set, grumbled about the irrationality of it all. At a December 7, 1985, meeting on the Iran initiative, President Reagan delivered some lines about encouraging our friends the moderates. McMahon, according to his testimony to the Tower Commission, "pointed out that we had no knowledge of any moderates in Iran, that most of the moderates had been slaughtered when Khomeini took over." He went on to say that the weapons "would end up at the front and that would be to the detriment of the Iran-Iraq balance." After the finding was signed he remarked, "Giving TOW missiles was one thing. . . . Giving them intelligence gave them a definite offensive edge, and I said that can have cataclysmic results." Among other aspects of the operation that McMahon found distasteful was the involvement of North, who he considered deserved a lot of the blame for the disastrous Nicaraguan mining operation. Despite this carping, however, McMahon did as he was told.

By early 1986 Richard Secord had solidified his position—and his control of the funds—in the Iranian arms supply operation. North and Casey agreed on January 14, 1986, that Secord should be in charge of buying the weapons from the Pentagon that were to be resold to Iran. He did this as an "authorized agent" for the CIA, causing him some embarrassment later on, when the Iran-contra committees asked him how he, as a CIA agent, could have been making so much money out of the deal.

At that same January meeting Casey and North discussed high finance. North reported that Ghorbanifar, who was still involved as a middleman, could probably come up with $10,000 per TOW. The Pentagon initially said that their TOWs were priced at $6,000, but when North said that he would take older models the price came down to $3,407 apiece. The gross profit on an initial batch of one thousand therefore would be about $6.6 million. North, displaying his usual unquenchable optimism, then worked out a schedule by which "all U.S. hostages" would be released by February 9.

As it turned out, the operation proceeded relatively smoothly, except that no hostages were released. Ghorbanifar induced Saudi businessman Adnan Khashoggi to front the $10 million that North & Co. were asking for the missiles. Khashoggi, who had in turn borrowed the money from various British and Canadian investors, paid the money into Secord and Hakim's Lake Resources account in Switzerland. Lake Resources then sent $3.7 million to the CIA to give to the army.

The U.S. Army duly handed over one thousand TOWs at Redstone Arsenal, Alabama, on February 13–14 to Southern Air Transport, a Miami-based ex-CIA proprietary operating, according to an army report on the transaction, "under the control of General Secord and Colonel North." The missiles were then flown to Israel for transmission to Tehran.

The middlemen and investors made a profit on the deal of $3.2 million. The "enterprise," as Secord called his operation, enjoyed a far more handsome profit of $6.3 million.

Ever since Attorney General Meese's famous press conference of November 25, 1986, the matter of the diversion of funds from the Iran arms sales has occupied a preeminent position in the scandal. A review of Albert Hakim's admirably clear account ledger, among the most fascinating and little-noticed documents released by the Iran-contra committees, makes it clear that from the point of view of the enterprise, the Iran sales were just another item of income for an ongoing financial operation, which had outlays for the contras and for other, more personal items.

In the weeks before the Khashoggi money arrived, for example, the ledger carries items such as $10,000 for contra leader Alfonso Robelo, $4,000 for Rafael Quintero, $165,000 (noted as an "advance") for Hakim. In the weeks after the money went into the bank, payouts included $3,500 for contra leader Arturo Cruz, another $10,000 for Robelo, $5,000 for Quintero and $28,000 to Hakim (noted as "cash"), $50,125 for "unknown," and an "advance" to "Korel," which was Richard Secord's personal account, of $165,000. Straitlaced bureaucrats who knew what was going on were inclined to look askance at Hakim's involvement. The chief of the CIA's Near East Division told the Tower Commission that he "thought Hakim had a potential conflict of interest arising from his own business relationships" and that Hakim had been involved in arms deals "that might or might not be legal." Hakim, in his congressional testimony, was more straightforward. He and his partner, Secord, he said, were in it for the money.

Once the first thousand TOWs had been delivered, North received a note of congratulation from McFarlane: "Roger, Ollie. Well done—if the world only knew how many times you have kept a semblance of integrity and gumption to [*sic*] U.S. policy, they would

204

make you Secretary of State. But they can't know and would complain if they did—such is the state of democracy in the late 20th century."

There is a curious aspect to this effusive message. Since North had just delivered one thousand missiles to the terrorist mullahs and had nothing whatever to show for it (no hostages were released), it is not clear why the lieutenant colonel suddenly deserved to be made secretary of state. There are two possible explanations; either North had done some yeoman service with the Iranians in persuading them to continue sitting on Buckley's testament and other unholy secrets, or McFarlane knew a lot more than he afterwards admitted about this novel method of contra fund-raising.

By March 1986 the Iranians had set their hearts on spare parts for Hawk missiles rather than more TOWs. In early April, North drafted a long memo to Vice Adm. John Poindexter, who was now national security adviser, "to forward to the President." The memo lays out a schedule of money transfers for a Hawk parts sale, "subject to Presidential approval."

Toward the end of this master plan, North noted that "the residual funds from this transaction are allocated as follows:"

> —$2 million will be used to purchase replacement TOWs for the original 508 sold by Israel to Iran for the release of Benjamin Weir. This is the only way we have found to meet our commitment to replenish these stocks.

(North was rewriting history here. The Israeli TOWs had of course been sent in the hope of getting William Buckley, not Benjamin Weir.)

The next paragraph gave the game away.

> —$12 million will be used to purchase critically needed supplies for the Nicaraguan Democratic Resistance Forces. This materiel is essential to cover shortages in resistance inventories resulting from their current offensives and Sandinista counterattacks and to "bridge" the period between now and when Congressionally-approved lethal assistance (beyond the $25 million in "defensive" arms) can be delivered.

The entire document, entitled "Release of American hostages in Beirut," was left undated and unsigned. At the bottom there was a space for the president to "approve" or "disapprove" the above, but that too was left blank. North later claimed that his memo was similar to four others he had written for the president, seeking approval for the use of secret arms sales to help finance an illegal war. Poindexter testified that although there was very little he could remember on points of material interest, he did recall not showing any of these memos to the president in order to preserve Reagan's "deniability." Whether or not he was telling the truth, deniability was preserved. The ensuing official inquiries, the Tower Commission and the congressional Iran-contra select committees, were able to conclude that there was no evidence that the president had approved the diversion.

The April memo also contained details of hopes and plans for a longer-term relationship with Tehran, one not necessarily concerned with the grubby exigencies of suppressing secrets, releasing bodies, and peddling weapons. The Iranians were to be reenlisted as full members of the anti-Soviet alliance. As North wrote to his commander in chief, "We have convinced the Iranians of a significant near term and long range threat from the Soviet Union. We have real and deceptive intelligence to demonstrate this threat during the visit. . . . We have told the Iranians that we are interested in assistance they may be willing to provide to the Afghan resistance and that we wish to discuss this matter in Tehran."

The "visit" alluded to here was an integral part of the new Hawk deal. McFarlane, North, NSC staffer Howard Teicher (North's titular superior), George Cave (an old CIA Iran hand), and a CIA communications specialist were to go to Tehran in person to negotiate and resolve all outstanding issues.

Whether Reagan was or was not given this memo, he approved the proposed trip. On May 25 the delegation arrived in Tehran. The group had expanded to include Amiram Nir, an Israeli who had graduated from TV announcer to Prime Minister Shimon Peres's personal adviser on counterterrorism. They carried fake Irish passports; McFarlane's alias was Sean Devlin. Richard Secord had come with the team as far as Israel, where he had remained. Democracy Inc., as the enterprise was sometimes called, furnished the aircraft and crews for the trip.

The delegation came bearing gifts. Apart from a pallet of spare parts for Hawk missiles, they brought small arms—six Blackhawk

.357 Magnums in presentation boxes—and a key-shaped chocolate cake from a kosher bakery in Tel Aviv.

The excursion went badly from the start. Ghorbanifar had messed up the reception arrangements and the group waited in their plane for an hour and a half before anyone arrived to meet them. One of the presents did not survive the attention of the youthful Revolutionary Guards at the airport; as Speaker Rafsanjani later explained, "The kids ate the cake."

Once the delegation had checked into their luxury suites at the Independence Hotel, formerly the Tehran Hilton, discussions got under way. The Iranians were upset that the Americans had brought less than half the quantity of Hawk parts promised. McFarlane, at least, was angered that neither any live hostages nor the body of Mr. Buckley materialized as promised. Both Ghorbanifar and Nir were anxious that the Americans quell Iranian suspicions about the price they were being charged for the Hawk parts, which involved a markup of more than 400 percent over the amount being charged by the U.S. Army. On May 27 the group flew home, leaving their four-thousand-dollar hotel bill unpaid.

There are a number of conflicting reports on the trip, some of them from the same people. (McFarlane long denied the existence of the cake and his false passport.) Overall, the American delegation has portrayed the mood on the homeward flight as downbeat. McFarlane claims that North tried to cheer him up by pointing out that at least the deal had generated more cash for Central America, and that this was the first McFarlane had heard of the diversion.

A report in the *London Observer,* on the other hand, once again quoting a "senior Iranian diplomat" and "well-placed Iranian sources," says that McFarlane actually did meet with Rafsanjani himself, and that the meeting was fruitful. McFarlane agreed to supply high-level intelligence on the Iraqi order of battle (which is indeed what happened). Rafsanjani, for his part, agreed to continue to keep the Buckley confession quiet, and to suppress the latest products of the Tehran shredder team, the dedicated literary archaeologists who had spent years piecing together intelligence documents shredded during the embassy takeover in 1979. The latest deshredded pile allegedly contained accounts of the exploits of George Cave, the CIA man who was the interpreter for the trip.

Whatever the truth of that account, and despite the fact that the Americans and Iranians bilked each other on hostages and spare parts, the enterprise itself profited immensely. According to the final accounting for the trip, there was an $8.5 million surplus. Adnan Khashoggi had furnished $15 million to finance the deal. Lake Resources gave the CIA $6.5 million to pay off the army for the parts. Unfortunately for the Saudi, the Iranians refused to pay for the parts they had not received, so Khashoggi only got $8 million back. He was left complaining that he was $10 million short ($3 million for "costs and financing").

The principals of the enterprise were in a happier position. Business was humming at the host of interlocking companies, Lake Resources, Hyde Park Square, Albon Values, Udall, and the many others crafted by Hakim and Secord. Four days after the last part of Khashoggi's payment arrived in the Lake Resources account, Albon Values paid $26,490 to Korel, where Secord's nest eggs were lodged. Four days later Hyde Park Square dispensed $200,000 as "capital" for "Button."

Hakim, one of the more beguiling witnesses to testify, later explained to the Iran-contra committees what Button was all about. Giving a good imitation of the late actor Peter Lorre, the Iranian fixer purred to the stony-faced congressmen and senators that out of "love" for Oliver North he had suggested that the enterprise should make provision for the colonel's family. As Hakim eloquently described his emotions, "I saw a man dissipating so much love for his country and his associates that the radiation of that love really immediately penetrated to my system." Since, as Arthur Liman pointed out, Hakim had only met North once at that point, this was a case of "love at first sight."

Hakim had thought that half a million dollars would be about right, but Secord had said that was too much, so the Iranian had paid two hundred thousand dollars into an account with CSF, the Bellybutton account. He had, indeed, sent his Swiss lawyer, Willard Zucker, to confer with Mrs. Bellybutton (Betsy North) about it. In his own testimony Oliver North deployed his full powers of rhetorical eloquence to state that he knew that provision was being made for his family in the event of something going wrong with the May trip to Tehran, but that he had lost interest afterwards. He was unable to explain why Mr. Zucker was still trying to find a legal way of getting the money to Betsy as late as October 1986.

According to Hakim's accounts for the enterprise, the Iran deals yielded a total of $30 million in gross income. After expenses there remained about $15 million in profits, which was expended on supplies for the contras, stipends for their leaders, and "capital" for the principals' outside business interests.

Overall, according to the ledger, the enterprise had a turnover of $47,734,093 between December 21, 1984, and November 28, 1986. (The last recorded item of expenditure was $20,000 for "Attorney".) Thirty million dollars of that had come from the financiers of the Iranian deals; over $10 million was paid in by Adolfo Calero (presumably the fruits, or some of them, of the donations from Saudi Arabia and other U.S. allies); the remaining $7 million came variously from wealthy individuals like beer magnate Joseph Coors, professional fund-raisers like Spitz Channell, and directly from the CIA.

In his testimony to the Iran-contra committees, Secord claimed that the contras had garnered $3.5 million from the Iran arms sales, though nearly $8 million made its way from the accounts "for the benefit of the contras." He also claimed that a further $4 million had been set aside as "insurance" for the Israelis should one of their aircraft be lost in Iran while ferrying the weapons. As there were no mishaps, that money remained in the account. Secord could not, however, produce any documentary evidence of an insurance agreement, which means that the Israelis would have had trouble collecting, if such an agreement in fact existed. In all, at close of business in November 1986, a total of over $8 million remained squirreled away in the network of shell companies, a large portion of it, by mid-1987, in an account at Merrill Lynch. In the event of the death of both Secord and Hakim, Oliver North was to inherit $2 million set aside in a reserve account. Secord refused to grant authority to Congress so that investigators could examine the books of these entities and satisfy themselves that everything was aboveboard, as the general claimed.

What did emerge from Secord's testimony, and from the documents obtained by the committees, was that $2.1 million marked in the books as money designated "CIA" were for contra weapons. On September 24, 1986, the enterprise sold these items to the CIA for $1.2 million. Since, however, the weapons had already been given to the contras, and remained with them, this would seem to constitute a violation of the Boland Amendment, with the CIA supplying weapons to the contras. Hakim referred to this CIA transaction as the "stranded arms." The enterprise partners took a hefty commission on the sale. Secord, Hakim, and Tom Clines each pocketed $258,000.

Before the untimely exposure of the enterprise, Secord, according to his former employee, retired air force colonel Robert Dutton, had nurtured plans to sell off more of its property, including aircraft and the secret Santa Elena airstrip, to the CIA. The listed owner of these assets was the Panamanian company Udall Research, which retained, according to a company document, Richard Secord as its "U.S. representative." When confronted in the hearings with this document, and the inference that he planned to make a tidy profit out of the transaction, Secord prevaricated. He said first that the document had to be "wrong" and then that it was "irrelevant." He stoutly denied charges of profiteering, claiming that he had given his word to the late William Casey that the "assets" would be turned over to the CIA free of charge.

Secord admitted that the tangled web of shell companies and accounts was designed to "confuse anyone who might start poking around" (Hakim claimed he sometimes got lost himself). Nevertheless it emerged clearly that the dividing line between the supposedly private "enterprise," as Senate Counsel Arthur Liman invariably called it with ironic relish, and the U.S. government was fuzzy, at best.

During all the time that Secord, as Arthur Liman put it, was "selling arms for profit" on behalf of the U.S. government, he was reportedly the head of operations for an official counterterrorism task force, as designated by President Reagan under NSDD 138. It was American taxpayers' money that had built the arms shipped off to Iran, and American taxpayers' money that had been paid to the enterprise by the CIA. CIA Director William Casey had agreed that Secord be designated an "agent for the CIA" in his dealings with the Defense Department. Secord, uniquely for a private citizen, had been allowed to consult CIA lawyers on whether his enterprise violated the Neutrality Act. Secord was able to communicate in secret with his managers in the field, such as Dutton, thanks to the KL-43 encryption devices furnished free of charge by the National Security Agency.

The most vivid example of the degree to which foreign policy had been delegated to semiprivate citizens and a marine lieutenant colonel is to be found in the transcript of the conversation between an Iranian envoy (the so-called second channel) and North, Secord, and Hakim on October 29 and 30, 1986. This channel of communication with Iran through an unnamed relative of Rafsanjani had been opened by Secord. So well had all concerned got on that the Relative, as he was code-named, had earlier come to Washington and had been taken for a tour of the White House by North and Hakim.

Hakim, the self-professed former bagman for bribes in Iran arms deals, had now been vested by North with the responsibilities of a secretary of state. (He had been originally involved in negotiations back in February, with Ghorbanifar present. Since he and Ghorbanifar were old enemies, Secord and North sent him out to get a disguise. He rushed around Frankfurt trying to buy a wig. Eventually, and suitably tonsured, he returned to fool his compatriot.) At one point, when negotiations with the second channel were breaking down, Hakim on his own had worked out an agreement that included the release of terrorists imprisoned in Kuwait; the handing over of the Buckley "debriefing"; and a reduction of the demand for the release of all hostages to a promise of freedom for "one and a half." When Hakim communicated that point to North, the colonel accused him of being drunk. When it was made clear that this actually meant one hostage for certain and a possible second, North agreed to all nine points with alacrity, and told Hakim that the president did too. Poindexter later confirmed the president's agreement, though Secretary of State George Shultz said it wasn't so. There was, it should be noted, an urgent political deadline fast approaching. President Reagan was campaigning ardently to retain Republican control of the Senate, and North was anxious to do his bit. Hakim, who was interested in the profits he could collect if people stopped fussing about the hostages and got on with a long-term deal, was irritated at North's short-term agenda: "I did not approve of Colonel North's focusing on hostages . . . because his prime objective at that time was to support the President in connection [with] . . . the elections."

In the late-October meeting, which took place in Frankfurt, the parties united in denigrating Saddam Hussein, the Iraqi president. From the tenor of the conversation as recorded and transcribed by the CIA, it appears that there had already been talks about getting rid of Hussein. At one point in the meeting Hakim interprets the Iranian as saying: "We both agree that the foundation and base of an honorable victory means for Saddam to go. We have said enough and we both understand that. What they [the Iranians] need to know now is what should they do for us [the U.S.] to take the next step towards that and how. . . . Explain to us very clearly the method that we have to achieve this."

North replied that "We also recognize that Saddam Husayn [*sic*] must go."

It might be inferred from this colloquy that in previous conversations with the Relative there had been discussions on how the U.S. might cooperate in getting rid of President Hussein, a man who has given every sign that he is unlikely ever to leave office other than feetfirst. Later on in the conversation, in the course of discussing the date when the three remaining American hostages in Lebanon might be released, Secord introduced a lighter note. "We're going to be negotiating about the new hostages by then," he remarked. The CIA transcript notes that this pleasantry drew laughter.

Contra dignitaries were also an integral part of this public/private mechanism. The directors of UNO, the United Nicaraguan Opposition, all received paychecks from the Swiss accounts. Alfonso Robelo got a regular $10,000 monthly stipend, Arturo Cruz received $7,000 a month, and Adolfo Calero, who himself controlled large pools of cash, received $200,000. Thus the men selected by North and his colleagues on the Restricted Interagency Group as contra "leaders" were salaried employees of the U.S. government via the commercial cutout of the enterprise. In the case at least of Cruz's wages, so North informed Calero at one point, the enterprise took over the job directly from the CIA.

In fact, the only difference between the enterprise and a duly authorized government operation was that those involved were making money out of it.

As with the arrangement with the cocaine traders like Ocean Hunter, and with the Costa Rican mercenary operation, the Iran arms business left some potentially embarrassing loose ends lying around. It may be remembered that the money for the Hawk shipment that accompanied McFarlane and company to Tehran had been raised by Khashoggi from investors in Canada and elsewhere. When the Iranians failed to pay the full amount, the Canadians, reputed to be tough customers, began to pressure Ghorbanifar. Discovering that the White House and CIA were dumping him as middleman in favor of the Relative, a frantic Ghorbanifar threatened to blow the whistle.

This was a potent threat. "He has too much documentary evidence that implicates US interests," noted North in a memo, "clearly there are some personal things that can be done for Ghorbanifar—arrange permanent alien residency for his girlfriend in California." North was also prepared to offer visas for Ghorbanifar's family, as well as to find the discarded middleman a job. "These steps will not alleviate Ghorbanifar's financial problems—regardless of their merit—but may dispose him more kindly to the US government and lessen his inclination to expose the Iranian initiative. There is also," noted North presciently, "likely to be material alleging poor judgment and shabby conduct" by the lieutenant colonel and his associates.

William Casey did not need to be told that the Iranian chickens were coming home to roost. In October it had been learned that leaflets describing the McFarlane visit were flooding Tehran. At the same time, Roy Furmark, an associate of Khashoggi's (and an old friend of Casey's), had told the CIA director that Ghorbanifar was saying that he thought "the bulk of the original $15 million price tag was earmarked for Central America." The word was out on Iran. Meanwhile, deep in the Nicaraguan jungle, a wrecked airplane was yielding damning evidence to the world of what the enterprise had been doing for the contras.

Chapter Twelve
HASENFUS

"This company has no connection or affiliation with the CIA, period."

—William Langton, president of Southern Air Transport
December 18, 1986

On October 5, 1986, a Southern Air Transport C-123 transport plane carrying seventy automatic rifles, one hundred thousand rounds of ammunition, and seven RPG grenade launchers was shot down over southern Nicaragua. It had taken off at nine-thirty that morning from Ilopango military base in El Salvador, flown down the Pacific coast of Nicaragua to the Costa Rican border, then veered east and north again into enemy territory. For the crew, it was just another routine flight.

As the plane neared the drop zone where the munitions would be parachuted out to waiting contras, it was flying dangerously low over the steaming jungle. Down below, a patrol from the Gaspar Garcia Laviana Brigade of the Sandinista army was astonished to see the big plane heading straight toward them. In a reflex action, one of the infantrymen raised his rocket launcher to his shoulder and fired. No one was more astonished than he to see the rocket hit a wing of the plane, which went into a dive. When he realized what had happened he began to scream, "I can't believe I did it. I can't believe it." One parachute floated to earth; dangling at the end was Eugene Hasenfus.

Hasenfus had been one of the three-man American crew on the plane (there was also a Nicaraguan contra on board). His humble but necessary specialty was "kicker"—that is, kicking the pallets of cargo attached to parachutes out the door at precisely the right moment. The two pilots, Buz Sawyer and William Cooper, had teased Hasenfus for being the only one to bring along a personal parachute.

All three men were right at home with dangerous missions over enemy territory. They had cut their teeth flying secret missions for secret wars in Southeast Asia for Air America, the CIA airline, running guns and anything else that would fit inside a plane. Back in those days they and the other crews had been dubbed "the cowboys." They wore civilian clothes and heavy gold bracelets.

Hasenfus had left the marines to join the cowboys. "I could stay in the marines being Joe Blow the grunt, running up and down the hills with a rifle, but here you can go out and you can fly," he explained later. "You get paid more money and you don't have to sleep in the mud." Air America had been a walk on the wild side. "Vientiane [the Laotian capital] was a fun town. . . . It was fast moving all the time. Vientiane was a place where it seemed like at night everybody forgot about what was going on. Everybody would come in, go to the same places, and get drunk together, then the next day go out and fight each other." The work had been hazardous: "The war was de-escalating very much, and when the unilateral cease-fire took place we were going into more and more dangerous places with no cover, no nothing, and they were just literally blowing us out of the sky."

The crews called these flights "spook" missions and the standard orders were for them to leave their I.D. cards behind to preserve deniability. Usually they carried them anyway, for in the tradition of black operations over the years, no one wanted to die anonymously. Over Nicaragua, thirteen years later, it was the same. Along with the ten thousand pounds of weapons they had picked up at Ilopango on the morning of their last flight, the veteran crewmen were carrying enough documents to compile an operations blueprint for the entire secret war.

Hasenfus, a tall and rugged figure with red hair and ruddy skin, was a bit old at forty-five for such missions, but he was part of the old-boy network from Southeast Asia and he could be trusted. Five months before the crash he had been roused from the torpor of small-town life in Marinette, Wisconsin, by a call from pilot Bill Cooper offering Hasenfus the chance to relive his past. "I said, 'I don't really know, it don't really sound that good,'" Hasenfus recalled. "But it dug at your soul a little, and you start thinking more on it and you say, 'I hate to throw it aside.' You wake up in the middle of the night and say, 'I wonder what's really happening. Let's give it a try.'" Hasenfus left behind his wife, Sally, "three beautiful children," and a construction job in June 1986, and by July 10 he was en route to El Salvador with a salary of $3,000 a month and a bonus of $750 for every flight into Nicaraguan airspace. He was now part of the enterprise, or Project Democracy as Oliver North liked to call it, flying with fellow veterans of the old days in planes belonging to Southern Air Transport.

Hasenfus earned his bonuses. Between July and early October he flew ten missions, four of which were night runs from Aguacate air base in Honduras. Aguacate had been set up by the CIA on behalf of the contras, and was the strip where Mickey Tolliver claimed he had delivered twenty-eight thousand pounds of weapons in exchange for a twenty-five-thousand-pound load of marijuana back in March. The other six flights had been directly out of Ilopango, ferrying supplies to Oliver North's beloved southern front. On one or two occasions Hasenfus had landed at Santa Elena, the secret air base in Costa Rica owned by Richard Secord's front company and managed by the trusty Rafael Quintero.

Secord's aerial supply operation for the southern front had arisen out of the high-level meeting between North, Secord, Calero, Quintero, Enrique Bermudez, and other members of the contra leadership in Miami on July 1, 1985. As Secord later related, there had been general agreement that a new supply route for the south was needed. "After the meeting, I was asked by North whether I could put together this operation." He later said ruefully, "My partners [Clines and Quintero] told me I was crazy to do it."

Secord did not have the time himself to organize the southern operation, so he had turned to some old colleagues from Air Force Special Operations for the day-to-day management work. One of these was a retired air force lieutenant colonel, Richard Gadd, who, like many others in this story, had already discovered that government covert operations could be a profitable private enterprise.

Before leaving the service in 1983, Gadd had worked as a liaison officer between the Joint Chiefs of Staff and the Joint Special Operations Command at Fort Bragg, home of unconventional warfare. At

Bragg, Gadd had gotten to know the inner workings of the "zoo," as Army Special Operations headquarters was popularly known. The zoo had a staff of twenty, an annual budget of $100 million, and was on call to provide paramilitary assistance to the CIA when required. Gadd learned from his army friends that, rather than having to rely on the air force for air transport, they hankered after an air fleet of their own. He saw his window of opportunity.

Rather than accept a promotion to full colonel in 1982, Gadd went private to provide the zoo with a small but efficient air wing. As one of his friends told a reporter, "Dick Gadd was smart enough to see a market opportunity." A sales brochure for his company, American National Management Corp., described the firm as providing "discreet and expedited services which transcend military discipline." Just prior to the Grenada invasion in October 1983, for example, he was contracted by Army Special Operations to ferry helicopters and pilots from a covert aviation unit based at Fort Eustis, Virginia, to Barbados. Covert units were used in the first wave of the invasion, sustaining heavy casualties that the Pentagon refused to acknowledge (much to the annoyance of at least one bereaved parent, who was told that his son had died in Lebanon).

Gadd was a sole-source contractor for such missions, a happy blend of private initiative with public service that ended in 1984 about the time, according to the *Washington Post,* that Pentagon officials started investigating "mishandling of covert funds by some army officials. Although there is no indication that Gadd's companies were involved, government records list no more army contracts with ANMC after 1984."

The loss of army business does not seem to have discommoded Gadd's business career. A 1984 brochure for Gadd's operation lists Southern Air Transport, the ex-CIA proprietary in which Richard Secord kept a close interest, as a client. By the fall of 1985 he was gathering planes, pilots, and crews for Secord and North. One of his companies, Airmach, garnered a contract for $182,000 from the Nicaraguan Humanitarian Assistance Office.

The other deputy selected by Secord for day-to-day management of the air supply business was an old colleague from the Air Force Military Assistance Advisory Group in Iran. Col. Robert Dutton had served under Secord there, selling weapons to the insatiable shah. When Dutton returned to Washington, he had served as assistant director of the Air Force Office of Special Plans, and as such had been a planner for a projected second Iranian hostage rescue mission, code-named Rice Bowl, under the watchful eyes of his superior, Gen. Richard Secord.

In April 1986, Dutton became "Staff Director" at Stanford Technology Trading Corp., Secord's operating company in Vienna, Virginia, at a salary of five thousand dollars a month. This was a rather bland title for the job of running air drops for the contras inside Nicaragua. According to Richard Secord, Dutton took over management of the contra project because "Gadd was running the operation badly. I call it the five Ps," the general explained, "Piss Poor Performance from no Prior Planning. Dutton," said Secord, "turned things around." (In his testimony before the Iran-contra committees, CIA Central American Task Force chief Alan Fiers said that Gadd was pushed by North for the job, although Fiers's checks into the airlift operator set off "shyster alarms."

Dutton took enough professional pride in his air operation to produce a photo album chronicling its exploits. Oliver North thought it a fine idea and promised he would show the album to the "top boss." "It was my assumption," Dutton later told Congress, "that it was the president."

In his testimony Dutton described how instructions on where and when to drop supplies would come from CIA Costa Rican station chief Joe Fernandez. "Joe was critical to us throughout the operation," explained the former staff director. "Joe was coming up with new commandantes that he wanted us to support and new drop zones that he wanted us to fly to and put loads on. All we had to do was go in, make the drop, call Joe, and say, 'There's another load on that drop zone; where do you want the next load?' " Unfortunately, what should have been a smooth-running operation was marred by the inability of Fernandez's commandantes to accurately chart their own whereabouts, making it difficult for the supply pilots to find them. "We would get instructions," explained Dutton, "that they would have three bonfires" to mark the drop zone. But when the pilots found the map reference, "there would be no fires."

Thus, for the operational end of the enterprise in Central America, Secord was able to call on a staff seasoned in the black arts of covert operations and who knew how to take advantage of the U.S. military system, in even small ways such as by getting free gas. It appears that active-duty military personnel in Central America were routinely refueling Secord's planes. "I don't ask whose plane it is," remarked one American sergeant, "my job is to fill it up and get it out again."

*   *   *

None of this elaborate support system was much use to Eugene Hasenfus the day the Sandinista missile hit his plane. The parachute he was wearing when he climbed through a window and jumped had been his own idea and had earned him the ridicule of his crewmates when he brought it along. When Hasenfus floated down into the dense undergrowth he was alone with the deafening cicadas and the sweltering heat.

The kicker stayed put until a patrol stumbled across him the following day. Watched by scores of correspondents and camera teams hurriedly flown to the crash site by the Nicaraguan government, Hasenfus was led away with a rope around his neck, an American prisoner of war. He appeared to take his predicament stolidly, and within the next few days he had a lot to say to Sandinista military intelligence.

The administration's reaction to this disaster was to attempt a replay of the successful cover-up deployed when Dana Parker and James Powell had been shot down in the Santa Clara raid two years before. Spokespersons at the White House, State Department, Pentagon, and CIA spoke with one voice in affirming that the Hasenfus mission had been a private mission run by private citizens, with no ties whatsoever to the U.S. government. So anxious was U.S. officialdom to keep its distance that the embassy in Managua refused to unlock its gates to receive the coffins containing the bodies of Cooper and Sawyer.

As evidence mounted to the contrary, officials in Washington stuck to their story. They were not wholly bereft of believers. On October 12, 1986, a week after the plane had gone down, Assistant Secretary of State Elliott Abrams appeared on a TV show hosted by columnists Robert Novak and Rowland Evans. Asked by Evans whether he could give a "categorical assurance" that Hasenfus "was not under the control, the guidance, the direction or what have you of anybody connected with the U.S. government," Abrams, a member in good standing of the Restricted Interagency Group, smoothly replied, "Absolutely. That would be illegal. We are barred from doing that, and we are not doing it. This was not in any sense a U.S. government operation. None."

At the end of the program, as the two journalists mused on their guest's performance, Novak commented: "You know, I've seen a lot of cover-ups in this town, Rowland, and we both may end up with egg on our face before this is over . . . but this doesn't look like a cover-up."

A cover-up it was, and Elliott Abrams was in the thick of it. He and Pentagon official Nestor Sanchez cooked up a story for the press that retired Gen. John Singlaub had been the organizer of the contra supply flight. For a few days the media generally accepted this story, but Abrams had neglected to get permission from Singlaub, who was in the Philippines, to use him as the scapegoat. When the general returned he gave a press conference and angrily denied that he had had anything to do with the Hasenfus mission. Abrams then tried to deny that he had originated any of the leaks naming Singlaub.

North himself had been on a flight to Frankfurt when Hasenfus went down. He was on his way to a meeting with the Relative, carrying a Bible inscribed by Reagan. When he returned he went to work trying to repair the unraveling situation. On October 12 he wrote to McFarlane, the very active former national security adviser, on how the tide might be turned: "We urgently need to find a high-powered lawyer and benefactor who can raise a legal defense for Hassenfus [*sic*] in Managua. If we can find such persons we can not only hold Gene and Sally Hassenfus together (i.e., on our side, not pawns of the Sandinista propaganda machine) but can make some headway of our own in counter-attacking in the media." This was a sensible move. Up to that point the State Department had offered no help to Hasenfus's family; the only offer to fly Mrs. Hasenfus down to Managua had come from our team at CBS News. "By Tuesday," North went on, "a Swiss lawyer, retained by Corporate Air Services [one of Secord's shell companies, which had garnered three hundred thousand dollars from enterprise funds], should be in Managua. We should not rely on this person to represent the whole case since he is supported by covert means. We would be far better off if we had an overt mechanism here in the States which represented USG/Hassenfus' [*sic*] interests, and who would not have to respond to questions regarding the origins of Corporate Air Services Inc. or its other ongoing activities. Can you help? If need be, I can meet w/you/others tomorrow or Tues. Believe this to be a matter of great urgency to hold things together."

North then went on to indicate that Ronald Reagan was slightly more of a hands-on President as far as contra supply efforts were concerned than subsequent public White House statements would indicate: "Unfortunately, RR was briefed that this plan was being contemplated before he left for Iceland [for the Gorbachev summit] and am concerned that along about Wednesday when people begin to think of things other than meetings in cold places, he will remember this and nothing will have been done. Any thought will be much appreciated." It appears that Abrams was also fully abreast of the plan: "Elliott Abrams willing to sit-in any time after Yom Kippur fast is finished tomorrow night. Pls advise."

Unfortunately for the crisis managers in Washington, there was a tide of damning evidence pouring out of Managua. The documents on the plane, for example, indicated that this operation had some remarkable contacts. There was a memo from "The Desk of William Langton," the president of Southern Air Transport, noting the name of "David Passage, Deputy Chief of Mission U.S. Embassy" in El Salvador. There was a phone number for Jack Jennings, the supervisor for stores at Southern Air Transport. (Southern Air Transport management was telling their employees that the crashed plane had absolutely nothing to do with them in any way, shape, or form.) There were notes on warehouses used by Corporate Air Services in El Salvador. There was a business card with the phone number of the operations coordinator of the Nicaraguan Humanitarian Assistance Office in the State Department. Robert Owen's business card was on board. The plane itself was equipped with sophisticated and costly navigational instrumentation for finding drop zones, which Hasenfus told his captors had been put there by the CIA. There were also the addresses for the safe houses of the crew in El Salvador. When reporters in El Salvador rushed to these addresses they found that they had been hurriedly vacated, but enterprising pressmen elicited records from the local phone company listing the calls made from these houses. They made interesting reading, showing, among other connections, regular calls to Secord and his man Dutton at their headquarters in Vienna, Virginia.

The flight records found on board showed that this was a crew that had gotten around a bit, flying in and out of U.S. military bases as far afield as Ramstein, West Germany, and Cyprus. Fittingly enough, the wreckage even yielded an Air America operator's manual dating from the Vietnam War. The logs showed that pilot Buz Sawyer had flown at least fifteen drop missions between March and August 1986, and had used both Aguacate, the contra supply base in

Honduras, and Mocoron, another Honduran dirt strip. Both had been built and improved by the U.S. Army between 1984 and 1986, for the sole purpose, so spokesmen had solemnly maintained, of giving U.S. soldiers practice in field construction techniques, and neither would not nor had not been used to aid the contras.

The plane itself had an interesting history. It was registered to Corporate Air Services, which was reportedly based at the same address as Southern Air Transport at the Miami airport. It had once belonged to the late drug smuggler and DEA informant Barry Seal, who had christened it the *Fat Lady* and used it in the CIA-inspired scheme to implicate the Sandinistas in cocaine smuggling. Seal's *Fat Lady* was later passed on to a Harry L. Doan, of Doan Helicopter. Doan had then sold the plane for $475,000. The identity of the buyer—or buyers—raises some interesting questions about the relationship between Richard Second and the ex-CIA proprietary Southern Air Transport, which remained the airline of CIA choice in supplying the contras in the days before the aid cutoff in 1984.

Doan was paid with a cashier's check signed by "Udall Research Corporation (Southern Air)." Udall Research was owned by Richard Secord. Southern Air received nearly $2.5 million in contracts from the enterprise. If Udall and Southern Air were part of the same overall organization, which Secord had consistently denied, then it would appear that Secord might in some way have been awarding large contracts to himself. Secord explained away the curious combined signature of Udall and SAT: "The plane was bought under the auspices of Southern Air Transport. Then Udall took title. It took a while for the papers to go through."

What Hasenfus himself had to say was even more explosive. Four days after he was shot down he appeared before the press and declared that he had worked with people he believed were from the CIA and were operating with the knowledge and blessing of Vice President George Bush. He said the CIA men were two Cuban-Americans, Max Gomez and Ramón Medina.

Within a week, the Nicaraguans concluded that Hasenfus had told them all he knew. He was charged with heinous crimes, put on trial in front of a People's Anti-Somocista Tribunal, and swiftly given a draconian sentence. Although this procedure elicited noisy protests from Washington, the Sandinista leadership were letting it be known that they had no reason for holding him and would send him home in time for Christmas, which is what happened. He returned to obscurity and bankruptcy, since his former employers abandoned him as they did other humble foot soldiers of the secret army, such as Peter Glibbery or Jesus Garcia. Having promised to pay the Hasenfus family's expenses, Elliott Abrams's office promptly reneged, leaving Eugene and Sally with an outstanding bill of thirty thousand dollars.

Meanwhile, it had swiftly emerged that "Gomez" and "Medina" were actually cover names for two sanguinary veterans of CIA covert operations.

Max Gomez was in fact Felix Rodriguez, the Shackley shooter team alumnus who had killed Che Guevara, solicited the aid of cocaine accountant Ramón Milian for the contra cause, and who liked to shoot out streetlights on his nights off. Ramón Medina was Luis Posada Carriles, wanted in Venezuela for the terrorist bombing in 1976 that had blown a Cubana airliner and seventy-six innocent people out of the sky. (The real identity of Gomez was leaked by sources in the Salvadoran military; Nicaraguan intelligence identified Medina as Posada Carriles.)

Hasenfus had said that Gomez/Rodriguez had been in charge of the operation in El Salvador, and he quickly became the center of attention, though his whereabouts were unknown. However, staff at the CBS News bureau in San Salvador turned up a long-forgotten tape featuring a proud-looking Rodriguez in the act of receiving a medal from a Salvadoran general. Beside him there stood the beaming figure of Col. James Steele, chief of the Milgroup, the U.S. military advisory mission in El Salvador. It soon became apparent that Rodriguez's connections ranged far higher than mere colonels—all the way up to the vice president of the United States. That was the reason George Bush's office had been the very first people in Washington to hear the news about the Hasenfus plane, even before North's staff on the NSC.

Between 1970 and 1972 Rodriguez had served in Vietnam for the CIA. His boss was Donald P. Gregg. Gregg in turn reported to the CIA station chief in Saigon, who at that time was Theodore Shackley. As Gregg told the *New York Times*, Rodriguez "developed under his direction a system using low-flying helicopters, warplanes and small airborne squads for destroying entrenched Vietcong positions." Other administration sources recall that Rodriguez also developed a great interest and expertise in the proper employment of napalm while in Vietnam, which he later put to good use in El Salvador.

In October 1986, Gregg was assistant to the vice president for national security affairs, and had an autographed photograph of Rodriguez on his desk. When Hasenfus started talking, and reporters started calling about his old friends, Gregg was suddenly rather anxious to put some distance between himself and his former colleagues. He said that he only bumped into Shackley occasionally at "weddings" and social functions around Washington. Gregg did admit to keeping in touch with Rodriguez by phone and letter. For a while he lied stoutly about the fact that his office had been the first to hear (from Rodriguez) that the Hasenfus plane had been lost.

By Gregg's initial account the conversation between these two old covert operators invariably steered clear of the contras. Instead, insisted Gregg, they had discussed only El Salvador, where he had helped Rodriguez find work as a counterinsurgency adviser to the local military. "Felix knows more about low-intensity insurgency than almost anyone else alive," he explained. So far as the contras were concerned, however, Gregg continued to insist that they had discussed the matter only once, in August 1986. Even that admission came after Gregg had first neglected to mention it to reporters and then blamed a lapse of memory for the omission. He said that Rodriguez had called him to share worries that the private resupply efforts might be abandoned before the Congress would once again authorize legal support. Gregg acknowledged that he did set up a meeting in the Executive Office Building with Rodriguez and "CIA officials."

Throughout, claimed the vice president's assistant, Rodriguez had remained absolutely silent about his employment with the resupply network. "He was down there, he's a dedicated anticommunist, and a lot of the arms supply stuff was going on. He knew some of the people, I'm sure. I don't feel he pulled the wool over my eyes. We still talk a lot; we're still fast friends."

In the late fall of 1986 George Bush was already a front-runner for the 1988 presidential nomination, so any contact with Rodriguez and the illegal contra aid effort was extremely damaging. His problem was that he too knew Rodriguez, who had bragged about the friendship to a number of people in El Salvador. Rodriguez broadcast his Bush ties "to anyone who would listen," as Richard Secord remembered. "He was trying to impress our people."

The Bush office frantically assembled a chronology of their con-

224

tacts with this contra illegal resupply officer. Rodriguez, it appeared, had first contacted Gregg in December 1984 to ask for help in getting a job in El Salvador. Gregg had obligingly called a number of high-ranking officials. The following month Rodriguez (this would be just a few weeks after he reportedly tapped the cocaine cartel for $10 million in contra aid) met with Bush himself. According to the Bush office chronology, the topic was Rodriguez's desire to help out in El Salvador, where he finally moved in March 1985.

Rodriguez was back for another visit with Gregg in June, bringing with him Colonel Steele of the Salvador Milgroup. According to Richard Secord's testimony before the Iranian-contra committees, Steele was so key to the supply network that he was given one of the KL-43 encryption devices for secure communication with the other leading lights. It therefore seems strange that these two partners in the contra supply operation would not discuss this important effort with their friend Mr. Gregg.

The Bush office said Rodriguez's next contact with Don Gregg was a Christmas party at Gregg's Washington office, where he was introduced to the rest of the staff. Gregg's deputy, Col. Samuel Watson, then traveled to San Salvador in January to meet with "Mr. Rodriguez, Col. Steele and others in El Salvador to discuss counterinsurgency operations," according to the official statement. "This was part of an orientation trip to the area for Col. Watson." The statement failed to mention that Watson went on to visit two contra bases in Honduras.

In May of 1986, Rodriguez, Watson, and Gregg met with the vice president "for approximately ten minutes," said the statement. "Lt. Col. North joined the group in the Vice President's office." At this point North was working seven days a week on the Iran arms traffic, not to mention the contra supply effort out of El Salvador. It is hard to believe that the conversation steered clear of the contras, since there was no reason to keep the vice president in the dark. From the warm tone of letters turned up by investigators later on, it is clear that North and Rodriguez were on close and friendly terms.

Nevertheless, Gregg insisted right up to the start of the Iran-contra hearings that North and Rodriguez united to keep him in the dark. He claimed that he could not remember whether he had been the one who introduced Rodriguez to North, but admitted, "Ollie got to Felix because of my relationship with Felix." He said that North "explicitly" ordered Rodriguez not to inform him about what was going on. "Felix is a trained intelligence officer. So am I. We believe in the need-to-know principle. I had no need to know. It was not a subject we had ever talked about," he told the *Washington Post,* ". . . and I suspect that it smelled bad to him and he probably didn't want me to get involved in it."

As it so happened, the operation did smell bad to Rodriguez, and Gregg was the first to hear about it.

By the summer of 1986, this fanatical anticommunist, who was known in Miami as "the ayatollah of the contra movement," was becoming concerned about corruption in the covert network, as well as the shipment of "shoddy" goods to the men in the field. For this he blamed Richard Secord.

By the end of June 1986 relations between Rodriguez and the rest of the secret network's high command were so strained that North insisted that Rodriguez come to Washington for a showdown. North claimed that he had National Security Agency phone intercepts "that had Max on the phone talking about our operation with unauthorized people," according to Robert Dutton, who attended the meeting. These "unauthorized people" turned out to be Tony Avirgan and Martha Honey in Costa Rica. Rodriguez thought North was bluffing, but the confrontation was a serious one in view of the big guns being deployed on both sides. As North noted after the meeting, it was "time we talk to Max [as they called Felix in deference to his code name of Max Gomez] . . . possibly because of Max's other connections w/i [within] the United States Government which he flaunted." As they might have expected, "Max" lost no time in taking the matter up with his "other connections"—that is, Vice President Bush.

A meeting in the vice president's office in August, which was later claimed by Bush's staff to have been concerned merely with Rodriguez's worries about the private aid money for the contras running out, was, according to Secord, a rough argument in which Rodriguez denounced the general to both Gregg and Bush for shipping "old munitions."

The way Secord explained it to the Iran-contra committees, the problem was that Rodriguez "wanted control of the operation. He believed it belonged to the contras." In an interview after the hearings were over, however, Secord said he believed that the real motive behind the denunciation was that Rodriguez had allegiances to a rival arms dealer. Ronald Martin had made a fortune selling weapons through his Tamiami gunshops in Miami. The contra war opened up a new market for the arms merchant, and Rodriguez was, according to Secord, his emissary. "Felix was working for Ronald Martin. I was also paying Felix." Martin, as Secord saw it, was determined to sew up the weapons trade in Honduras. "Martin bought Honduras," said the general matter-of-factly. "It only takes a few million dollars to buy Honduras. Martin had his supermarket down there [arms warehouses]. Martin expected Felix to promote his arms supermarket." Secord says he was suspicious of where the profits had come from to pay for Martin's "thirty-million-dollar supermarket." "I sent investigators to check it out. They thought some of the money was coming from drugs." This Rodriguez/Martin alliance was causing problems for Secord's enterprise. In the spring of 1986, after Secord had ferried in a load of weapons through the American Palmarola air base, he met with the Honduran high command. Their message was blunt. "The chief of staff said, 'From now on you will buy from us.' That meant Ron Martin," who had by that time presumably paid out his "few million dollars."

Rodriguez kicked up enough of a fuss that Secord was, at one point, ordered to abandon all of the Project Democracy assets so that they could be turned over to the contras. Secord, who was planning to sell, not give, these same assets to the CIA, fought back. "I wasn't about to turn them over to that gang of Yahoos," Secord recalled in an interview. "They had no qualified flight instructors, no good maintenance, no experience. The contras couldn't handle them." He argued that the property under discussion belonged to Udall Research Corporation, which he controlled. Secord eventually won the argument—he was, after all, also a vital part of the Iranian goings-on and could hardly be dispensed with. Rodriguez was able to push Secord so far because of his close ties to Gregg and Bush, who were drawn repeatedly into the murky affairs of the enterprise.

Alan Fiers, the CIA Central American Task Force chief, talked in his secret testimony before the Iran-contra committees about a meeting in Don Gregg's office in mid-August 1986. Gregg and his staff were principally concerned with extolling the shining moral character of Felix Rodriguez as opposed to "unsavory" individuals like Tom Clines and others in the rival Secord organization. As Fiers, the perennially cautious and frightened bureaucrat, testified: "I got badly beaten up for my assessment of Felix Rodriguez. A lot of time was spent there by Don Gregg . . . convincing me Felix Rodriguez was a 'good guy' and [I was] . . . unjustly critical of Felix Rodriguez and, secondly, going into the fact that the people running the private benefactor operation were no-goodniks of various ilk. . . . And don't you dare buy those airplanes or don't get involved with those people,' says Don Gregg, who was pressing me for assurances that I would not buy those airplanes, and going into the corrupt nature of the people in a generic, broad sense behind the operations."

So blatant indeed was the Bush-Gregg relationship with Rodriguez that it moved General Singlaub to write to North in September 1986 expressing his concern about Rodriguez's "daily contact" with the vice president's office. Singlaub believed this could "damage President Reagan and the Republican Party."

This was not the first time that someone sponsored by Bush had caused trouble in contra operations. In 1983 Gustavo Villoldo, yet another Bay of Pigs and CIA veteran, had turned up in Honduras armed with a letter of introduction from Don Gregg. He was to act as a "combat adviser" to the contras. The arrangement was that Villoldo could use the CIA station for whatever support he needed but he would be off the payroll and out of the CIA's control. According to one report, quoting former intelligence agents who had worked with the vice president's office, Villoldo was only one of several such people recruited by Gregg and put to work outside CIA channels. He certainly came from the same small world as many other familiar figures. He had been with Felix Rodriguez on the 1967 mission to Bolivia to track down Che Guevara, and his son had been a partner of Dago Nunez's in two of the latter's many Miami companies.

Bush's active involvement with the covert operation in Central America is more easily understood in the light of the Byzantine White House covert organization chart. North, for example, served on the Inter-Departmental Group on Terrorism and on the Terrorist Incident Working Group, both of which reported to the Crisis Pre-Planning Group and the Special Situations Group, both of which in turn shared the same chairman: Vice President George Bush. The Special Situations Group had, according to one authoritative report, "oversight authority for public and covert actions related to terrorism policy." Since so much of Reagan's foreign policy was couched in reference to terrorism (Nicaragua, Libya, Iran), control of terrorism policy was a position of great power in the Reagan administration. That was why Bush, in a hard-fought turf battle, wrested it away from Secretary of State Haig early on.

Though he and Bush may have had their own turf fights, North venerated the vice president. As Bruce Cameron, an associate of professional fund-raiser Spitz Channell, told Alan Nairn of the *Pro-*

gressive, North "was very high on the role of Bush. . . . North saw Bush as the person to go down to Central America and consecrate the democracies that were emerging there." But in December of 1986, as the secrets of two years of illegal operations were being unearthed, Bush and his team were getting as far away as they possibly could from Felix Rodriguez, the contras, and Oliver North.

The Hasenfus crash had not only laid bare vital components of the involvement of Southern Air Transport, Richard Secord, and even the vice president of the United States in supplying the contras. It also provided further confirmation of Oliver North's central role.

North's operation had been well known in press circles for two years prior to Hasenfus, and he had been specifically named in published and broadcast media stories many times. Yet congressional watchdogs had always preferred to take the mendacious colonel's denials at face value. In August, two months before the Hasenfus crash, Congressman Lee Hamilton led his House Intelligence Committee over to the White House to hear North tell them that he had never given the contras military advice, had no knowledge of their military operations, and had never had more than casual contact with Robert Owen. Hamilton announced that he was completely satisfied with these answers.

The phone records of the Salvadoran safe houses exposed by Hasenfus now raised once again the unpleasant possibility that North might not have been telling the truth. There were several calls to North. The House Intelligence Committee duly called North's office for answers, and duly received a flat denial: "LTC North has never received any of the calls referred to."

Prior to the fall of 1986 the cover-up had always worked. Congress had not wanted to know the truth, and the press, with some notable exceptions, had maintained an unworthy discretion. But by October of 1986 the dikes were being breached in too many places for this situation to continue. Leaflets were being distributed in Tehran detailing the McFarlane visit in May; the financiers who had lost money on the arms deals were making their knowledge and displeasure known; Hasenfus had exposed the contra supply operation. The guilty parties set out to cover their tracks.

Richard Secord later testified that he began destroying evidence as soon as the Hasenfus capture forced him to shut down the air supply operation: "I had some telephone logs shredded . . . that related to the contras. . . . I was trying to conceal any documentary evidence linking us to the contras."

Oliver North shredded many, many documents concerning his activities. One he missed, or chose to overlook, directly implicated the attorney general in a cover-up of the contra supply operation that had been unveiled by the Hasenfus crash.

The Justice Department, as we have seen, had long been doing yeoman's service in keeping law enforcement off the back of the network. John Mattes had discovered that when he tried and failed to interest the Miami U.S. attorney in investigating the evidence presented by Jesus Garcia. Assistant U.S. Attorney Jeffrey Feldman had made the same discovery when his boss, Leon Kellner, reportedly followed orders and dropped plans to open a grand jury investigation into "the guns, the drugs, and John Hull." Immediately after the news of the Hasenfus crash came through in Miami, an attorney in the U.S. attorney's office went to see Kellner and suggested that it was now time to put Southern Air Transport in front of a grand jury. Kellner's response, according to the attorney, was, "Do you want me to lose my job?" It is clear from the memo left behind by North that Kellner was correct in interpreting the Justice Department policy on the matter. It would seem that Attorney General Meese was resolutely obstructing justice right up to the end, as is shown by the following memorandum.

The secret memo, which was never raised in the hearings, was written by North and dated November 14, 1986. It was headed "Memorandum for the record," and the subject was "Investigation of Southern Air Transport."

At 11:30 A.M., November 14, Major General Richard Secord, USAF (Ret.) called his office to advise that the President of SAT had just called him to inform that U.S. Customs officers had again requested all of the company's financial records. This request was being made pursuant to an investigation regarding SAT's role in supporting the Nicaraguan democratic resistance.

Because SAT is involved in supporting the January 1986 Covert Action finding on Iran, MGEN Secord was concerned that providing the company records for the Nicaraguan resistance investigation would reveal SAT's role in supporting the Iran covert action.

SAT aircraft and pilots were used to support the six deliveries to Iran in 1985 and 1986 and company records would reflect these activities.

This problem was discussed with Mr. Oliver Revell, Associate Director of the FBI, at 12:00 noon on November 14. He advised that ten days ago he had received guidance from Attorney General Meese to "suspend" the investigation of Major General Secord's involvement in support of the Nicaraguan resistance and that the Attorney General had discussed the Customs' investigation of SAT with Treasury Secretary Jim Baker. On Mr. Revell's advice, North called Associate Attorney General Stephan Trott to solicit his advice on this matter. . . .

Trott informed that he would discuss the matter immediately with Attorney General Meese and indicated that he (Trott) fully understood the need not to divulge SAT or Secord's roles in support of the Iran covert action."

It is therefore evident that when Ed Meese later claimed that the news of the diversion of funds from Iran to the contras came as a huge shock to him, and he immediately resolved to pass on the information to the American people, he was hedging on the facts. It was not the only time in the coming months that officials would stray from the truth.

Chapter Thirteen
FALL GUYS

"I asked John [Poindexter] what in the world was going on. He said, 'It's too late, they've already built a wall around the president.'"

—Gen. Richard Secord
November 25, 1986

hen Attorney General Meese went public on November 25, 1986, with the news that funds had been diverted from the Iran arms sales to the contras, the administration's damage-control machinery had already been working overtime. The announcement came during what had already been weeks of bad news for the Teflon presidency. The slide had begun on October 2, when Bob Woodward reported in the *Washington Post* that the White House had carried out a disinformation campaign on the American press regarding Muammar Qaddafi's terrorism plans. Thus the media were reminded that not everything their high-level sources told them was necessarily true.

The Hasenfus capture, and the official denials of any involvement with the plane and its mission, deepened this atmosphere of distrust. On top of Hasenfus came the failure of the Iceland summit with General Secretary Gorbachev, which the administration, rather too obviously, tried to pretend was a success. Then the Democrats, despite energetic campaigning by the president himself, captured control of the Senate in the elections on November 4.

When the U.S. press picked up the report in the Lebanese magazine *Al Shiraa* that Robert McFarlane had been negotiating with the terrorist Iranians in Tehran, the dam burst. The administration's efforts over the years to whip up public hysteria over terrorism now came back to haunt it. The Meese admission was the final blow. The White House could no longer control the terms of public debate.

The mood in government offices at this time was one of panic. Officials started to spend much of their day conferring with legal counsel, and in their spare moments they discussed who would have to go, who was sure to be indicted, and who would be left to twist in the wind. There was a surge of applications for inconspicuous government jobs in places like Brussels where guilty bureaucrats might hope to be forgotten.

The problem was that the investigations into the administration's covert foreign policy in the press and Congress did not go back to all the evidence that had been available to them for the previous two years. For example, the contra component of the Iran-contra scandal had first been revealed by Peter Glibbery and Steven Carr in July 1985. As noted, the subject had not been thought worthy of further investigation by the bulk of the press. The few reports that did appear were dismissed by all but the staff of one senator and, of course, the White House, CIA, State Department, and the Department of Justice.

The government agencies had taken action at the time to discredit or otherwise frustrate overinquisitive journalists. Tony Avirgan and Martha Honey, for example, were warned by a State Department official in June 1985 that if they got "too close" to the truth about the bombing at La Penca, the CIA would frame them as agents of the KGB or Cuban intelligence.

John Kerry, the junior Democratic senator from Massachusetts, had come under attack both from his colleagues and from various government agencies as soon as he opened his own investigation in early 1986.

Jack Terrell, the mercenary and former military commander in Civilian Military Assistance in Honduras, was branded a liar and an opportunist for disclosing that he had met with North's representative, Robert Owen, and top contra leaders to discuss the opening of the southern front and the assassination of Eden Pastora.

The trouble was that the key question, so far as journalists and congressional investigators in Washington were concerned, became, "What did the president know and when did he know it?" Of course this phrase harkened back to the days of the Watergate investigation, but the central issue of that probe had been the cover-up of a crime (the Watergate burglary), not the crime itself. This time the central issue was what had actually been done. While the question of what Ronald Reagan knew about the plan to use the Ayatollah Khomeini to finance the contras was an important point, it meant that what was actually carried out in the president's name received less attention than it might otherwise have. Furthermore, the chairmen of the committees knew throughout the public proceedings that the results would be inconclusive, since Admiral Poindexter informed them two days before the hearings commenced that he had never told Reagan about the famous diversion. In addition, the White House, by suggesting that the Boland Amendment had not actually meant what it said in cutting off aid to the contras, introduced an extra element of confusion by suggesting that there were no more than "possibilities" of illegal acts.

While witnesses at the hearings were prepared by their attorneys to argue the supposedly abstruse constitutional issues raised by Boland, they were adamant in denying that they had actually broken any old-fashioned laws, such as illegally exporting arms directly from the United States. As General Secord summarized their position, "not a beebee" had gone south. Unfortunately none of the committees' members, or their counsels, inquired into such pertinent questions as why, for example, Mario Calero, brother of Adolfo, had been granted an arms export license. The actual document in question was found on board a cargo plane impounded and searched by a suspicious Florida sheriff's office in April 1987 after someone noticed that the plane carried a phony tail number. The license was issued by the State Department to a company owned by Mario named Hondo-Caribe. The stated "end-users" were not of course the contras, but the Honduran military—not an organization traditionally averse to turning over military supplies to the forces led by Mario Calero's brother, Adolfo.

The plain fact of the matter was that there were witnesses who had been trying to tell the world about very definite illegalities for months before Mr. Meese declared open season on Oliver North. Danny Sheehan and the Christic Institute, for example, had filed their lawsuit detailing the dimensions and personnel of the illegal arms supply network six months before its existence was officially acknowledged in November. John Mattes and Jesus Garcia had a lot to say about the plot to blow up the U.S. embassy in Costa Rica, not to mention direct shipments of arms from the U.S. to the contras and foot-dragging by the U.S. attorney's office in Miami. Joe and Hilda Coutin had been talking to the FBI and others for three years about Rene Corvo's involvement with the cocaine trade.

Strange to say, these people and their evidence received hardly more attention after it was officially accepted that there had been a secret network shipping arms to the contras than they had before. They were not, so to speak, on the approved list of witnesses— Terrell, Garcia, Steven Carr, or many others. (The Iran-contra committees were happy to hear from CIA Central American Task Force chief Alan Fiers that Garcia's story was made up "of whole cloth.")

Carr had direct knowledge of the southern front operation, from the loading of arms in Miami, to a flight from Fort Lauderdale to Ilopango. He had watched the arms unloaded in Ilopango under the eyes of the American military, who acted "like it happened every day." He had sat in on meetings to discuss the Costa Rican embassy provocation, and he had seen the cocaine at Paco Chanes's house. He had trained the White House–approved contras in Costa Rica and taken part in a raid inside Nicaragua with another American citizen (Corvo). He would have made an interesting congressional witness, but by December 1986, three years short of his thirtieth birthday, Steven Carr was dead.

Carr had served his short sentence at the Collier County jail in Naples, Florida, where he had landed after his adventures in Central America. By November of 1986, six months after he had left Costa Rica, he was free to go.

We had spoken throughout the summer. Carr called often for news of any movement on Capitol Hill, since his promised hearing there kept getting postponed. He was anxious about Peter Glibbery, who had landed back in La Reforma prison after John Hull had convinced the court to revoke his bond. Carr's refrain on the telephone was that he had more to say, but that it would have to wait until his release. He was ecstatic about the prospect of not being in one prison or another for a change, but he was also afraid.

The precise object of Carr's fear was Felipe Vidal, who, he believed, was waiting to kill him. He remembered well how Vidal had boasted of doing "John Hull's dirty work for him." He suspected, correctly, that Vidal worked for the CIA. He also knew that Vidal had been caught by the Costa Rican Rural Guard with arms and drugs in the summer of 1986 and had escaped back to Miami. That made Carr even more anxious to get out of Florida.

Carr had been scared of Vidal and Hull for a long time. He had said as much in a letter written to his mother from the Costa Rican jail on September 10, 1985:

> Dear Ma
>   Just found out today; I'm supposed to be shot upon my return to Fla. It seems a guy named Morgan/Felipe ["Morgan" was Vidal's code name of choice] who worked for the FDN and John Hull has been given orders to shot [*sic*] me and Pete because we spoke out against John Hull. . . .

A month later the subject was still much on his mind, as he wrote his mother, ". . . I'm supposed to be eliminated very soon. One of John Hull's hired guns is in Miami awaiting my return."

Steven's letters were not the only ones Mrs. Carr had been getting from Costa Rica. At the end of October 1985, John Hull had decided to get in touch. Showing a somewhat indelicate lack of concern for a mother's feelings, Hull portrayed Steven as violent, possibly insane, and certainly not telling the truth about kindly old John Hull.

> Dear Mrs. Carr,
>   Due to Steve's strange behavior and threats to kill guards, kill me etc., the prison guards have held his mail and asked me to interpret for them. . . . [This may not be quite the way Hull got hold of Carr's letters.]
>   I have no idea why Steve thinks I am his boss or why he thinks I want to kill him.
>   My only connection with Steve was to let him stay at my house a few days as I have done with a great many people over the last few years.
>   The only advice I ever gave Steve he ignored completely and that was under no circumstances should he go with the cuban [*sic*] that brought him here to participate in a border raid into Nicaragua from Costa Rica as this would do little damage to the communist [*sic*] and would only bring the wrath of the Costa

Rican Govt down upon them. Two days later they raided La
Esperanza, Nicaragua, and killed a number of Nica miliciamen
[*sic*].

The US reporters convinced Steve to talk openly of his participation in the raid and to say they received help from Costa
Rican authorities. In efet [*sic*], they talked Steve into openly
admitting that he was actively engaged in murder of Nicaraguan
citizens, that they started the raid in Costa Rica and returned to
Costa Rica. So, the charge would be murder one. . . .

I will continue to do what I can to help Steve as I feel he is
sick and needs help.

Sincerely,
John Hull

Carr's body was found in a driveway in Van Nuys, California, on
December 13, 1986. He was pronounced officially dead at four A.M.
The police report filed later that day stated that "decedent is a
27-year-old who may have overdosed on cocaine. . . . I noted decedent's eyes were dilated but found no tracks or trauma to the decedent. No paraphernalia was found and no drugs." The report noted
that Carr had been staying with a woman called Jacqueline Scott and
her daughter Jackie Perry at 8728 Cedros Avenue. The women told
police that Carr had arrived home around ten and retired to his
room. According to the report he had come downstairs just before
3:30 A.M., apparently drunk, and told the daughter, "Just stay with
me, I drank too much." As the women further told police, Carr said
he was going to get something from the car. As they walked in the
driveway he suddenly collapsed. Perry ran back to wake her mother.
When they both came out, Carr, according to the police report, told
them, "I paranoided out, I ate the whole thing.' They then observed
the decedent foaming at the mouth and start to shake violently
(Convulse)."

Carr's dying words were carried in press reports as testimony
that he had swallowed three bags of cocaine, which had killed him.
The autopsies were to prove otherwise. In all, there were no less than
three autopsies on Carr's body. The first, carried out routinely by the
local police pathologist, found no alcohol at all in the body and only
small traces of cocaine. The cause of death was listed as "deferred."
The second autopsy was undertaken at the insistence of Danny
Sheehan, who had rushed to Los Angeles on hearing the news. This
time the cause of death was listed as "acute cocaine intoxication."
When the body was shipped back to Naples, Florida, Carr's family

commissioned yet a third autopsy. This pathologist decided that marks behind Carr's left elbow (which the first report had said were scratches, possibly from a fall in the driveway where he died) were needle marks from an injection.

Therefore, although all three postmortems contradicted each other, all were unanimous in reporting that there was no sign that Carr had swallowed three bags of cocaine, as press reports quoting police sources had indicated. Nor did the pathologists find any trace of burn marks on his throat from ingesting crack, as had been similarly reported. No one ever explained why Carr should have been injecting himself behind his left elbow. (He was not a habitual needle user).

There were an equal number of conflicting stories as to where Carr had come by the cocaine. The final police report stated that he had bought it in San Diego and had driven back with a friend, snorting on the way, arriving home "very intoxicated." Yet Carr had arrived home alone, and the women he was staying with had not thought he was intoxicated when he got in. He talked to Mrs. Scott in a rational way about TV programs for between thirty and forty-five minutes before going to bed. He was excited about starting a new job on Monday.

Despite all these intriguing discrepancies, the case was considered officially closed in April 1987, when John Mattes got an agitated phone call from Peter Glibbery. Glibbery was calling from La Reforma prison in San José, where he languished, waiting in hope of a promised presidential pardon, for which Senator Kerry's staff had been lobbying. Glibbery told Mattes that he had just had a visit from John Hull, who, according to the Englishman, "was ranting and raving." Hull demanded yet again that Glibbery sign a statement recanting all that he had ever said about the goings-on on the southern front. Glibbery told Mattes that when he refused, Hull issued a threat, shouting, "The CIA killed Steven Carr, and they can do the same to you."

While no evidence has been produced to back up ex–CIA operative Hull's claim about the CIA, this does not signify that the official Iran-contra investigations in Washington ever looked for any. In fact, none of the investigations, not the Senate Intelligence Committee, nor the Tower Commission, not even the select Iran-contra committees, showed anything more than the most timid interest in what the Central Intelligence Agency had been up to throughout the period they were supposedly investigating.

The last of these investigative bodies, the combined Senate and House Iran-contra select committees, was to have been the public forum through which the American people would "get the facts." But a telling appointment when the Senate committee was set up suggested that some facts were very definitely not going to be brought out.

Among the investigators hired by the Senate panel was Thomas Polgar. Polgar certainly knew a lot about covert operations, for he was a thirty-year CIA veteran. He had worked his way up the bureaucracy, climaxing his career with an appointment as station chief in Saigon, where his immediate superior as head of the Far East Division was Theodore Shackley. Polgar had not distinguished himself in Saigon, since he had continued to send rosy reports on the durability of the American-backed government almost up to the moment in 1975 when he fled for the helicopters, just ahead of the advancing North Vietnamese tanks. Nevertheless he had shown loyalty to the agency, and on his return from Asia he was given the plum posting of station chief in Mexico City.

After his retirement Polgar became active in CIA lobbying activities, ever ready to support his old employers. In December 1986, for example, he wrote in the *Miami Herald*, "I think the CIA is telling the truth that it was not involved in the flight on which the Hasenfus plane was shot down." The airlift had, he declared, been run by people with no connection to the government. As it turned out, the CIA had a very strong connection indeed with the Hasenfus and similar flights, if only because they were being coordinated by the CIA station chief in Costa Rica, Joe Fernandez.

Polgar was chosen for the Senate job by the committee's Republican vice chairman, Senator Warren Rudman of New Hampshire, because, as the senator explained, they needed an intelligence expert to guide them through what would obviously be a complex probe of a covert operation. The fact that Thomas Polgar, Jr., worked as Rudman's legislative aide may have influenced the decision.

The investigator was quick to reassure his friends in the community that they need have little cause for alarm. Don Gregg has been quoted as having been reassured by Polgar that the hearings "would not be a repeat of the Pike and Church investigation."

Although there were six investigators in all on the Senate committee's staff, it was Polgar who drew the job of going to Costa Rica to talk to such pertinent figures as Eden Pastora and John Hull. The trip does not appear to have been marked by any excess of investigative zeal. Polgar's interviews were arranged for him by the local embassy, not, as we have seen, the most disinterested party in the whole affair.

Polgar did not see John Hull, claiming no one could find the man. (It was around this time that Hull started making himself available for press interviews in Washington.) If he had caught up with the rancher, it is unlikely that Hull would have found the experience especially testing. As Polgar told a journalist in Costa Rica: "Don't you think it would be absurd for a conservative American rancher to smuggle drugs?"

The intrepid investigator did talk to Eden Pastora, an experience that made the survivor of La Penca highly suspicious. "Was that man really from the Senate?" he asked later. "He didn't ask me anything, all he wanted to talk about was the weather." Perhaps unsurprisingly, Polgar asked none of the key players about La Penca, nor did he make any effort to interview Peter Glibbery or the Avirgans.

Polgar's apparent lack of curiosity about the darker aspects of U.S. Central American policy was not untypical of the approach taken by his colleagues on the staffs of the committees. "I can understand that they might not want to put Jack Terrell in the witness chair," remarked another congressional investigator not employed by the committees, "I can understand them perhaps not taking a deposition from him, but to not even interview this man, not even to call? That's unforgivable."

This is not to say that the committees did not go through the motions of examining the most explosive aspect of the entire contra scandal. Robert A. Bermingham, a staffer on the House select committee, notified Chairman Hamilton on July 23, 1987, that after interviewing "hundreds" of people his investigation had not developed any corroboration of "media-exploited allegations that U.S. government condoned drug trafficking by Contra leaders or Contra organizations or that Contra leaders or organizations did in fact take part in such activity."

It is not entirely clear whom in fact Mr. Bermingham and his trusty staff actually talked to. He is indeed happy to repeat the Justice Department's position that drug smugglers were claiming a U.S. government–contra connection in hopes of a lighter sentence, but he made no attempt to talk to some of the chief sources on this matter, which would have allowed him at least to make his own judgment. Michael Tolliver, the man who flew 25,360 pounds of marijuana from a CIA-controlled contra air base to a U.S. Air Force base in Florida, was not questioned, nor was George Morales. Ramón Milian-Rodriguez, the man who talks about delivering $10 million in cocaine money to the contras at the request of George Bush's friend Felix Rodriguez, had what he recalls as a "cursory" conversation with a select committee staffer who promised to return, but never did.

In his memo to Hamilton, Bermingham quotes Hayden Gregory, the chief counsel of a House Judiciary subcommittee that had been conducting an in-depth investigation of the drug issue for some time, in support of his thesis that there was and is no contra drug connection. Gregory is reported as dismissing the evidence he had so far gathered as "street talk."

Mr. Gregory, on the other hand, has stated for the record that he and Bermingham talked for the first and only time on July 21, just two days before the conclusive memo was written. Bermingham made it clear that his inquiries had hardly gotten beyond an exploratory stage and that he "had to make a recommendation on whether [the Iran-contra committees] should get into the drug issue. He certainly didn't seem to know much about it," says Gregory. Gregory also complains that his "street talk" remark was taken out of context in the memo, and that he told Bermingham that there were serious allegations against almost every contra leader, well worthy of further investigation.

Since Bermingham was unsure whether to proceed on July 21, and reported on July 23 that after interviewing "hundreds" of witnesses there was no corroboration of the "media-exploited" allegations, his investigation must have set an unbreakable record for speedy work.

Select Committee Chairman Hamilton, the man who accepted Oliver North's fraudulent denials of any involvement in contra supply in August 1986, is reported to have told Congressman Hughes, chairman of Gregory's subcommittee, "We're not going to get into this [drugs], that's not our baby." Yet again, it was a case of see, hear, and speak no evil.

In the course of the hearings themselves the members of the committees showed that they were no more anxious than Polgar and his colleagues on the staff to offend the CIA. Out of the many insults freely handed out by Oliver North to Congress during his testimony, none appeared to wound Chairman Daniel Inouye so much as the suggestion that Congress could not be trusted to keep intelligence secrets. (Typically, one of North's examples of a dangerous congressional leak, an account of the *Achille Lauro* affair, turned out to have been leaked by North himself). Inouye proudly recited how he had been assured by the director of the National Security Agency that there had been "no secrets" divulged by the committees, and listed the medals he had received from the intelligence community over the years as a reward for his responsible behavior.

Even when the committees did turn their attention to the CIA, the American public were locked out, for the witnesses were heard in closed session. Thus the TV audience never heard Joe Fernandez admit that "some of our people [Felipe Vidal and Rene Corvo] had a problem with drugs, but we had to protect them."

The roots of the committees' fear of taking on the CIA are almost certainly to be found in the Pike and Church investigations of the mid-1970s. These had been the only public examination, ever, of the activities carried out in the name of covert operations. The assiduous investigators of those bygone days had found evidence of assassination plots, profiteering, illegal domestic spying, and much else pertinent information. True, the tide of outrage and investigative fervor had quickly ebbed (ably assisted by Don Gregg, CIA liaison to the Pike committee, not to mention Robert McFarlane, who did the same job for the White House, and Antonin Scalia, who kept a watching brief for the Justice Department), but nevertheless the Congress had to bear the obloquy of having revealed secrets and crippled America's ability to fight the KGB on its own terms. None of the gentlemen selected to serve on the Iran-contra committees wanted to bear that particular cross again.

Thus the true role of the CIA as an institution in fighting a dirty and, during Boland, illegal war was one of the black holes of the televised hearings. It did emerge, particularly during Oliver North's depiction of himself as an officer who was only following orders, that the conveniently dead William Casey had been central to every aspect of the Iran-contra affair. However, as of August 1987, there was no apparent acceptance on the part of the committees that the agency as an institution had been systematically engaged in flouting not only the law as enacted in the Boland Amendment, but traditional statutes relating to arms export control, neutrality, narcotics, and, as the La Penca bombing suggests, murder.

The avenues the committees were prepared to pursue were the question of the extent of President Reagan's guilty knowledge of the use of arms sales to illegally finance a war, as noted, and the question of what happened to the money.

The pursuit of the money meant that Richard Secord came in for some rough handling. The general himself is bitter about the congressional strategy. As he complained, "The fix was in; they had decided to treat this like a small cancer that had a surgical cure: it could be excised. I was the cancer."

The other financial area regarded as fair game was the private fund-raising network that had flourished during the period of the Boland Amendment. The story of the fund-raisers' activities served to illustrate one key aspect of the whole contra operation—its essential seediness.

Among those serving the cause of the "freedom fighters," for example, had been Carl "Spitz" Channell. In May 1987, Channell pleaded guilty to "conspiring to defraud the government" by using tax-exempt charitable foundations to raise millions of dollars for weapons purchases. He named Oliver North as a coconspirator. Channell's indictment cited $2.26 million that had been raised for the National Endowment for the Preservation of Liberty, just one of Channell's stable of nine foundations, in 1986. The money, extracted mainly from elderly ladies, was earmarked for "Toys," which, as one of Channell's aides admitted, was a euphemism for guns.

Channell had learned his business at the knee of Terry Dolan, who died of AIDS in December 1986. Dolan, a homosexual like Channell, had made his name as the cofounder of the National Conservative Political Action Committee, which did much execution among liberal Democratic senators in the 1980 election partly by attacking them for their support of gay rights. Channell set up in business on his own in December 1984, and achieved instant success tapping the wealthy right for deserving conservative causes. The NEPL reported gifts of $3.36 million in 1985.

The technique was simple. Channell wooed the donors, especially the blue-rinse brigade he referred to, though not to their faces, as "Hamhocks," "Dogface," and "Mrs. Malleable," to give money for Nicaragua. The donors were rewarded with flattery, limos in Washington, "secret briefings" at the White House, and visits with President Reagan. The presidential access was arranged by former White House aide David Fischer, who was paid twenty thousand dollars a month for his pains, and by North. Channell and his coterie referred to North as "Mr. Green"—the color, as Christopher Hitchens observed in *Harper's* magazine, "of money, and of boyish innocence." It was assumed that everyone, including Ronald Reagan, knew what the money was for. As "Mr. Green" wrote to Poindexter at one point,

"The President obviously knows why he has been meeting with several select people to thank them for their 'Support for Democracy' in CENTAM." The president himself wrote Channell, "You and your organization have made a remarkable contribution to the course of democracy in Central America."

Not all the money thus raised went for "toys," however lethal. Channell subtracted a sizable amount, about one third, for overhead. Some of this money went straight into Channell's pocket. In 1985 he received over $130,000 from just two of his foundations. Other large sums went to his and his associates' friends. For example, in 1986 the National Endowment for the Preservation of Liberty paid $17,500 to Eric Olson, who did nothing for NEPL but was Channell's roommate. Ken Gilman was the roommate of the executive director of NEPL, Daniel Conrad. He was president of a San Francisco company that performed no identifiable services for NEPL, but nonetheless received $97,000 from the Endowment.

Roommates aside, however, the Channell diversions raised a more sinister issue, for some of the money was put to use in domestic political campaigns. In a hotly contested 1986 Senate race in Maryland, local TV stations carried political commercials paid for by the "Anti-Terrorism American Committee," which was headed by Spitz Channell. The commercials consisted of a highly personal attack on Democratic candidate Barbara Mikulski. The Republican candidate was Linda Chavez, a former deputy assistant to the president for public liaison, who had helped introduce at least one group of Channell donors in a presidential meeting. When the campaign began to receive complaints that the commercials were in bad taste, Chavez called on Oliver North to have the spots pulled off the air.

It seemed that the "Support for Democracy in CENTAM" covert action program was meddling in democracy at home, and not just through TV commercials either. It must be remembered that the administration plan had always been to get Congress to turn on the money tap again. Rather than mounting a frontal assault it was resolved that funding be restored, as North put it in testimony, "slice by slice." The first step was to allow the CIA to furnish intelligence to the contras, then to allow the $27 million for humanitarian aid, then, finally, the request for $100 million with no restrictions.

Channell and his friends played a key part in this domestic political offensive. International Business Communications, a company headed by Richard Miller, was hired by Channell to run a two-million-dollar lobbying campaign for contra funding in the spring of 1986. Miller later also pleaded guilty to "conspiring to defraud the government." While working for Channell, Miller's company received a $276,000 classified contract from the State Department, supposedly for assistance in debriefing defectors from the Sandinista regime in Nicaragua (not normally a specialty of PR companies). The company also functioned as a conduit for money going from Channell to Lake Resources, the Secord-Hakim company in Geneva.

The money trail uncovered by the investigators was not only unwholesome, as in the case of the roommates, or sinister, as in the deployment of North's fund-raising network to lobby the Congress, it was also petty, as with North's personal use of enterprise money in the form of traveler's checks.

North's safe contained thousands of dollars in traveler's checks given him, he claimed, by Adolfo Calero. Much of this was given to Robert Owen, who would cash the checks and then hand over the money to deserving individuals either in the U.S. or Central America. He told the committees of transactions on rainswept street corners, in "Chinese markets," in his apartment, or in the backseat of his car. Some of the money never made it south of the border, however, as it turned out that North had on occasion used the checks as petty cash for his groceries, clothes (Park Lane Hosiery), and snow tires. This last item was raised during the testimony of Adolfo Calero, who was asked, "When was the last time it snowed in Nicaragua?" Calero replied, "Well sir, it does not snow in Nicaragua, however, I'm sure there is an explanation. . . ."

It was a pity, while all this high finance was being discussed, that Peter Glibbery could not watch the hearings in his jail cell, or that Steven Carr had not lived to see a smirking Robert Owen confirm what they had long been saying. Owen described how Adolfo Calero had been instructed by North to put ten thousand dollars a month in Hull's Miami bank account, just as they had said.

If the committees showed no sign of interest in Glibbery, or Carr's death, the investigation that had begun with the La Penca bombing was still under way. As Owen took the stand, Danny Sheehan was gathering depositions in Costa Rica. One of these was from the DIS agent, Albert Guevara Bonilla, who told of having seen Hull and the La Penca bomber cruising the river toward La Penca, with the bomb case on board. Shortly after he gave this damning testimony, Guevara was picked up by Costa Rican security forces and disappeared. It appeared that any investigator who aimed at getting to the heart of the matter was living dangerously.

If Tony Avirgan and Martha Honey needed any reminder of this fact, they got it in mid-May 1987, when their Secretary, Carmen Araya, went to pick up a package at the post office. It contained two books and a letter, with a return address "T. Borge, Managua." As Carmen left the post office she was grabbed by the Costa Rican narcotics police, and when they opened the package, rather theatrically, before a judge, one of the books turned out to have been hollowed out and filled with cocaine. The letter was from the Nicaraguan minister of the interior, Tomás Borge. Choosing his name for this particular dirty trick was rather like naming CIA Director William Webster or Ed Meese as the author. That it was a fraud was obvious from the absurd language of the letter:

> . . . we are very thankful for all of your work in Costa Rica which is definitely producing good results. The Commandantes were very happy with your mission and want me to tell you that. . . . The shipment you made in February got to Miami alright and the Institute [apparently a veiled reference to the Christic Institute] already has advised us and soon we will pick up the money. What we don't understand is that what we discussed was a shipment of 500 kilos of top quality. Nonetheless the Reverend [again, apparently an intended reference to Father Bill Davis of the Christic Institute] told us there were only 400 kilos of quality not like the sample we received from Bolivia. . . . We are waiting for you to send us what your good friend J.K. [Senator John Kerry?] left with you in Costa Rica. Humberto [Nicaraguan Defense Minister Humberto Ortega] spoke with him by phone and everything is going just as planned here with Daniel [President Daniel Ortega].

It was indeed a ludicrous attempt at a frame-up. But even though the Avirgans were able to persuade the judge to stop the police ransacking their house, they were now forbidden to leave the country—disastrous for free-lance journalists covering Central America—unless they posted a bond that they could not afford.

That in a way was the story of the contra war, a crude and seedy operation that nonetheless wrecked lives, killed people, laid waste communities.

*   *   *

The hearings did indeed uncover a vast amount of information about how the operation to sell arms to the Iranians and to support the contras in defiance of Congress had actually operated. The televised hearings, and still more the documentation obtained and released by the investigators, laid bare much that would otherwise have remained hidden forever. Yet, by the time they ended, it seemed that the cover-up strategy concocted by North and Casey the year before, which North very frankly described in his testimony, had worked. North told of how he and the late CIA director had discussed a "fall-guy plan" in which someone would "take the rap." Casey, according to North, had suggested that North was not senior enough to be an adequate scapegoat all on his own, and that Admiral Poindexter might have to share some of the burden. Since this scheme was so freely admitted and discussed, it is ironic that the fall-guy strategy worked all the same. At the close of the hearings North had successfully convinced everyone that he had been merely following orders from his superiors, and he had offered a far more convincing culprit than either himself or Poindexter: the usefully deceased William Casey.

The Iran-contra scandal, so the general message of the hearings indicated, had been an aberration, the product of a "secret government" supplanting the normal, open government. But in the light of recent U.S. history, the administration appears to have been behaving in a traditional manner in pursuing a covert foreign policy and fighting a secret war. The war in Laos, where so many of the contra supply network had cut their teeth, had been carried out without reference to the American voter or Congress. Henry Kissinger would have had nothing to learn from Robert McFarlane or John Poindexter so far as obsessive secrecy was concerned.

The difference between the Iran-contra hearings and previous investigations of such government activities was the desire of the 1987 investigators to avoid the central controversy.

Even more than the CIA, or George Bush, or the narcotics business, the great unmentionable of the Iran-contra hearings was the war itself. The congressional leadership had made this clear when they selected the membership of the select committees at the beginning of 1987. Fully two-thirds of the House and Senate members chosen to probe this devastating scandal—seventeen out of twenty-six—had previously voted for contra aid. As Senator Inouye intoned at the commencement of the proceedings, "these hearings are not intended to be pro-contra, or anti-contra."

The predictable result was that the affair turned into a publicity coup for the contras as witness after witness, egged on by some members of the panel, orated on the just cause of the freedom fighters and the need to promote democracy in Nicaragua. The U.S. was meanwhile fully engaged in the promotion of democracy, contra style. Enrique Bermudez was in military command as always, unaffected by the jockeying for power and paychecks among the civilian contra "leadership."

In 1987, with the CIA openly back in charge and the $100 million flowing, released just as the Iran-contra scandal broke, the contra tactics turned more aggressive. Troops and supplies were dropped deep inside Nicaragua to blow power lines and bridges. Blackouts became common and the hardship in the country became even worse.

Increased aggression did not, of course, mean that the contras were actually taking on the Sandinista army, but that did not seem to be part of the American plan. At a congressional hearing on May 19, 1987, Gen. John Galvin, then head of the U.S. Southern Command in Panama, stated that he had become much more confident of a contra victory in recent months. After the session Galvin was asked by *Boston Globe* reporter Fred Kaplan what precisely he had meant. "They're going after soft targets," replied the general, with no sign of embarrassment or shame, "they're not trying to duke it out with the Sandinistas."

The American people had been given a good education in what the contras meant by a "soft target" six weeks before. Benjamin Linder was a mechanical engineer from Portland, Oregon. He had lived in Nicaragua since 1983, one of the thousands of *internacionalistas* who had come to work in the country. His project was to install and run a small hydroelectric plant to bring electricity to El Cua, a small town that had never had it before. Linder was popular with the townspeople. The local children called him "the Clown" because he juggled for them and rode a unicycle through the muddy streets.

El Cua is about sixty miles north of Jinotega in a magnificent patch of hill country that was also crawling with contras. There had been direct contra attacks in December 1983 and May 1984. On July

3, 1986, a private civilian truck was blown apart by a contra mine on the road between El Cua and San José de Bocay. Thirty-two civilians had been killed in that explosion, including twelve children.

Linder had no illusions about the dangers he faced. If his American passport had once been a security blanket, it was not any longer. In September 1986 he had written home to his family, "Recently Frank Arana, the FDN spokesman, is reported to have said that all international development workers, such as myself, will be considered as enemy. . . ."

The day he died, Linder was out with his crew, knee deep in a stream, measuring the water flow to see whether it was suitable to power a plant for San José de Bocay. Five grenades suddenly exploded around him and his helpers, followed by gunfire. One of the grenades wounded Linder, and as he lay there a contra came up and blew his brains out.

The White House responded with a statement that while Linder's death was regrettable, Americans who traveled to Nicaragua should "understand that they put themselves in harm's way whenever they're involved in any internal strife in another country."

At Linder's funeral service his father, Dr. David Linder, stated that his son was killed "by somebody paid by somebody paid by President Reagan."

That was a fair enough statement. President Reagan had stated that "I'm a contra too." He had stood beside their leaders on a podium, seemingly oblivious that these men, whom he fatuously compared to "the brave men and women of the French Resistance," had been hired by his administration to play the role. There was Arturo Cruz, holding up the "Contra too" tee shirt, and on the payroll at $84,000 a year. Alfonso Robelo, beaming at the president, was on a higher scale, $120,000 a year. Adolfo Calero, who bellowed, "Viva Reagan," had been given at least $200,000. And the other contra leaders, who could not be there that day, grabbed their cash from Rob Owen and his kind on dark street corners, in envelopes stuffed through car windows, or furtively, in the backseat.

These contra leaders were the beneficiaries of the president's policy, the necessary actors to sell the war. The other face of that policy was left offstage. The mercenaries, drug traffickers, and corrupt officials were hired to keep the production running. At the bottom of the heap, the soldiers roaming the hot, bug-ridden jungle were left to their own devices. No one tutored them in the principles of democracy, of which they were supposed to be the front line.

Back in the spring of 1985 I sat in a Connecticut coffee shop with an elderly nun. She belonged to the Maryknoll order, whose members were scattered throughout Central and South America. The nun was on leave from her post in the village of San Juan de Limay, a collection of whitewashed houses at the end of a dirt track deep in northern Nicaragua. There had been heavy contra activity in the surrounding hills. The road from Estelí was marked with painted crosses in remembrance of the dead.

The nun told me how she had caught a lift one day on a pickup truck full of farmers and housewives. When the contras attacked, some of the passengers were killed outright. The sister was released, and hurried back on foot to warn others in the village not to take the road. She was captured en route by another band of contras, who took her prisoner. Her most vivid memory of their appearance, aside from their weapons, was the patch that some of them wore sewn on their uniforms. It read, SOLDIER OF FORTUNE CONVENTION. She asked me if I knew what it meant. I explained that it was a memento, no doubt secondhand, of an annual gathering organized by a magazine, where mercenaries and would-be mercenaries gathered to swap stories and fantasize about war.

The nun asked the men why they had launched a raid on San Juan de Limay some days before and burned the town's only bus. She explained that it had taken a very long time to raise the money for that bus and for many it was the only means of transportation. If they won the war, she asked, would they buy the town another bus? "You won't need the bus," a soldier replied. "After democracy comes, everyone will drive a big car." It was the only definition of democracy they could think of.

In Washington they had had their own definitions of democracy, summarized by what Oliver North's secretary Fawn Hall called the "higher law," permitting secret wars without the approval of Congress or the voters. Yet all the effort had not brought the president's policy any nearer to fruition. The men of Oliver North's southern front, at the time he left the White House, were under house arrest in San José—in one house. While the contra leaders invested their takings in Miami real estate, and Richard Secord shopped for lumber investments in Washington State, the government in Managua was still firmly entrenched. For all the painted-out tail numbers, Swiss bank accounts, and kilos of cocaine shipped north, there had been no uprising in Managua. The government in crisis was at home.

NOTES

EPIGRAPH

"Fawn—next time with fewer people": Alan Rusbridge of the *London Daily News* and Alexander Chancellor of the *London Independent* asked Fawn Hall to autograph their programs at the 1987 White House Correspondents' Dinner. McFarlane snatched Rusbridge's program and wrote the above note to Hall. Rusbridge never got the autograph.

CHAPTER ONE

"giant animal": *Los Angeles Times,* March 3, 1985.

"push-pull": *New York Times/Washington Post,* September 3, 1984.

"Elephant Herd": *Washington Post,* September 15, 1984.

"for combat": Oliver North memo to Robert McFarlane, September 2, 1984 (exhibit OLN-254, Top Secret, released July 1984).

"instructed to take the credit": memo from North to McFarlane, March 2, 1984 (exhibit OLN-177, Top Secret, released July 1987).

"back to Aguacate": map on board helicopter showing route of O2s and 500MD.

"killed more civilians": initial Nicaraguan reports listed three children and one cook dead, September 2, 1984.

"burned beyond recognition": John Lantigua, *Washington Post,* September 3, 1984.

"fire from the other side": *New York Times,* January 14, 1984.

"mottled green camouflage colors": Lantigua, op. cit.

"Brown Brothers, bankers": Smedley Butler quoted in *The Plot to Seize the White House* by Jules Archer (New York: Hawthorn Books, 1973), p. 118. As well as in the letter to his wife, Butler reiterated this theme on August 21, 1931, in an address to the American Legion convention in Connecticut: "I helped purify Nicaragua for the international banking house of Brown Brothers in 1909–12."

"of course there were none": ibid.

"dynamited collapsed buildings": interviews with Guardia families, May 1985.

"Casey . . . Galtieri": *Los Angeles Times,* March 3, 1985.

"presidential finding": March 9, 1981 (Annex A, World Court Document), *Washington Post,* May 8, 1983.

"November 1981 NSDD": dated November 23, 1981, authorizes CIA to build a paramilitary force: *Washington Post,* May 8, 1983. In December Reagan signed a second finding authorizing "covert activities": *Washington Post,* January 1, 1983.

"military liaison in Washington": interview with Colonel Bermudez, June 1985.

"a terrorist group": DIA Weekly Intelligence Summary, July 16, 1982.

"Santivanez . . . murder of Archbishop": Santivanez interview in *New York Times,* March 22 and 24, 1985.

"still running contra intelligence": interviews in Honduras, June 1985.

"had indeed commissioned the manual": Senate Intelligence Committee Report 98-665, October 10, 1985.

"Chamorro . . . had censored it": interview with Edgar Chamorro, June 1985.

"our atrocities . . . routine": CBS News *West 57th,* June 21, 1985.

"use of terror": ibid.

"until people cry 'uncle' ": ibid.

"commando knife": Chamorro interview aired on CBS News, June 21, 1985.

"faces had been peeled off": interviews aired, ibid.

"gives them status": Edgar Chamorro interview, June 1985.

"routinely brutalized their own recruits": Chamorro interviews, June 1985. Chamorro had personally admonished commandantes in cases of multiple rape and poor treatment.

"they were exposed to all atrocities": aired on CBS News *West 57th,* June 21, 1985.

" 'isolated' cases": interview with Bermudez, Honduras, June 1985.

"escaped kidnapees": This included American nuns. Sandra Price, who was in the spring of 1985 working in the hamlet of Siuna in Zelaya Province, had been kidnapped more than once. In the Siuna area, a region of heavy contra activity at the time, whole villages were uprooted and forced to march to the northern border. North's memos make clear this was at a time when he was keenly interested in increased contra activity around Siuna: interviews, Siuna, May 1985; North memos, May 1985.

"bereaved and scarred victims": The author and a CBS News team spent several weeks during May 1985 in the areas around Río Blanco, Paiwas, San Juan de Limay, and Siuna capturing this on film, at times immediately after an attack. One victim outside Río Blanco had just had her breast blown off, and the six-month-old child in her arms was blown to pieces by a grenade. The woman had been in her home at the time.

"White House knew very well": Chamorro interview aired on CBS News *West 57th*, June 21, 1985.

"pouring money down a sinkhole": Robert Owen memo to Oliver North, March 1986, released by Iran-contra committees May 14, 1987. This is the memo in which Owen says with resignation, "[Calero] is a creation of the U.S. government, so he is the horse we chose to ride."

"overthrowing the government of Nicaragua": December 22, 1982. First Boland Amendment, P.L. 97-377, bars the use of FY 83 funds for the purpose of overthrowing the Sandinista government.

"overthrow the Sandinistas": In late November that year, CIA agents assured Edgar Chamorro that the FDN would march to Managua by July 1983: Chamorro interview, June 1985. See also *New Republic*, August 5, 1985, and Chris Dickey, *With the Contras*, pp. 112, 156–8. On December 6 there was a meeting of exiles in Miami where they vowed same: *New York Times*, December 7, 1982.

"dragged from his bed at two A.M.": *New Republic*, August 5, 1985. See also North memo on mining, March 2, 1984 (exhibit OLN-177, released by Congress July 1987).

"David MacMichael": interviews with Andrew Cockburn, October 1984.

"Elephant Herd": CBS News, December 8, 1986.

"Oliver North": ibid.

"you will never be abandoned": *New York Times*, January 21, 1987.

"export of arms": see chapters 2 and 3.

"narcotics": see chapters 9 and 10.

"recruitment of mercenaries": see chapters 2, 3, and 4.

"absolute stealth": McFarlane memo to North, August 1984, released by Iran-contra committees July 9, 1987.

"donate a helicopter to the FDN": North memo to McFarlane titled "FDN Air Attack of 1 September," September 2, 1984 (exhibit OLN-254, released July 1987).

"Dana Parker": interviews September 1984 with Huntsville Police Department; National Guard, Washington; National Guard, Huntsville; Tom Posey; Jim Turney; Cliff Albright; U.S. Customs, New Orleans/BATF, New Orleans; D.A.'s office, Huntsville. Local reporter was Rita McKannin. The police department refused to answer questions about their late employee. His colleagues had been informed they would be fired if they talked about him. But brother officers let slip that Parker had routinely bragged about the large sums of money he was making on the side. The figures mentioned ranged from $1000 a week to $10,000 every three months. Two weeks after the Santa Clara raid, Reagan administration officials told the *Washington Post* that the attack had killed "at least four senior Cuban military advisors": *Washington Post,* September 15, 1984.

"James P. Powell": interviews with his sister, Roseanne Blair; his ex-wife, Gerry Powell; *Airwolf* helicopter coordinator; Phil McNamara, flight instructor at Charles Baker Airport (who qualified Powell as fixed-wing pilot); Petroleum Helicopter records (company Powell said he worked for in the Gulf). Powell's Cessna 206 belonged to John Moreno of Key West. Powell went to Gainesville, according to his diary read to me by Mario Calero. Moreno's son, who had tied down the plane for some time in Gainesville, vanished without trace according to Sunny South, the aircraft company there. Their letters came back marked "return to sender."

"proposed press guidance": North memo to McFarlane, September 2, 1984.

"the agency was looking into the circumstances": *New York Times,* September 3, 1984.

"Tragic Latin Expedition": *Washington Post,* September 6, 1984.

"jam jars": Posey reiterated this to me in interviews September 1984.

"foot powder": *Washington Post,* September 3, 1984.

"Elephant Herd": *Washington Post,* September 15, 1984.

"$24 million": ibid.

"aerobics": interview with Anne O'Connor, Reuters, Tegucigalpa, May 1985.

"at least one neo-fascist party": Arms Control and Foreign Policy Caucus report, April 1985.

"Nicaraguan Refugee Fund dinner": see Robert Parry, *Newsweek,* April 20, 1987. Dinner cost $71,000. Another $50,000 went to the PR firm of Miner and Frazer. $10,000 went to fund-raiser Daniel Conrad, on the payroll of Spitz Channell. The fund's lawyer, Michael Schoor, complained about Channell. Channell's lawyer threatened to "take legal action" if the fund's lawyer informed donors "directly" that the refugees would never see the money.

"Singlaub . . . lightning rod": Singlaub testimony before Iran-contra committees.

"so easy to push open": *Washington Post* journalist, July 1987.

"Pentagon . . . $100 million": General Accounting Office report "U.S. Military Activities in Honduras," January 1986 (declassified).

CHAPTER TWO

"A standing joke": interview with John Hull, May 1986.

"$250,000": interview with Pastora, May 1986.

"the aid would be turned off": *New York Times,* May 31, 1984.

"as Pastora bitterly recalls": interviews with Pastora, San José, May 1986 and January 1987.

"five gringo trainers": interviews with Peter Glibbery and Steven Carr, San José and Florida, May and June 1986.

"keep their mouths shut": interviews with Robert Thompson, May and June 1986.

"pure make-believe": interviews with embassy staff, May 1986.

"FDN-CIA liaison": interviews with Carr and Glibbery, May and June 1986. Hull admitted in July 1987 that he had worked as a CIA operative from 1982 to 1986, *Newsday,* July 26, 1987.

"pathological liars": interview with John Hull, Costa Rica, May 1986.

Glibbery's personal history: interviews with Glibbery, May and June 1986.

"The way Hull tells it": interviews with Hull, May and June 1986.

"the small rebel camp": description from Glibbery interview, May 1986, and visit to border camps by author with CBS News team, May 1986.

"humanitarian aid": NHAO bank records from General Accounting Office investigation at the request of Congressman Michael Barnes, 1986.

"three days on the beach with his girlfriend": interview with Glibbery, May 1986.

"ten thousand dollars a month": interview with Glibbery, May 1986, aired on CBS News, June 25, 1986. Also confirmed by Robert Owen in testimony before the Iran-contra committees, May 14, 1987.

"Hull's friend was Joe Fernandez": interview with Glibbery, May 1986; confirmation of Hull/Fernandez relationship, interview with Pastora, May 1986, and testimony of Robert Owen and Joe Fernandez before Iran-contra committees.

"The FBI informed the agency": Robert Parry, Associated Press, February 2, 1987.

"FDN's public relations man in Washington": interview with Glibbery, May 1986. Owen had been with Grey and Co. in Washington before setting up his firm I.D.E.A. Inc.

"courier and bagman": interview with Jack Terrell, June 1986; testimony of Robert Owen before the Iran-contra committees, May 14, 1987.

"The $50,000 contract . . . 'payoff'": interview with source, June 1986; interview with Ambassador Duemling, in charge of NHAO accounts, June 1987.

"the big picture": interview with Glibbery, San José, May 1986. Owen's testimony before Iran-contra committee on May 15, 1987, confirmed he had been there to receive the weapons.

"Maule aircraft . . . Secord": CBS News, July 14, 1986.

"The Courier": April 4, 1985, memo from Owen to North (exhibit RWO-7, select committees release).

"Morale is good": Owen memo to North, "Update," April 9, 1985.

CHAPTER THREE

Carr personal data: Carr interviews, June through October 1986.

"discharged": Michael Fessier, Jr., "An American Contra," *Los Angeles Times,* May 31, 1987.

"Howard Johnson's": Carr's details confirmed in FBI reports to the extent of hotel registrations, payment of bills, January 1986.

"Corvo . . . CIA protection": confirmed in closed hearings of Iran-contra committees in testimony of CIA station chief in Costa Rica, Joe Fernandez.

"Chanes controlled the money": Carr interview, September 1986.

"FBI file on the shipment": *Wall Street Journal,* January 15, 1987; *Village Voice,* December 30, 1986.

"consistent supply": Carr interview, Naples, Florida, June 1986.

"Thompson . . . state trooper": Thompson interview, Costa Rica, May 1986.

"air force personnel": Carr interview, June 1986.

"embassy . . . comment on Carr's assertion": author demanding official response, Costa Rica, May 1986.

"Hilda and Joe Coutin": Coutin interviews, June 1986 through June 1987.

"drug smugglers": Cuban Legion members made a statement to the FBI in 1983 about Corvo's involvement with drugs. Joe Fernandez, former CIA station chief in Costa Rica, told the Iran-contra committees in closed hearings that he knew of Corvo's involvement with drugs but had to protect him because of his status as a CIA operative.

"someone is trying to hide something": While Corvo was officially wanted by the FBI in Miami in June 1986, the author and a CBS News team found him at home at nine A.M. one morning, certainly not on the run.

"blow the chances of forty million dollars": Glibbery interview, May 1986, with author and Jonathan Winer of Senator Kerry's (D-Mass.) staff.

"La Esperanza": details of raid from interviews with Carr and Glibbery, May and June 1986; raid mentioned in a letter from Hull to Carr's mother in the fall of 1985.

"brand-new Range Rover": Carr interview, Naples, Florida, June 1986.

"as a business": Owen memo to Lt. Col. North, March 1986 (select committee exhibit, May 14, 1987).

"two-thirds of the money had vanished": bank records subpoenaed by Barnes committee, obtained by author June 1986; General Accounting Office report, December 1986.

"Glibbery steadfastly refused": Glibbery letters to John Hull, obtained from Hull, May 1986.

"the ears of a U.S. senator": Senator John Kerry (D-Mass.), whose staff began investigating the arms pipeline in the spring of 1986 after a call from the sister of Miami public defender John Mattes.

"He did admit having met the mercenaries": Hull quote in "John Hull's Farm: Bordering on War," broadcast on CBS News *West 57th,* June 25, 1986.

"I'm a rancher, a farmer and absolutely nothing else": ibid. Hull did not admit to having received weapons shipments or to any military involvement with the contras until his role had been made clear in the testimony of Robert Owen before the select committees May 14, 1987, and Hull's relationship with North had been cited in the Tower Commission's report, which mentioned "several meetings" noted in North's appointment calendar.

"he carried Hull's gun": while in the presence of the author, May 1986.

"Pastora's war effort"/Hull role: Pastora interview, CBS News, June 25, 1986.

"Creaciones Fancy": *Miami Herald,* February 16, 1987; author interviews with State Department official Ambassador Duemling, June 1987; and other administration sources. The State Department claims to have tapped Adolfo Calero to make up the $15,000 shortfall.

"gratuitous hate": Pastora interview, Costa Rica, May 1986.

"I'll have to check my diary": North to Robert Parry and Brian Barger, then writing for the Associated Press, relayed to author June 1986.

"this troubled earth": poem in honor of North read aloud by Robert Owen before the select committees May 15, 1987, written by John Hull: *Wall Street Journal,* May 21, 1987.

"birthday check": CBS News investigation revealed that the Miami account did exist as of June 1986.

Feldman/Carr: Carr interview with staff of Senator John Kerry. For further details, Feldman memo, Owen memo to North, see chapter 8.

CHAPTER FOUR

"a hair from Castro's beard": Peter Wyden, *Bay of Pigs: The Untold Story* (New York: Simon and Schuster, 1979).

"million-dollar bribes": series of interviews with DEA officials for CBS News, 1986.

"Jesus Garcia": series of interviews with Jesus Garcia, Mercedes Garcia, Alan Saum, John Mattes, Carroll Doherty, Jack Terrell, Hilda and Joe Coutin, Rene Corvo, 1986–87.

"treated him special": interview with Jesus Garcia, Miami, June 1986.

"airport Howard Johnson's": interview with Steven Carr, June 1986; FBI reports on hotel records; interviews with John Mattes, September 1985 to July 1987.

"hit the American embassy": interview with Jesus Garcia, June 1986; statement of Mercedes Garcia to Miami police, August 1985; interview with Mercedes Garcia, June 1986.

"U.S. ambassador . . . warned the Sandinista government": July 1985.

"out of courtesy notify the CIA": The relationship between Brigade 2506 and the CIA has remained close since the Bay of Pigs.

"million-dollar bounty": By January 1985, Tambs had begun to receive death threats from the cocaine cartel families.

"Mr. Shrimp and Ocean Hunter": see chapter 9.

"March 6 arms shipment": interviews with Steven Carr, June 1986, Robert Thompson, May 1986, Rene Corvo, June 1986. Customs and FBI documents include the manifest and charter agreement. The CIA responded to the inquiries of Senator John Kerry by acknowledging the flight but insisting cargo was "web gear." Details of flight also in memo from Jeffrey Feldman, assistant U.S. attorney in Miami, to U.S. Attorney Leon B. Kellner dated May 14, 1986.

"Mac 10": details corroborated by Joe Coutin and by police reports. See U.S. District Court, Southern District of Florida, *United States of America* v. *Jesus Garcia,* October 31, 1985, Miami.

"recommendation from Tom Posey": According to the Garcias' phone records, Saum made calls to Posey from Miami during his stay. Saum interviews of May 1986 confirmed that Saum gave Garica Posey's name for entrée.

"I had known about Oliver North": Garcia interview, June 1986.

"Vernon Walters": phone records and numbers in Saum's papers left behind, obtained from Mercedes Garcia.

"I am working with the White House": U.S. District Court, Southern District of Florida, *U.S.* v. *Garcia,* p. 57, October 31, 1985.

"United States government couldn't find enough investigators": interviews, March 1986 and February 1987.

"as Glibbery tells it": interview with Peter Glibbery, Costa Rica, May 1986.

"gag order": Mattes was deeply shaken about this when interviewed by author just after the event. He made contact, through his sister, with the staff of Senator John Kerry, who questioned the Justice Department on this matter and subsequently pursued an investigation when they could not get satisfactory answers.

"President Reagan went on television": speech, March 16, 1986.

"hearing was abruptly called off": interview with Mattes, July 1987.

"Jensen": Murray Waas, *Village Voice,* April 21, 1987.

Saum letter: to author, April 8, 1987.

"Hilda Coutin": interviews, May 1986 through June 1987.

"Terrell past": interviews, May 1986 and June 1986.

"Terrell first met John Hull": confirmed by both Terrell and Hull, though they differ on the content of the meeting. Hull has switched his story on both the meeting, which in May and June 1986 he denied to CBS News had taken place, but which he now says took place, and his CIA role, which he denied strenuously until admitting it in July 1987 in a *Washington Times* interview.

"the bagman for Ollie North": Terrell's description of Owen as such in June 1986 was confirmed at the time by a senior administration source. When, in May 1987 before the Iran-contra committees, Owen described his function as courier and the man who carried bundles of cash to contra leaders, the description was once again confirmed. The "bagman" comment was broadcast on CBS News June 25, 1986.

"Owen's report": memo from Robert Owen to Oliver North, January 31, 1985, released by the Iran-contra committees as an exhibit May 14, 1987.

"This war has become a business": Robert Owen memo to Oliver North, March 1986, released by Iran-contra committees May 14, 1987.

"Jeane Kirkpatrick Brigade": *New York Times,* June 21, 1986.

"These people don't know they are even in a war": Owen memo to North, February 10, 1986, released by Iran-contra committees May 14, 1987.

"Flacko knows too much": Owen memo to North, January 31, 1985, released by Iran-contra committees May 14, 1987.

"Hiring mercenaries . . . conspiracy to murder": Terrell quote in "John Hull's Farm," broadcast on CBS News *West 57th,* June 25, 1986.

Terrell's diary: first shown to author by Carroll Doherty in the fall of 1985.

"La Penca": see chapter 5.

CHAPTER FIVE

"Costa Rican radio station": May 23, 1984, Radio Monumental. On May 22, Pastora, José Davila, and Donald Castillo placed an ad in *La Nación* stating, "We categorically condemn the manipulation of Pastora by interested sectors who try to make him look like an obstacle to unity." The unity issue had split ARDE's Democratic Assembly in heated debates on May 27 and 29.

"a warning from the CIA": *New York Times,* May 31, 1984.

"large aluminum camera case": see Honey and Avirgan, *La Penca: Report of an Investigation* (September 1985); also *La Penca: On Trial in Costa Rica,* edited by Avirgan and Honey (1987).

"CIA station chief": see testimony of Robert Owen before Iran-contra committees, May 15, 1987.

"Reid Miller": *New York Times* interview, June 1, 1984.

"Alan Fiers": Pastora meeting with CIA officer with code name "Alberto Fenton," reported in *Washington Post* July 3, 1986. Fenton is Alan Fiers.

"revolves around Oliver North": Pastora interview, Costa Rica, June 1986.

"Arturo Cruz, Jr." see *La Penca: Report of an Investigation,* statement made

May 31, 1984: "The perpetrator of the bombing may have been a news-woman who herself was blown up by the explosion." Cruz later admitted in an interview with Tony Avirgan, "I have no idea about the bombing."

"Curtin Winsor, Jr." quote: "Other diplomats, not myself of course, are saying that Tony has ties to ETA." No other diplomats were spreading this rumor.

"I was just sitting on a box": interview, San José, May 1986.

"Carlos Rojas Chinchilla": see Honey and Avirgan, *La Penca: Report of an Investigation;* also Rojas testimony, May 22, 1986, First Penal Court in San José. Author interviewed Rojas May 21, 1986, in Costa Rica.

"Garcia": see chapter 4.

"Bonilla, a former agent of DIS": May 1987 deposition for RICO conspiracy suit brought against John Hull and codefendants by Daniel Sheehan of the Christic Institute, Washington, on behalf of Avirgan and Honey. See chapter 6.

"Robert Owen": memo dated August 25, 1985, released by Iran-contra committees May 14, 1987.

"telephone death threats": interview, Costa Rica, May 1986.

"Felipe Vidal . . . drug running": *Miami Herald,* February 16, 1987. José Fernandez's closed-session testimony came from confidential sources in Congress.

"big friend and get a gun": Honey interview, May 1986.

"State Department had stepped up security": Brian Barger of Associated Press informed the author in June 1986.

"agents of the KGB": Hull interview, May 1986.

CHAPTER SIX

"Sheehan": personal details from interviews with author May 1986 through July 1987. For charges alleged, see Sheehan affidavit, filed December 12, 1986, Miami, available from the Christic Institute, Washington, D.C.

"Federal Emergency Management Agency": While North was testifying before the Iran-contra committees in July 1987, Congressman Jack Brooks asked pointed questions about North's plan to suspend the Constitution. He was cut off by the committee chairman and told the subject would be discussed in closed session. The *Miami Herald* ran details of the FEMA/suspension-of-Constitution plan (Alfonso Chardy) just prior to North's testimony. For details on the burgeoning agency see the *Progressive,* May 1985.

"introduced by Posey to Robert Owen": This "source" was a well-known Washington reporter who, after participating in many internal CMA meetings, confirms Posey's White House ties.

"exclude active U.S. government officials": There was much concern in May

1986 when the suit was filed that some of the witnesses were risking their lives to come forward.

"Fuck Communism": The author is well acquainted with Paul Hoven, who appeared in the CBS broadcast "The Pentagon Underground," produced by the author for *Our Times* with Bill Moyers, July 1983.

"Edwin Wilson": see Peter Maas, *Manhunt* (New York: Random House, 1986).

Quintero testimony: ibid.

arms shipments to Somoza: James Ridgeway, *Village Voice* interview with Wilson, February 24, 1987.

"mission of assassinating Castro": see Select Committee to Study Governmental Operations with Respect to Intelligence Activities, "Alleged Assassination Plots Involving Foreign Leaders" (November 20, 1975), pp. 71–190. Includes details of CIA recruitment of underworld gangsters such as Momo Salvatore Giancana and John Rosselli as well as Trafficante. A $150,000 fee was to be paid to the successful assassin. By July 1960 assassination plots were under serious consideration, though as early as March 1960 the CIA was experimenting with chemicals to be sprayed in Castro's broadcasting studio with a similar effect to LSD. The author's favorite mode of murder under discussion was Desmond Fitzgerald's exploding seashell, an elegant idea that was deemed impractical.

"shooter team": This term comes from Sheehan's intelligence sources, though the notion of using a select group of Cuban exiles for the dirty work is borne out in the Church committee report. One of the chosen few met with President Kennedy, Robert McNamara, and the then chairman of the Joint Chiefs on April 19 and 20, 1961, along with other Cuban exiles. FBI memos on the Cuban in 1960 and 1961 tied him with Trafficante assasination plots, and later, in 1962, with mobster John Rosselli in one of the "poison pill" attempts on Castro. At least one of the CIA/mobster meetings to discuss means of offing Castro was held just outside of the Boom-Boom Room of the Fontainebleau Hotel in Miami, a hotel that would be used at the height of the contra program to discuss guns-for-drugs runs (see chapter 10).

"Felix Rodriguez was a Batista Cuban": Wilson interviewed by James Ridgeway, *Village Voice*, February 24, 1987. Rodriguez was named by Eugene Hasenfus as his control agent in October 1986 under the pseudonym Max Gomez.

"Shirley Brill": *Newsweek*, February 9, 1987, p. 35. Brill, from author's own investigation, was known as "Don't Ask, Shirley," a nickname acquired when the inquisitive blond would ask Clines and his companions why she must remove her suitcases from certain charter flights to make room for mysterious cargo, or why she must donate her makeup case for stacks of bills. Ms. Brill says she and Clines, Quintero, etc., spent a good deal of time relaxing on the luxurious grounds of estates belonging to Miami drug dealers. Her favorite night spot in Washington was the Black Orchid, a CIA hangout. She now fears for her life because of her wealth of anecdotes on the members of the "enterprise."

"Posada Carriles": *New Republic,* November 24, 1986.

"Dolly Parton look-alike contest": from Shirley Brill interview with Lee Aitken, April 1987.

"twelve thousand operatives": see Joan Didion, *Miami* (New York: Simon and Schuster, 1987).

"the opium business": see Alfred McCoy, *The Politics of Heroin in Southeast Asia* (New York: Harper & Row, 1972).

"Special Operations Group": Sheehan affidavit filed December 12, 1986, Miami, available from the Christic Institute, Washington, D.C.

"gold or opium": series of interviews with military and CIA veterans of secret war in Laos, 1987.

"Hasenfus": Many of the pilots tapped for the contra airlift were veterans of Air America. An old Air America manual was found in the rubble after the Hasenfus C-123 was shot down in Nicaragua in October 1986.

"Phoenix program": see Ralph W. McGehee, *Deadly Deceits* (New York: Sheridan Square Publications, 1983). According to 1971 testimony of William Colby (the initiator of the Phoenix program), 20,587 "suspected Vietcong" were killed in the first two and a half years of the program. The Vietnamese estimate is 40,994. Shackley's successor as Saigon station chief was Tom Polgar, who McGehee reports deliberately suppressed accurate CIA reports on the numbers of South Vietnamese personnel and civilian government employees who were defecting to the Vietcong. He wanted no gloomy reports on the large number of provinces where communist control was increasing. Thus reports were suppressed saying that the South Vietnamese government was in danger of collapse. Polgar's past deceit was of no consequence when he was appointed chief investigator for the Senate side on the Iran-contra committees.

"Nugan-Hand": Commonwealth–New South Wales Task Force on Drug Trafficking, presented to Australian Parliament March 1983. Also see Jonathan Kwitny, *Crimes of Patriots* (New York: W.W. Norton, 1987).

"Baksheesh": Testimony of Albert Hakim before Iran/contra committees, June 3, 1987.

"Wilson . . . Somoza": James Ridgeway, *Village Voice,* February 24, 1987. See also Sheehan affidavit.

"Clines . . . Somoza": Peter Maas, *Manhunt,* p. 138.

"Israel . . . Somoza": interviews with author: Israeli arms dealers, 1981–82; Somoza family, 1981.

1981–1984: see chapter 1.

CHAPTER SEVEN

"Marine Corps records": Lt. Col. John Shotwell, Marine Corps spokesman, told Art Harris of the *Washington Post,* "He could have gone to the moon and it wouldn't be in the file." (Published December 13, 1986.) North colleague Andy Messing said North talked about "classified missions" in Laos.

"Blue's Bastards": Art Harris, *Washington Post,* December 13, 1986. The Randy Harrod section also comes from Harris.

"medals": Charles Mohr, *New York Times,* December 4, 1986.

"accidentally opened fire": Rod Nordland, *Newsweek,* November 17, 1986.

"Firing Line": North and two marine colleagues appeared on the broadcast of July 21, 1971.

"Peers Inquiry": see Seymour M. Hersh, *Cover-Up* (New York: Random House, 1972). My Lai quotes in this section all come from Hersh. Proper title of Peers Inquiry is "The Department of the Army Review of the Preliminary Investigation into the My Lai Incident."

"reports of atrocities in Nicaragua": see "Nicaragua: the Dirty War," CBS News *West 57th,* broadcast June 21, 1985.

"bayoneting infants": Stephen Kinzer, "Contras Raided Civilian Target," *New York Times,* March 10, 1987. Kinzer reported that the contras "bayoneted a nine-month-old infant."

"the altar boy": R. S. Greenburger, *Wall Street Journal,* December 31, 1986.

"premed at Rochester": North said this while testifying as a character witness in the Thomas Reed stock fraud case: Harris, *Washington Post,* December 13, 1986.

"studying South America": *Washington Post,* December 23, 1986.

"jumping off his roof": R. S. Greenburger, *Wall Street Journal,* December 31, 1986.

"twist slowly in the wind": author's interview with confidential source, April 1987.

"It's good to die with our leaders": author's interview with administration official, March 1987.

"however unwise or foolhardy": author's interview with a marine lieutenant colonel and colleague of North's, November 1986.

"FEMA": Alfonso Chardy, *Miami Herald,* July 5, 1987.

"ask the president": Andy Messing interview, June 1986.

"loose cannon": North testimony before Iran-contra committees, July 9, 1987.

"appetite for self-promotion": It was well known among Washington journalists that North was selectively leaking news of major operations. John Berry of *Newsweek* described the scene for me when North came in to leak the *Achille Lauro* affair. This later came out after North chastised Congress for being a primary source of leaks. *Newsweek* and the *Washington Post* both named North as a source for breaking stories.

"I sought approval": North testimony before Iran-contra committees, July 10, 1987.

"the hand of one superior": On March 25, 1987, D. Rosenbaum quoted congressional sources in the *New York Times.* "Casey's fingerprints are everywhere," one lawmaker said. Another said, "North surely needed the expertise and the help of the CIA to do all the things he did in Central America."

"Ollie's like a son to me": *Wall Street Journal,* December 31, 1986.

"He's like a kid you would like to have for your own": ibid.

"McFarlane . . . 'like a son of mine' ": *Newsweek,* November 17, 1986.

"Casey was for me a man of immense proportions": North testimony before Iran-contra committees, July 9, 1987.

"plenipotentiary for Ronald Reagan": Stephen Engelberg, *New York Times,* December 3, 1986.

"United Methodist Church congregation": ibid.

"the old man loves my ass": testimony of Felix Rodriguez before Iran-contra committees, May 27, 1987.

"commie bastards" and "advance man for the invasion": Tom Morganthau, *Newsweek,* December 8, 1986.

"dedication to work": North once reportedly worked forty consecutive weekends, and took his first vacation in five years in August of 1985: John Wolcott, *Wall Street Journal,* November 26, 1986.

"Ms. Hall . . . mother": David Ignatius at the *Washington Post,* on November 30, 1986, quoted an administration official as saying, "If Ollie wanted to get in to see Bud, it was just a question of the daughter calling up her mother to set up an appointment."

"Casey . . . 1983": North testimony before the Iran-contra committees. Administration officials had been leaking a later date for North's involvement and a different superior. On November 26, 1986, John Wolcott, in the *Wall Street Journal,* quoted "senior officials" as saying it was McFarlane who, in 1984, "directed Lt. Col. North to keep the Contras armed, financed, and afloat—without involving the U.S. government."

"a chamber-of-commerce type": Helms interview with author and Bill Moyers, June 1984.

"RIG": see Keith Schneider, *New York Times,* January 3, 1987. Article notes that North's RIG duties brought him to the attention of Congress. " 'It was the first time Col. North's name came across our desks,' said a former member of the Senate Intelligence Committee." Also, author was kept apprised of RIG activities by administration officials.

"Special Activities in Nicaragua": NSC memorandum N44842, March 2, 1984 (committees exhibit OLN-177).

"traveling frequently to the contra camps": see David Ignatius, *Washington Post,* November 30, 1986. Also several North memos released by the Iran-contra committees bear this out. See chapter 1.

"off-the-shelf, stand-alone entity": Oliver North testimony before Iran-contra committees, July 9, 1987.

"North . . . drafted an operational plan" and "verbal approval": This was revealed by both Alfonso Chardy of the *Miami Herald* and Brian Barger/Robert Parry on the Associated Press wires almost simultaneously in June of 1986. AP had been holding the story for some months, much to the disappointment of its authors. AP was in a delicate position as its Beirut bureau chief, Terry Anderson, had been kidnapped, and North was the NSC point man for the hostages. Barger believed North was pressuring the AP not to run the story about North's contra operation (and presidential approval) by threatening not to help on the Anderson front. As of this writing (August 1987), Anderson is still a captive. Details of the AP wire story were repeated by Parry and Barger in the *New Republic*, November 24, 1986.

"those liberals in Congress": North quoted by Parry/Barger, *New Republic*, November 24, 1986.

"memo to . . . Moreau": North memo to Moreau, released by Iran-contra committees July 9, 1987.

"Secord had had to resign": Secord stated this in his May 5, 1987, testimony to the Iran-contra committees with some bitterness, saying that he had hoped to rehabilitate his image and stature after the Wilson affair by his participation—without pay, he claimed—in the "enterprise."

"presidential directive": *Miami Herald*, March 8, 1987, and interview by Ty West (CBS News) with Rand. As of writing, Freedom of Information Act request is outstanding.

"Director Casey is the one who suggested Secord": North testimony before Iran-contra committees, July 9, 1987.

"scheduler type": Secord testimony before Iran/contra committees, May 5, 1987.

"Secord . . . first meeting with North": Secord testimony before Iran-contra committees, May 5, 1987.

"weapons and ammunition captured from the PLO": *New Republic*, November 24, 1986.

"Owen . . . cutout": see Owen testimony before Iran-contra committees, May 14 and 15, 1987.

"San José Declaration": NSC document N40754.

"the document was written by Calero, Cruz and North": North memo to McFarlane, April 1, 1985, released by Iran-contra committees July 9, 1987.

"Sea Goddess": Los Angeles Times service reprinted in *New York Post*, March 21, 1987.

"My Friend" letter: undated; NSC document, released by Iran-contra committees July 9, 1987.

"Tambs . . . RIG": *Tower Commission Report,* New York Times Books/ Bantam Books edition, p. 471.

"one mission in Costa Rica": ibid.

"Fernandez . . . Casey": *Wall Street Journal,* May 1, 1987.

"air base . . . meeting in Miami": testimony of Richard Secord before Iran-contra committees, May 5, 1987. The "program review" meeting began with a "hard note" about who was "lining their pockets." The meeting broke up at dawn.

"the money was being 'wasted . . . squandered' ": Secord testimony, ibid.

"I was asked by North whether I could put together this operation": ibid.

"the strip": author's personal observation, January 1987. There is a second strip there that is also restricted. It is not clear whether the "enterprise" built it or bought it with the property.

"Udall Research": registered in April 1985 by lawyer Julio Quijano in Panama. Quijano was busy incorporating several companies for "enterprise" including Lake Resources and Stanford Technology. See *Washington Post,* December 14 and 21, 1986. Secord talked at length about Udall during his congressional testimony on May 5 and 6, 1987. Albon Values Corp., another company account prominent in the Hakim ledger, was also incorporated by the Panamanian lawyer Quijano. Albon was used regularly to transfer funds to ACE, another shell company, controlled by Southern Air Transport. It is no wonder that moneyman Albert Hakim admitted to Congress he had trouble keeping his accounts straight. Secord acknowledged his Udall role in his testimony before the committees May 5, 1987: "We set up Udall."

"pointing fingers at each other": Fernandez and Tambs interviews, in the *Tower Commission Report,* Times Books/Bantam Books edition, p. 471.

"BG: FOR YOUR EYES ONLY": Owen memo, August 1985, released by Iran-contra committees as Owen exhibit May 14, 1987.

"Mr. Abrams . . . well informed": *Tower Commission Report,* p. 472.

"Ambassador Tambs was equally blunt": Lewis Tambs's testimony before Iran-contra committees, May 28, 1987.

"it had never quite gotten into operation": *Tower Commission Report,* p. 472.

"If CBS knew about Santa Elena": I received a call June 26, 1986, giving details of Santa Elena, from a pilot known as "Tosh." In the course of several interviews, he gave a very accurate description of the strip and surrounding area.

"These guys are trying to save their jobs": Joel Brinkley, *New York Times,* May 3, 1987.

"fry lower-level officers": ibid. In the Brinkley interview, Tambs went on to say, "Now the people who gave us the orders are trying to paint us as running amok . . . it's insane."

"local residents later reported hearing C-130s": Tony Avirgan interviewed

the local residents right after the strip became public knowledge in
Costa Rica, October 1986.

"call Costa Rican President Arias": *Tower Commission Report,* p. 473.

"there would be no press conference": North memo to Poindexter (prof
note), ibid., p. 473.

"I was well beyond my charter": North prof note to Poindexter, ibid., p. 473.

"the approval of either Weinberger or Casey": Interviews with high-ranking
NSA staffers revealed that such encryption devices were "state-of-the-
art." The fact that North got them without the usual bureaucratic delays
caused a certain amount of jealousy within the intelligence ranks. NSA
Director Odum, said the sources, would never have turned over equipment at the request of a lowly lieutenant colonel but required high-level
approval. The KL-43 devices, according to Secord, were spread among
his men, SAT, and two embassies.

"Blackie's troops": *Tower Commission Report,* p. 463. Blackie Chamorro,
according to Owen memos to North, had a serious drinking problem and
a staff known for drug trafficking and stealing from the "USG," the U.S.
government.

"Lecayo . . . John Hull's payroll": see chapter 2. Also, Owen memos to North
released by the Iran-contra committees May 14, 1987, mention Lecayo
as part of the operation. Owen acknowledged in testimony that Hull was
receiving ten thousand dollars a month via Calero.

"a sudden flurry of death threats": El Negro Chamorro ("Blackie") contacted
CBS News in March 1987, hoping to do an interview disclosing corruption in the upper levels of the FDN. When my CBS colleague Ty West
got to the house where El Negro was staying in Miami, it was swarming
with police. The accountant in San José was trying to peddle his story
to every journalist in town, including CBS.

"2500 man force": Fernandez to North, message quoted in *Tower Commission Report,* p. 464.

"Robert Dutton . . . drops": When Dutton testified before the Iran-contra
committees in June 1987, he made it clear that Joe Fernandez was
directing American flight crews where and when to make drops: "Joe
was critical to us throughout the operation. Joe was coming up with new
commandantes that he wanted us to support and new drop zones that
he wanted us to fly to and put loads on. All we had to do was go in, make
the drop, call Joe, and say, 'Where do you want the next load?' "

"launch a major offensive": *Tower Commission Report,* p. 466.

"it could well become a political embarrassment for the President": North
prof note, quoted in the *Tower Commission Report,* p. 468.

CHAPTER EIGHT

"the guns, the drugs, and John Hull": see chapter 3. The quote is from a
taped interview with Steven Carr. Feldman, in his memo of May 14,

1986, to U.S. Attorney Leon B. Kellner, makes it clear that he is indeed interested in these three subjects.

"Hull had asked him why the agents and myself were in Costa Rica": memorandum to Leon B. Kellner, United States attorney, from Jeffrey D. Feldman, Assistant U.S. attorney. Subject: Costa I. Dated May 14, 1986. In the memo, Feldman goes into the cast of characters from chapters 2 and 3. He identifies Rene Corvo as leader of CANAC, Comité Ayuda Nicaragua Anti-Communista, cofounded by Juan Perez-Franco. Franco, says Feldman, is a Brigade 2506 member who runs an insurance business in Miami: "The FBI has observed CANAC related activities take place at this address" (1890 Southwest 57th Avenue, Suite 103).

"the whole operation was 'in jeopardy' ": Murray Waas, *Village Voice,* March 31, 1987.

"Robert Owen, who kept himself fully up to date": Owen memo to North, April 7, 1986, document released by Iran-contra committees May 14, 1987.

"a box of food": author's interview with Carr, June 1986.

"disinformation experts": Owen memo to North, April 7, 1986.

"Godless Communists": ibid.

"We's in too deep now to turn back": Owen memo to North, April 7, 1986.

"receiving copies of all FBI files": Robert Parry, *Newsweek,* April 20, 1987.

"possibly from the antiterrorist specialist": A memo from George Kiszynski was seen in North's office according to Iran-contra committee sources, though this memo was not released with the North documents.

"Mattes . . . complained to his sister": author's interview with Mattes, March 1986.

"answers from the CIA and the Justice Department": details of the meeting of the Kerry staff and the CIA in interviews with the author, June 1986 and March 1987.

"Justice . . . had found no evidence": Author was present when the Justice Department called the Kerry staff to break the news.

"Meese assured Poindexter that he would 'get on top of the situation' ": This story was broken by Murray Waas, *Village Voice,* March 31, 1987. Meese, according to documents released by the Iran-contra committees, was comfortable with squelching investigations into the efforts of the NSC to secretly aid the contras. North, for example, wrote a lengthy memo on November 14, 1986, detailing how Meese called off both the FBI and U.S. Customs, who were eager to unmask the involvement of Southern Air Transport in the Hasenfus affair. Meese, according to North, pressured Jim Baker, secretary of the treasury, to stop the Customs investigation. Meese personally called off the FBI. For more details see chapter 12.

"a source inside Kellner's office": To date, the source has given a statement to Special Prosecutor Walsh. Another source inside the U.S. attorney's

NOTES

office has given details to Walsh of the suspension of the SAT investigation, corroborated by North.

"Hull wrote to two FBI agents": see Waas, op. cit. Hull was, as he told the author in June 1986, quite friendly with George Kiszynski of the FBI in Florida.

"Don't you know there's a vote coming up?": This source has not yet gone public but has given a statement to Special Prosecutor Walsh.

"a fishing expedition": The revised memo was dated May 14, 1986, though it states that "on May 30th, 1986, in the Southern District of Florida (86-1146-Civ-KING), Martha Honey and her husband Tony Avirgan, have sought damages against 30 defendants. . . ." Thus, the revised memo was produced at least two weeks later than it was dated.

"The memo was waved before the committee": interviews with congressional staffers, June 1986 and March 1987. Also see Waas, op. cit.

"the doors of La Reforma prison in San José": Details of this scene are from Peter Glibbery, May 1986, and Martha Honey and Tony Avirgan, May 1986.

"install Glibbery in their home": For this and the scene that follows, author was present, May 1986.

"Carr . . . Kirk Kotula": interviews with Carr, June 1986 through September 1986. Carr also relayed this information, with full details of his ordeal getting out of Costa Rica, to Ron Rosenblith of Senator Kerry's staff.

"until the politicians say you're going to get out": ibid.

"killed civilians": see chapter 3.

"John Jones turned up": interviews with Carr, June 1986 through September 1986. Also interview with Carr conducted by Ron Rosenblith of Senator Kerry's staff.

"You know John Hull's lying": ibid.

"I'm being set up or something": ibid.

"It's decision time": ibid.

"Robert Thompson returned to the Hull ménage": author's interviews with Thompson in San José courtroom, May 1986, and at Hull's ranch, May 1986.

"paid by the Avirgans to lie": author's interviews with Thompson, San José, May 1986.

"appraised each newcomer to the house": author's observations, May 1986.

"old and curious ties to the Korea lobby": author's interview with Terrell, April 1986.

"a plant from the other side": as told to the author by Glibbery, May 1986.

"Its a cancer, its like Watergate": interview on CBS News *West 57th*, broadcast June 25, 1987. Also stated in conversation with author, May 1986.

"Glenn Robinette": Robinette testimony before Iran-contra committees, June 1987.

"Steven Carr disappeared": Author was present for the frantic calls to the court on May 20 and 21, 1986.

"the courtroom": author's personal observations, May 22, 1986.

"Smith . . . a veteran of the administration's propaganda battles": When the author produced a broadcast on contra human rights abuses in June 1985, the State Department swiftly dispatched Smith's report. This was after authenticity had been called into question by Brian Barger from AP in a press conference, and Smith had admitted his questionable methods. The report is almost certainly still available at Elliott Abrams's office.

"I.D.E.A. Inc.": Owen testimony before the Iran/contra committees, May 14, 1987.

"training contras for John Hull": see chapter 2.

"who would do anything for pay": interviews with John Hull, May 1986.

Mattes in court: Author was present in courtroom, May 1987. More details on Mattes's testimony are with the public defender's office in Miami. Also see chapter 4.

"what the hell the State Department was cabling [Mr. Kellner] for": *National Law Journal,* March 16, 1987.

"Danny Sheehan filed suit": see chapter 6.

"box of food": CBS News interview, June 1986.

"The mystery of Carr's disappearance": interviews with Carr, June 1986 through September 1986. Also, interviews with Carr conducted by Ron Rosenblith of Senator Kerry's staff, June 1986.

"with the key thrown away": interview with Carr, Naples, Florida, June 1986.

"hacking through the jungle": Jane Wallace, Manny Alvarez, George Bouza, and I went with Glibbery to the border camps to verify their existence, May 1986.

"no scruples about a blind girl": Carr was terrified that one of his enemies, particularly Felipe Vidal, might try to harm his sister. Interview, June 1986. Carr's lawyer, Jerry Berry, was equally alarmed.

"glutted Miami market": The price of cocaine was at a low ebb in Miami in February and early March 1985.

"The head of Hugo Spadefora": Prior to Spadefora's death in 1985, he had been a close associate of Eden Pastora's and a well-loved contra leader. He was, according to his old associates, upset about drug smuggling and corruption in the war effort. His murder has not been solved, though Panamanian leader General Noriega has been implicated by a whistle-blower in his top command.

"friend at the NSC" call: interviews with Glibbery and Carr, May and June 1986.

"Hull . . . drug trafficking": see chapters 9 and 10.

CHAPTER NINE

"the CIA having connections with drugs": interview with Ramon Milian-Rodriguez, June 1987, aired on CBS News *West 57th* July 11, 1987.

"$200 million a month": ibid.

"Pablo Escobar and Jorge Ochoa": are often said to control up to 80 percent of the world's cocaine market, though Milian-Rodriguez says the figure is much closer to 40 percent.

"Noriega $4 million a month": This figure was, according to Milian, calculated along the lines of market share. He estimated that Noriega received a total of $10 million per month from various drug interests.

"*Forbes* magazine cover": April 1986.

"$5.4 million in cash": see *Forbes*, April 1986.

"chief orderly in the hospital": Butner, North Carolina.

"his dealings with the CIA and the contras": Milian-Rodriguez had never been pegged publicly with a contra operation, so that when I and my CBS colleagues Jane Wallace and Ty West came in with hard evidence of his involvement with one Miami contra supplier, Milian was quite surprised, not only that we knew of his operation, but that we had details of one very specific case: Ocean Hunter.

"over three and a half million dollars boldly labeled 'CIA' ": government exhibit 12F, November 25, 1985.

"Some said . . . that I condoned drug trafficking to generate funds for the contras": testimony of Oliver North before Iran-contra committees (opening statement, July 7, 1987). North was asked on July 13, 1987, about the CBS News broadcast two days earlier on Milian-Rodriguez and Ocean Hunter, but the subject was quickly dismissed. The drug issue was also briefly raised during the testimony of Robert Owen in May, but the committee, according to Senate sources, had decided to deliberately avoid questions on matters involving CIA proprietaries and assets.

"unwholesome allegations of a CIA-contra-narcotics link": The Senate Foreign Relations subcommittee convened in July 1987 with two days of closed hearings with Ramón Milian-Rodriguez. I and my CBS colleagues convinced Senate investigator Jack Blum to interview Milian, which resulted in the hearing. Senators Jesse Helms and John Kerry were in the midst of their own investigations on the drug allegations. After Milian's testimony, the committee issued eighteen subpoenas, including those sent to Felix Rodriguez and John Hull.

"$30 to $40 million . . . Somoza": interview, Butner, North Carolina, June 1986.

"Manuel Artime": Artime is a major figure in all accounts of the Bay of Pigs. See Peter Wyden, *Bay of Pigs: The Untold Story.*

"$200,000 individual payments for the Cuban burglars . . . Watergate": interview with Milian-Rodriguez, June 1987. He later testified to this before the Senate Foreign Relations Committee in closed session, July 1987.

"Felix Rodriguez": ibid.

"$180,000 in campaign contributions": interview with Milian-Rodriguez, June 1987. The money was laundered through 180 different contributors, who each gave $1000.

"Reagan was our kind of candidate": ibid.

"Giro Aviation Corp.": see *The Chronology* (New York: Warner Books, 1987), November 1984 entry; and the *Miami Herald,* November 2, 1984.

"George Bush": According to a chronology assembled by the office of the vice president after the downing of the Hasenfus plane, the vice president met with Felix Rodriguez in January 1985, two months after his former business partner was indicted on cocaine-smuggling charges, and an attempted assassination.

" 'look favorably' . . . Ocean Hunter": interview, with Milian-Rodriguez, June 1987.

"cash money . . . to a designated courier": aired on CBS News *West 57th,* July 11, 1987.

"three kilos" and "Carr": see chapters 3 and 8.

"Headquarters was a hole-in-the-wall": I first visited the corporate offices in June 1986. Also see CBS News *West 57th,* July 11, 1987.

"Luis Rodriguez . . . Panamanian records": from exhibits in the Ramón Milian-Rodriguez case in Miami. For Ocean Hunter records, see 1983 state of Florida incorporation papers.

"Rosell": interviews in June 1986 and January 1987.

"It was just a front. What they wanted to import was cocaine": CBS News *West 57th,* July 11, 1987.

"The CIA have a lot of front companies": aired on CBS News *West 57th,* July 11, 1987. Several sources corroborated this claim of Ocean Hunter operating as a CIA front, including contra leaders, Senate sources, and a high U.S. government official.

"ten feet away from Oliver North's arms shipment": CBS News *West 57th,* July 11, 1987.

"We're investigating him for drugs": ibid.

"Joe and Hilda Coutin": interviews, June 1986 and March 1987.

"arms shipment and the cocaine shipment": interview, March 1987.

"Jack Terrell": interviews, April 1986 through June 1987.

"what the hell were you doing with the information?": Mattes interview, March 1987.

"somebody's back pocket": ibid.

"General Accounting Office audit": accounts obtained by author from Congress, July 1986.

"BAC . . . the contras' bank": see Dan Morgan, *Washington Post,* April 21, 1987.

NOTES

"Frigorificos is the Costa Rican sister firm": bank records obtained by author from Congress. For more details on the companies see CBS News *West 57th,* July 11, 1987.

"Nunez... a friend of John Hull's": Hull volunteered this information in June 1986 at Muelle, Costa Rica.

"$231,587": documents obtained by author from Congress: GAO/Barnes committee audit, 1986.

"when we paid a call on Frigorificos": CBS News team, January 1987.

"Robert Owen as its watchdog": internal NHAO reports obtained by author. For more on this see CBS News *West 57th,* July 11, 1987.

"when Owen reportedly picked up a fraudulent receipt": *Miami Herald,* February 16, 1987. The staff of Creaciones Fancy recognized Owen. As he is several inches taller than any Costa Rican (and most Americans), he was apparently not difficult to spot.

"Pastora and his aide Carol Prado": interview, San José, January 1986.

"Chanes . . . supplying weapons shipments": see chapter 3.

"With the shrimp, they were shipping cocaine": interviews, June 1986 and March 1987.

"They were covering up for the CIA": ibid.

"Kerry took the case to FBI headquarters": interview with Senator John Kerry, April 1987.

"We shouldn't be involved with these kinds of people": see CBS News *West 57th,* July 11, 1987.

"checked that out": ibid.

"Ambassador Duemling . . . checked out": interview, Washington D.C., July 1987.

"FBI . . . ongoing investigation.": CBS News *West 57th,* July 11, 1987.

"General Accounting Office": In the course of their investigation into the mismanagement of humanitarian assistance funds, the GAO reported to the State Department that Ocean Hunter was under investigation by the DEA, according to a State Department official questioned on the matter.

"bounty hunters": interview, Los Angeles, February 1987.

"The bounty hunters had first gotten wind of Ocean Hunter": Charles Stewart, a producer for ABC News at the time, briefed Valis and Hanks.

"took their information to Hayden Gregory": interview with Valis and Hanks, February 1987; confirmed by the House Judiciary subcommittee. Gregory did arrange the meeting at DEA headquarters. The DEA later denied to CBS News that there was such a meeting.

"It was sort of like the Paris peace talks": interview, February 1987.

"selling national security secrets": ibid.

"the 2506 group": see chapters 3 and 4.

"a little pin on the map": interview with Valis and Hanks, February 1986.

"Miami customs officials": interviews with customs officials for CBS News, February 1987.

"I don't like interference": interview with Brian Barger for CBS News, February 1987.

"John Denby": interviews with Carr and Glibbery, May and June 1986. See also chapters 2 and 3.

"due to lack of interest": ibid.

"I'm not in the shrimp business": CBS News *West 57th,* July 11, 1987.

"I've been out to Puntarenas": interview with Hull, May 1986.

CHAPTER TEN

"Nice group the Boys chose": Robert Owen memo to Oliver North, February 10, 1986, referring to the CIA's recommendation of former drug pilots to be used in a State Department humanitarian assistance airlift.

"George Morales": CBS News *West 57th,* April 6, 1987.

"the ruling Duvalier family": By the time the Duvaliers fled Haiti in February 1986, that island had become a major transshipment point for cocaine entering the United States. (Interviews with Haitian drug enforcement officials and U.S. embassy staff, March and April 1986.) According to drug enforcement officials, Michelle Duvalier's father was heavily engaged in the trade. In one amusing incident in 1985, American smugglers miscalculated their "drop point" and kicked several duffel bags full of cocaine out of an aircraft onto the Île de la Gonâve, where villagers tried the white powder first as whitewash, then foot powder, and finally as a soothing cure for raw baby bottoms. Drug enforcement officials found them selling the cocaine to neighboring villages for this purpose.

"1986 report": internal DEA memo obtained by CBS News, November 1986.

"$250,000 every three months": interviews with George Morales for CBS News, November 1986 through July 1987.

"Octaviano Cesar": interview with Octaviano Cesar, Costa Rica, January 1987. See CBS News *West 57th,* April 6, 1987.

"high-level Washington people": ibid.

"operative of the Central Intelligence Agency": Cesar lost this job after the story of his relationship with Morales was aired on CBS on April 6, 1987. He was also forced to resign his post as director of international relations for the Southern Opposition Block (BOS) in San José. His brother Alfredo was later elevated to the contras' civilian directorate, a post he holds as of August 1987.

"a trip to the Bahamas": CBS News obtained confidential customs documents in Miami that both recorded Octaviano Cesar's declaration of $400,000 from the Bahamas trip and listed Cesar, Morales, and "Popo" Chamorro on the flight manifest (October 1984). Cesar had claimed in an interview in January 1987 that he had met Morales at the drug smuggler's Opa-locka office just after his indictment and had immediately boarded a plane for the Bahamas. Customs records show that there was an interval of several months between the first meeting and the flight.

"we had a hamburger, and then we came back": interview with Octaviano Cesar, Costa Rica, January 1987.

"Pastora . . . one Morales suitcase": interviews with Pastora, Costa Rica, June 1986 and January 1987.

"Adolfo ('Popo') Chamorro": interview, Miami, February 1987. Chamorro is Octaviano Cesar's cousin and another official of the Southern Opposition Block, having defected from the Pastora camp. Pastora's comments on him are taken from an interview in January 1987.

"$300,000 per flight": interview with Morales, aired on CBS News *West 57th* April 6, 1987.

"a thousand kilos of cocaine": interview with Betzner, January 1987, aired CBS News *West 57th* April 6, 1987.

"six ship mines": interview with Betzner, January 1987.

"How much will I be paid?": ibid.

"John Hull's strip is a little short": interview, CBS News, January 1987.

"stacked all the way to the ceiling": interview, January 1987, aired on CBS News *West 57th* April 6, 1987.

"The call sign was a whistle": CBS News *West 57th*, April 6, 1987.

"thirty-three-hundred-foot strip": interview, January 1987. See also the map Carta Aeronáutica de la República Costa Rica, May 1984.

"Cessna Titan": a model 404. T-O run: 1,788 feet. T-O to 50 feet: 2,367 feet. Landing from 50 feet at max landing weight: 2,130 feet. (Source: Jane's *All the World's Aircraft*, 1979–80, p. 326.) This was not the same aircraft purchased with the funds from the Bahamas trip in October 1984. That aircraft, #N5273J, was bought "under the supervision of Cesar and Chamorro" and given to Pastora. Flight logs show the plane was flown from Ilopango air base in El Salvador to Hull's ranch four or five times in December 1984 and early 1985, flown by Geraldo Duran. Cesar eventually took the plane back and had it flown to Ilopango. While in Costa Rica, the plane was based for a time at Pavas Airport in San José. Morales gave other planes to the contras. A C-47 was donated on October 21, 1984 (registered in Brazil PPCED). At Ilopango, military personnel stripped and repainted the plane and put new tail numbers on. Morales also donated a Beach Baron N666PF that crashed on February 3, 1985, on a flight from Pavas to Ilopango. Flight logs show that plane was flown by Duran and John Hull to Miami on July 26 and 27, 1984. Pastora had another Titan given to him by the CIA (identification number HP978) that crashed during a 1984 raid on the Managua airport.

"John Hull was there": interview with Betzner, January 1987, aired CBS News *West 57th* April 6, 1987. See CBS News "John Hull's Farm: Bordering on War," June 25, 1986, for Hull's denials of drug activity and for Pastora interview where the contra leader states that he knew that drug planes were flying in and out of John Hull's farm. In an interview with Pastora in May 1986 in Costa Rica, he specifically remembered drug planes on the Hull ranch in August 1984.

"unaccounted-for cash": CBS News *West 57th,* April 6, 1987.

"clearing four million off that load": interview, January 1987.

"Los Llanos": Author visited the strip in January 1987.

"east of Hangar One": see CBS News *West 57th,* April 6, 1987. Hanger One is famous for CIA activity there.

"George Morales is a very, very careful man": interview, January 1987.

"for the Costa Rican narcotics people": interview, aired on CBS News *West 57th* April 6, 1987.

"Pat Korten": interview, April 1987.

"lie-detector test": interview with Jack Blum, Senate Foreign Relations Committee investigator, August 1987.

"DEA . . . one of their agents made him an offer": A DEA supervisor, according to Miami public defender John Mattes, made the offer. The DEA man reportedly said, "We can get you under the ten-year mandatory minimum." April 16, 1987. Morales had passed this news to both CBS and to the Senate Foreign Relations Committee.

"Blum shored up the drug dealer's resolve": interview with Jack Blum, July 1987.

"related to narcotics trafficking": interview with Eden Pastora, aired on CBS News *West 57th* June 25, 1986.

"I wrote a letter to the DEA": interview, Costa Rica, May 1986.

"Dea men in Costa Rica": interview, May 1986.

"Santa Elena": see chapter 7.

"Duran . . . drug runs": interviews with Duran, January 1987, and George Morales, November 1986, by Brian Barger for CBS News.

"Duran . . . friend of John Hull's": conversation with Jonathan Kwitny, May 1987.

"copies of gas receipts": hearings, July 1987; interview with Jack Blum, August 1987.

"Tosh": interview, June 1986.

"The word came down from Washington": interview aired on CBS News *West 57th* April 6, 1987.

"seventy to eighty percent": interview, January 1987.

"contra war . . . a 'business' ": ibid.

"Robert Owen brought up the drug issue": February 10, 1986, memo released by Iran-contra committees May 14, 1987. Owen was questioned on this point during the hearings, where he elaborated that "the group had been recommended to NHAO [State Department] by the CIA." There were, remarkably enough, no further questions.

NOTES

"Mickey Tolliver": see CBS News *West 57th,* aired April 6, 1987, and *CBS Evening News with Dan Rather,* April 6, 1987.

"Barry Seal": During his illustrious drug career, Seal worked for both the CIA and DEA, in between runs for his own profit. He was the pilot used for the famous Sandinista sting, contrived by the CIA to pin drug-smuggling charges on the Sandinista government. What is not common knowledge about this sting effort is that representatives of the Colombian cocaine cartel had previously met with CIA antiterrorist expert Bill Wagner (pseudonym) in a Miami restaurant to offer the cartel's services to sting the Sandinistas directly. This offer came with other perks: use of the cartel's two-thousand-man guerrilla army and hundreds of millions in cash to overthow the Sandinistas. The CIA failed to tell the cartel about the Seal operation in process. When the druglords discovered the agency's duplicity, they killed Seal "to teach them a lesson."

"anything from Campbell's soup to dead babies": interview, February 1987.

"Rafael Quintero": CBS News *West 57th,* April 6, 1987.

"Who's they?": interview, February 1987.

"Hi, my name is John Doe": ibid.

"As an extra added bonus": CBS News *West 57th,* April 6, 1987.

"marijuana, cocaine": ibid.

"IBM situation": ibid.

"my man": testimony of Richard Secord before the Iran-contra committees, May 6, 1987.

"GI discount": interview, February 1987.

"my expenses were high": ibid.

"Colombian cocaine cartel": see note "Barry Seal" above.

"little old lady from Pasadena": CBS News *West 57th,* April 6, 1987.

"Homestead": ibid.

"Follow me": ibid. The "Follow me" truck was shown on the broadcast.

"Taxicab": ibid.

"top four, three slots of the CIA": ibid.

"basically a whore": interview, February 1987.

"Customs . . . CIA": Stephen Kurkgian, Mark Hosenball, *Boston Globe,* April 27, 1987.

"We think he did land at Homestead": ibid.

"Vortex . . . Palmer" Steve Stecklow, *Miami Herald,* March 22, 1987.

"Dioxa": investigation by Carroll Doherty, July 1987, for CBS News.

"let the matter drop": The Customs/CIA squabble was reported on CBS News, Rita Braver, April 1987.

"it happens to be true": quoted by Kurkgian and Hosenball, *Boston Globe,* April 27, 1987.

"collective refusal to accept it": Senate investigators were particularly exasperated at the failure of the general press as of August 1987 to pick up the story. One major newspaper had delegated the story to an intern.

But the *Boston Globe, Newsday,* the *Christian Science Monitor,* and the *Miami Herald* had all run strong stories on the subject. In spite of these papers' weighing in on the drug story, the *New York Times* reported on July 15 (when George Morales was before the Senate) that CBS News *West 57th* was the only place the story had appeared. According to the *Times,* "The charges have not been verified by any other people."

"business as usual": confidential interview, Washington, March 1987.

"half a million dollars": interviews with Morales, November 1986 and January 1987.

"the early 1950s": Just before CBS News correspondent George Polk was murdered in Greece by British intelligence with American backing, the journalist had told Edward R. Murrow that there was evidence the Greek leadership was involved in the drug trade: Ann M. Sperber, *Murrow* (New York: Freundlich, 1986).

"money to fight the communists": interview, January 1987.

CHAPTER ELEVEN

"Americans will never make concessions to terrorists": press conference, June 18, 1985.

"ayatollah is helping us with the contras": Lieutenant Colonel North to Richard Armitage, quoted in the *Tower Commission Report,* Times Book/Bantam Books edition, p. 54.

"We did not . . . trade weapons or anything else for hostages": Ronald Reagan, address to the nation, November 13, 1986.

"Americans in chains": Reagan, address to the nation, August 1987.

"not telling the truth": according to all major polls taken between December 1986 and August 1987.

"finding": March 9, 1981. Authorized the CIA to undertake "covert activities" against Nicaragua. See chapter 1.

"CL-44 transport plane": arrangement revealed was that Israel planned to sell Iran 360 tons of American-made tank parts and ammunition, a $30 million contract. It came out that Israel had been supplying Iran for several months. See *Washington Post,* July 27, 1981; *The Chronology,* p. 8; Zbigniew Brzezinski, *Power and Principle* (New York: Farrar, Straus & Giroux, 1983), p. 504.

"BBC": *Panorama,* February 1982.

"Evans and Novak": *Washington Post,* May 21, 1982.

"Arens": David Nyhan, *Boston Globe,* October 21 and 23, 1982. Robert Levy, *Boston Globe,* October 22, 1982.

"FBI's 1984 investigation": Federal Bureau of Investigation, Washington Field Office, "Factfind," Major Case #48, March 7, 1984.

"Wexford": ibid.

"Reagan Debate Practice Tape #2": ibid.

"subcommitte . . . debate papers": Christopher Hitchens, *The Nation,* July

4–11, 1987; Subcommittee on Human Resources release, May 23, 1984, chaired by Congressman Donald Albosta. "The better evidence indicates," the report states, "that Carter debate briefing materials entered the 1980 Reagan/Bush campaign through its Director, William J. Casey, and that Casey provided Carter debate briefing materials to James A. Baker III." The subcommittee recommended the appointment of an independent counsel. The materials, they concluded, "most likely came from the National Security Council."

"Bani-Sadr": interview with the author, August 1987, confirming earlier interview with Alfonso Chardy, *Miami Herald,* April 12, 1987.

"meeting": ibid. Chardy got confirmation from the three officials. Bani-Sadr told the author that he knew of the meeting, and told Rafsanjani he believed it was "dangerous" to undercut the Carterites and go with Reagan. Bani-Sadr said he also complained to Khomeini.

"judged to be a fraud and dismissed": Alfonso Chardy, *Miami Herald,* April 12, 1987.

"Dick cut a deal": Honneger quoted by Hitchens, *The Nation,* July 4–11, 1987. Interestingly enough, in Casey's affidavit (March 2, 1984) for the Albosta committee, he states, "Information about negotiation for the release of the hostages came to me from many sources. . . . I do not specifically recall Richard Allen's memorandum of October 15, 1980, or the identity of 'ABC–XYZ' referred to in that memorandum": committee report, p. 1109.

"arms shipments had been assured": interview with author, August 1987. See also Alfonso Chardy, *Miami Herald,* April 12, 1987.

"Mansur Rafizadeh": Rafizadeh, *Witness* (New York: William Morrow, 1987).

"or the deal is off": Honneger quotes Allen on *MacNeil-Lehrer Newshour.*

"Buckley . . . 'an expert on terrorism' ": North testimony before Iran-contra committees, July 10, 1987.

"eliminating hostile terrorists": see chapter 6.

"National Security Decision Directive 138": *Miami Herald,* March 8, 1987.

"Secord denies any association": interview, August 19, 1987.

"drafted by Oliver North": *Miami Herald,* March 8, 1987.

" 'fantastic' contacts in Iran": *Tower Commission Report,* pp. 106–107

"using Ghorbanifar as a middleman": ibid.

"via other channels": ibid., p. 107.

"Leslie Aspin": Simon de Bruxelles, *London Observer,* July 26, 1987. On the eve of Oliver North's testimony, Karen Burns of ABC News also did a series of stories that said that North had begun the arms business in 1984.

"North didn't know what the hell he was on about": Simon de Bruxelles, *London Observer,* July 26, 1987.

"back into business with Ghorbanifar": *Tower Commission Report,* p. 123.

"widely believed to be an Israeli agent": North testimony before the Iran-contra committees, July 9, 1987.

"Murder Incorporated": *Washington Post,* December 7, 1986; *New York Times,* December 25, 1986.

"Drug Enforcement Administration": *Tower Commission Report,* p. 125.

"Kattke": Senate sources; FBI report: Washington Field Office to FBI Director, Priority Report, July 18, 1985, Iran-contra committees exhibit OLN-264.

"old crap": Aspin interview, *London Observer,* July 26, 1987.

"$3 million on the deal": *Tower Commission Report,* p. 149.

"contingency plans for extracting hostages": ibid., p. 149.

"asked to play God": testimony of Robert McFarlane before the Iran-contra committees, May 11, 1987.

"William Buckley 'might be released' ": *Tower Commission Report,* p. 149.

"Buckley . . . died of a heart attack while under torture": Farzad Bazoft and Simon de Bruxelles, *London Observer,* May 3, 1987.

"Vernon Walters": Senate Intelligence Committee report, January 29, 1987.

"North . . . personally viewed a tape": North testimony before the Iran-contra committees, July 10, 1987.

"we have been very patient with you people": *Tower Commission Report,* p. 158.

"Clarridge deserves a medal": ibid., p. 163.

"One hell of an operation": ibid., p. 164.

"McMahon": ibid., p. 188.

"a lot of the blame for the disastrous Nicaraguan mining operation": North pointed this out in one of his own memos, released July 9, 1987, by the Iran-contra committees. North knew McMahon disliked him because of the mining fiasco.

" 'authorized agent' for the CIA": testimony of Richard Secord before the Iran-contra committees, May 9, 1987.

"under the control of General Secord and Colonel North": "Support for Intelligence Activities," army report quoted in *Tower Commission Report,* p. 247.

"account ledger": exhibit OLN-17, released by the Iran-contra committees during the testimony of Oliver North, July 9, 1987.

"profit": In a note to himself cited in the *Tower Commission Report,* p. 253, North says the cost per missile was $13,200. Ten thousand dollars per missile is what is reflected in the Hakim ledger. It is possible that Ghorbanifar spread the profit between two or three people, though Ledeen, for example, denies he received any profit, though North noted that he would receive $50 per TOW. North has also denied since that Ledeen received any profits.

" 'Korel . . .' Richard Secord's personal account": Iran-contra committees exhibit OLN-17, Hakim ledger. Hakim confirmed in his testimony on June 3, 1987, that Korel was the personal Secord account. As of that date, the Korel account was worth $1,578,000.

"Hakim . . . potential conflict of interest": quoted in the *Tower Commission Report*, p. 257.

"Roger, Ollie. Well done": McFarlane to North, ibid., p. 254.

"to forward to the President": ibid., p. 267.

"Presidential approval": ibid., p. 269.

"chocolate cake from a kosher bakery": *Tower Commission Report*, p. 296.

"A report in the *London Observer*": May 3, 1987.

"Button": Iran-contra committees exhibit OLN-17, Hakim ledger.

"dissapating so much love": testimony of Albert Hakim before the Iran-contra committees, June 3, 1987.

"and directly from the CIA": Iran-contra committees exhibit OLN-17, Hakim ledger.

"nearly eight million . . . contras": testimony of Albert Hakim before the Iran-contra committees, June 3, 1987.

"Oliver North was to inherit": Iran-contra committees exhibit OLN-169, CSF Investment Bank document.

"stranded arms": testimony of Albert Hakim before the Iran-contra committees, June 3, 1987.

"CIA free of charge": testimony of Richard Secord before the Iran-contra committees, May 7, 1987.

"sometimes got lost": Hakim testimony, June 3, 1987.

"late-October meeting": CIA tapes among the North exhibits, released by the Iran-contra committees July 9, 1987.

"trying to buy a wig": Hakim testimony, June 3, 1987.

"His prime objective . . . the elections": deposition of Albert Hakim read by Arthur Liman at the Iran-contra hearings, June 4, 1987.

"all received paychecks": Iran-contra committees exhibit OLN-17, Hakim ledger.

"Cruz . . . CIA": North letter to Calero, exhibit OLN-258, released by the Iran-contra committees July 1987. Cruz had been on the CIA payroll in 1984.

"He has too much documentary evidence": memo dated October 24, 1986, exhibit OLN-196.

"poor judgment and shabby conduct": ibid.

CHAPTER TWELVE

"no connection or affiliation with the CIA": William Langton, quoted in the *Los Angeles Times*, December 18, 1986.

"Gaspar Garcia Laviana": Alfonso Chardy, *Miami Herald*, July 12, 1987.

"I can't believe I did it": author interview, Nicaragua, October 11, 1987.

"you don't have to sleep in the mud": Peter Ford, *Christian Science Monitor*, November 3, 1987.

"blowing us out of the sky": ibid.

"$3,000 a month and a bonus of $750" and "ten missions": flight logs from downed plane obtained by CBS News, October 9, 1987. Hasenfus disclosed his pay at the time. See also Hasenfus's press conference, Managua, October 9, 1987.

"put together this operation": Secord testimony before Iran-contra committees, May 5, 1987.

"told me I was crazy": author interview with Secord, August 19, 1987.

"mishandling of covert funds": Dan Morgan, *Washington Post,* March 22, 1987. Other Gadd details here are also taken from Morgan's investigation.

"Piss Poor Performance": interview with author, August 19, 1987.

"shyster alarms": Fiers testimony before Iran-contra committees, August 5, 1987.

"my job is to fill it up": *New York Times,* April 24, 1987.

"refused to unlock its gates": from CBS News cameraman who fell on one of the coffins in the crush of people backed up against the locked gates.

"not in any sense a U.S. government operation": Evans and Novak transcript, October 12, 1986.

"this doesn't look like a cover-up": ibid. See also Iran-contra committee exhibit OLN-135.

"leaks naming Singlaub": Singlaub press conference, October 9, 1986; *New York Times,* January 15, 1987.

"flight to Frankfurt": *Tower Commission Report,* Times Books/Bantam Books edition, p. 425. See also Secord testimony, May 7, 1987, and North testimony, July 10, 1987. (Bible quote released with North exhibits.)

"a high-powered lawyer": North prof note to McFarlane, October 12, 1986, in *Tower Commission Report,* p. 546.

"only offer . . . CBS News": As the the administration was taking no steps to arrange for Sally Hasenfus to see her husband, I offered to book her a seat on our flight, and explained to her that she had clearance to go. The State Department suddenly rushed to her side and arranged for her flight. They told her they would pay all costs, which they later conveniently forgot.

"urgency to hold things together": *Tower Commission Report,* p. 546.

"RR was briefed": ibid.

"documents on the plane": CBS News and the *New York Times* were the first to get the documents. We pored over them in a Managua hotel room October 9 and 10, 1987.

"practice in field construction techniques": *Washington Post,* October 17, 1986.

"Doan Helicopter": FAA records and *Miami Herald,* October 9, 1986.

"airline of CIA choice": Department of Transportation records. See also *CBS Evening News,* July 9, 1984, and AP, July 10, 1984.

"Udall . . . Southern Air": National Security Archive. Published in *The Chronology,* p. 321.

"auspices of Southern Air Transport": interview with author, August 19, 1987.

"two Cuban-Americans": Hasenfus press conference, Managua, October 9, 1986.

"Hasenfus had told them all he knew": Sandinista military intelligence chief Captain Wheelock told us in Managua, "We couldn't get him to shut up": October 9, 1986.

"send him home . . . Christmas": told to Mike Wallace, October 1986.

"outstanding bill": By the summer of 1987, the Hasenfus family was locked in a bitter dispute with the administration and were threatening to sue.

"Gregg told the *New York Times*": *New York Times,* December 12, 1986.

"Gregg . . . Hasenfus plane": CBS News and *Washington Post,* December 16, 1986.

"we're still fast friends": *New York Times,* December 12, 1986.

"to anyone who would listen": author interview with Richard Secord, August 19, 1987.

"tapped the cocaine cartel": see chapter 9.

"Steele . . . KL-43": Secord testimony before the Iran-contra committees, May 5, 1987.

"Bush chronology": quotes taken from "Statement from Bush's Office," *Washington Post,* December 16, 1986.

"Ollie got to Felix": *Washington Post,* April 26, 1987.

" 'shoddy' goods": Secord brought this out in his testimony, May 5, 1987.

"National Security Agency phone intercepts": testimony of Robert Dutton before Iran-contra committees, May 27, 1987.

"old munitions": Secord testimony, May 5, 1987.

"Martin bought Honduras": interview with author, August 19, 1987.

"gang of yahoos": ibid.

"Fiers": testimony of Alan Fiers before Iran-contra committees, August 5, 1987.

"damage President Reagan": Singlaub, quoted in *Washington Post,* February 26, 1987.

"Villoldo": Alan Nairn, the *Progressive,* May 1987.

"Bruce Cameron": ibid.

"North has never received any of the calls": exhibit OLN-139, released during North testimony along with details of the calls.

"some notable exceptions": Alfonso Chardy, Robert Parry and Brian Barger, Pat Lynch, Karen Burns, and Knut Royce come to mind.

"evidence linking us to the contras": Secord testimony, May 6, 1987.

"the guns, the drugs, and John Hull": see chapter 8.

"Do you want me to lose my job?": source told this to the special prosecutor.

North memo on Meese (November 14, 1986): As of August 24, 1987, this memo had not surfaced in the press, though it was released with the North exhibits: memo #N9127/OLN-205.

CHAPTER THIRTEEN

"wall around the president": repeated in testimony of Richard Secord before Iran/contra committees, May 5, 1987.

"Al Shiraa": The issue was published November 2. The following day Rafsanjani made a speech to the Iranian Parliament confirming the visit.

"Tony Avirgan and Martha Honey . . . were warned": The warning was privately conveyed through a U.S. journalist visiting Costa Rica.

"John Kerry . . . had come under attack": author interview with Justice Department officials and Kerry staffers.

"Hondo-Caribe": documents obtained from impounded cargo plane, April 1987.

"Danny Sheehen and the Christic Institute . . . had filed their lawsuit . . . six months before": The lawsuit was filed in Miami on May 29, 1986.

"made up of whole cloth": testimony of Alan Fiers before Iran/contra committees, August 5, 1987.

"We had spoken throughout the summer": Carr would call me collect almost every week from the Naples jail.

"Dear Ma": Carr's letters obtained both from him and from members of his family.

"Decedent is a 27-year-old who may have overdosed on cocaine": LAPD report, December 13, 1986.

"Just stay with me. . . . I paranoided out. . . . (Convulse)": ibid.

"The final police report stated that he had bought it in San Diego. . . . He was excited about starting a new job on Monday": Reports of Supervising Investigator Dean Gilmore, LAPD, December 26, 1986, and January 20, 1987.

"Autopsies": L.A. County Coroner Autopsy Report 86-16321.

"John Mattes got an agitated phone call from Peter Glibbery. . . . The CIA killed Stephen Carr": private communication from Mattes.

"Polgar had not distinguished himself in Saigon": Frank Snepp, *Decent Interval* (New York: Random House, 1977).

"he was given the plum posting of station chief in Mexico City": *In These Times,* June 10–23, 1987.

"he wrote in the *Miami Herald*": *Miami Herald,* December 14, 1986.

"Polgar was chosen . . . by Rudman": *Legal Times,* February 23, 1987.

"Don Gregg has been quoted": ibid.

"Don't you think it would be absurd for a conservative American rancher": *In These Times,* June 10–23, 1987.

"Was that man really from the Senate?": author interview with Pastora aide Carol Prado.

"I can understand that they might not want to put Jack Terrell in the witness chair": author interview with Senate investigator.

"Bermingham": memo to Congressman Lee Hamilton dated July 23, 1987, released by Iran/contra committees August 1987.

NOTES

"Inouye proudly recited": Iran-contra hearings, July 14, 1987.

"Hayden Gregory": interview with Gregory, August 27, 1987.

"that's not our baby": Gregory interview, ibid.

"some of our people . . . had a problem with drugs": congressional sources.

"ably assisted by Don Gregg . . . Robert McFarlane . . . Antonin Scalia": Interview with former senior Pike committee staffer.

"The fix was in": telephone interview with Richard Secord, August 19, 1987.

"$2.26 million . . . raised for the National Endowment for the Preservation of Liberty": *Washington Post,* February 28, 1987.

"Dolan, a homosexual like Channell": Christopher Hitchens, *Harper's,* August 1987.

"The President obviously knows": *Tower Commission Report,* p. 476.

"In 1985 he received over $130,000 from just two of his foundations. . . . Eric Olson . . . Daniel Conrad": Christopher Hitchens, *Harper's,* August 1987.

"In a hotly contested 1986 Senate race . . . Chavez called on Oliver North": *Washington Post,* December 20, 1986.

"slice by slice": North testimony before the Iran-contra committees, July 10, 1987.

"traveler's checks . . . 'When was the last time it snowed in Nicaragua?' ": Iran-contra hearings, May 20, 1987.

"Owen described how Adolfo Calero": Iran-contra hearings, May 14, 1987.

"Guevara was picked up . . . and disappeared": information from Tony Avirgan.

"two books and a letter": account of episode and translated copy supplied by Tony Avirgan.

"At a congressional hearing on May 19, 1987, Gen. John Galvin": House Foreign Affairs Subcommittee on Western Hemisphere Affairs, May 19, 1987.

"They're going after soft targets": Fred Kaplan, *Boston Globe,* May 20, 1987.

"Benjamin Linder was a mechanical engineer": *New York Times,* April 30, 1987.

"The White House responded": ibid.

"There was Arturo Cruz . . . on the payroll at $84,000 a year . . . Alfonso Robelo . . . Adolfo Calero": Hakim ledger.